THE TALE OF THE CLASH

BOOK FOUR

THE CXNTERBURY TALES

MICK N BAKER

To Chris, Jess and Abbie

For Mum and Dad
With life comes understanding

Rest in peace Alan,
The brightest of lights burns so much faster. After you left,
The world was a poorer place.

Rest in peace Phil,
I don't know where you are now, mate, but wherever it is I bet
you're still giving people a laugh.

Special thanks to Andy Lane, Richard Lane, Paul Smith, Dave Russ, Irena Halder, Malcolm Paul, Matthew Burgin, Mickey 'Penguin' Baxter, Paul 'Forgotten' Glory, Neil Frederick Roberts, Dave Lusby, Stephen Dearman, Stig Miller, Jackie Gizzi, Mickle John, Mart McIver, Darren 'Latty' Latimer, Andrew Keeble, and finally and by no means least Jessica Keeble, I couldn't have done it without you!!!

The Cxnterbury Tales - Book Four
The Tale of the Clash

"Purity in body and heart,
May please some – as for me,
I make no boast."

Geoffrey Chaucer

Chapter One

George Best's Hairy Chest

In 1983, on a wave of nationalism after the Falklands War, the Tories were on target for a second term in government. If that wasn't bad enough, spring had stalled, like mother nature had passed her judgement on The Mori polls. It was sad, she had gone cold on the U.K., and it's wishes for a second coming of Maggie Thatcher; and it was all about jingoism. I had talked to the old man on many occasions about the war, and he had outdebated me on nearly every level, certainly, the most important ones. Not that I would have admitted such a thing at the time.

When he said it wasn't right for any country to send soldiers to another country, another country where the people and government didn't want those soldiers - despite their geography, I just didn't have the words to answer him back. How could I? It was an invasion, a military invasion, with tanks and troops, perpetrated by a fascist junta. No way could I condone an invasion by fascists, but of course, that gave me a huge dilemma - I could be seen to be supporting Thatcher and her nationalist policies. Crass and other anarcho Punk bands, had no qualms about criticising the government for fighting, and OK, it was great watching Diane Gould rattling The Iron Bitch on Nationwide, but the fact remained. If you were against fighting, then in effect, and by default, you were supporting the military dictator General Leopoldo Galtieri. It was an almost impossible decision to make, but in a world of only variants of right and wrong. I had to choose Thatcher… No, no way, I couldn't; it was the unthinkable, she was the unspeakable evil. To choose the milk snatcher, the loathsome heartless old bitch, who had told the world that destroying people's lives would be better for them in the long run, and all the while, silently, behind closed doors, her rich friends had made millions more for themselves in the public utilities fire sale. No, no, no, no way, but hold on, General Leopoldo Galtieri was a fascist dictator who took over Argentina in a military coup, a fascist dictator who tortured and executed thousands of people in his so called 'dirty war'; it was time to think about something else.

I had been broken up with Cerys getting together with Mark, and during one of our car port conversations, Dave had assured me that time heals all – all but… syphilis. In the months that had followed, I had found out that was only partially true, sure, time had helped patch me up again, but I wanted to be in a relationship, be with someone, have a girlfriend who I could have a laugh with, share those precious times. I suppose when it came down to it, I wanted to have sex and lots of it. It just wasn't happening for me, though. Clare, the girl in the orange arc, had fallen foul of The Pillock just once too often, and was under complete control now. Phil had told me that as The Pillock worked close to where she worked, he would drop her off in the morning and then pick her up on his return that evening. He would only let her out to come up to his posh golf club, near the private school of Heath Mount, so he could get her in with the rich club members. Sadly, from my point of view, it had worked perfectly for the careerist asshole, as she was now going out with a local businessman's son.

Karen Corker, or little girl lost, as I thought of her, really was lost now. The news was out. Stampy of the Wolf Pack was now officially going to be a dad. I couldn't believe it; I knew her Mum was bad news, but Stampy? Stampy the dad, I couldn't see it. Oh well, I thought, she had made her bed, got in it, got knocked up by a violent skinhead bastard, and now she was nothing to me - a no one in my life. Cerys Ash, it always came back to her, the Punk rocker, my ex-girlfriend. Dave had made some encouraging sounds about her getting bored with musk man Mark, but the reality of the situation was, I had about as much chance of getting her back as I did going on a date with Diana, the princess of being a doe eyed, fucking parasite by royal appointment. It was time to think about something else.

On the work front, things were moving in a sinister direction, too. Mum's kind offer of helping out with my driving lessons had certainly put the whole issue of me getting a full-time job back a bit - even the old man had stopped hassling me about it – but it was only a stay of execution, though. Once I had passed my driving test, there was no way that I would be able to dodge it anymore. It was only a matter of time now. It was time to start thinking about something else, time to start thinking about the most important something; the next gig. On the day of the gig, we would be focused on what we did best. On the day of the gig, we would be thinking that this one might be the one that gets us signed. On the day of the gig, Andy, Whiff, Dave and me would be buzzing, ready for a laugh, ready to make a racket, ready for the chaos of it all. Fuck the whole world for today. This is our world, I thought.

*

On the day of the gig, early, around five o'clock in the evening, I picked up my guitar in its case, leads, effects boxes, said my goodbyes to Mum and the old man, who wished me the best of luck, and went down to Dave's, where we loaded up his van, and set off in good spirits down the A10 towards Ware College. It was so good to be gigging again, especially after the Bowes gig. It had given us a look at what we wanted for the future of the band. A packed-out venue full of pissed up Punks, Skinheads and other reprobates ready to have a laugh, cause mayhem, smash it up, using our music as their catalyst.

I sat back in the shotgun seat as the trees whirled past us in a green haze, watching Dave drive, hoping to learn something that would help me with my up-and-coming driving lessons; our soundtrack Rudimentary Peni's Death Church album. Dave sometimes used to wind me up by almost hitting the keep right signs at the bottom of Kings Hill, I wondered whether he was going to do it again today.

"Whoa fucking hell Dave, that was close," I exclaimed.

Dave cracked a grin, "It always looks a lot closer on your side, Skin."

"If you say so, mate," I said, totally unconvinced.

"So Skin, did you rescue any snared cats on the way down to mine?" Asked Dave, as Nick Blinko, bellowed 'Holy matrimony is a blissful myth, wholly based on tradition, wholly based on bullshit' out of the van's tinny speakers.

I creased up, "No mate, it was all quiet on the god front… You haven't told anyone that I got punched by Malcolm, have you? …What am I saying, of course you have."

Dave braked hard at the build-up of traffic on Ware High Street, "Don't worry about it, Skin, you had him, didn't you?"

"Yeah, I beat up a twelve-year-old, sounds good, doesn't it?" I said, sarcastically,

"The silly little twat, I reckon I've delayed his balls dropping by at least two years… I kicked them so hard they must have been up under his armpits."

Dave cracked up in his seat. "Up under his armpits," he repeated, "Jesus, that's got to have hurt."

"Yeah, that's why he needed his booby milk, to heal his burst sack."

Dave shook his head, getting back to the snake of slow-moving traffic ahead.

Nick Blinko sang, 'There's nothing as slimy as a member, obscene as a prime cut.'

"You still don't believe me, do you?"

"I don't know, Skin. I can't get my head around that."

I cackled, "Oh, I see, you just don't want to believe it."

"I don't, it's well… Unbelievable… Euuugghgh, Jes… Us," he said, shaking like a shitting dog.

"Dave, I can understand that mate, it's like a video nasty, isn't it? …It's like the sequel to 'I spit on your grave' …I suck my Mum's tits."

In a deep voice, Dave intoned, "In cinemas nationwide. A new terror. Malcolm was just a normal twelve-year-old boy until he started sucking his Mum's tits. Now he wreaks havoc upon the feline world. I suck my Mum's tits, the long-awaited sequel to I spit on your grave. Cats be afraid, be very afraid."

I fell forward, creasing up laughing, helplessly, slapping my hands on the dashboard.

"You know what? I've been having some pretty lucid dreams recently, I bet I dream about that, I know I will. If I do, I'll puke the bed," I said, gaining a bit of composure.

Dave laughed, "Oh, look who it isn't, it's the whiskey in the box kid."

I looked up past the metal and glass snake to see Danny walking along Ware High Street towards us. So, I gave him the wankers sign, and we pulled out of the traffic into a parking space next to him.

"Wanker," I shouted, "Alright Danny, what you up to?"

Danny laughed, "I'm waiting for the man, and you?"

I smiled, "We've got a gig at the college; you want to come, mate?"

"No, sorry Skinner, I would have done. If someone would have told me about it," he said, accusingly, holding my gaze steadily.

"Oh yeah, sorry mate, I should have said something, I had a lot on my mind that day though… That fucking job interview…"

"Did you get it?" Danny asked.

Dave interrupted. "Yeah, of course he did; he's the managing director of the company now. We're just off to Jewson's to pick out some new wallpaper for his office," his voice dripping with sarcasm.

"I'm chairman, of the bored out of my fucking head, mate," I added, backing him up.

Danny laughed, "So you fucked it up then? …Nice one, knew you could do it Skinner."

I smiled magnanimously, putting my palms up, "What you up to then Danny boy? Waiting for the man, is that man Ashley, by any chance?"

"Yeah… Ashley's that man, we're going up The Frontline, get some sensi," He grinned.

I smiled knowingly, "Hey, hey, sounds like a plan."

"I love it when a plan comes together," said Danny, rubbing his hands together.

"And a few Rizlas," I quipped.

Danny guffawed, "When you going to come up again, Skinner? Ashley's been asking about you."

Dave gunned the engine, hinting playfully.

"I don't know, maybe next week; we'd better get on mate, I'll see you about, Danny," I said.

Danny mimed smoking a spliff, laughed, and we pulled away.

"What's that all about? Who's this Ashley?" Dave asked.

"Oh, nothing really… Ashley's a gypsy bloke I know, we smoke a bit of dope together."

Dave put the van into first. "Oh right," he said, rolling his eyes.

A few minutes later, we were at the venue. Unloading the gear quickly, we ferried it past the obsolete, for now, job centre at the back of the college and into the vast main hall at its front. Inside, we were pleased to see there were quite a few people in already, and there was a buzz of conversation coming from the scattered groups. In amongst them, I saw Whiff standing at the bar talking to Mark Harper and some of his Skinhead mates, while Andy was over near the stage with a couple of his mates, chatting avidly.

I walked up behind Whiff, gave him a playful shove in the back, "Whiffters, old chap, you alright?"

Whiff spun around, "Mr. Baker, how's it going? You know Mark, don't you?"

"Yeah, a fellow lazy sod from the dig, how are you mate?" I smiled broadly.

"You alright Skinner, how's it going? You heard anything about another one?" Mark asked.

I shook my head sadly, "Nah nothing really mate, a few rumours. I'd love to get back there, though, that was a fucking laugh, wasn't it?"

Mark smiled, wistfully, "Yes mate, some good days, good days there. So, you're playing tonight, then?"

"Yeah, we are, should be a good night." I looked around as another group of students dressed in black sauntered in through the main doors, "Oh, by the way, Mark, you know I told you we sound like the Cockney Rejects?"

Mark snickered, showing a row of battered yellow teeth, "Yeah… I remember," he replied.

"I think you might be in for a surprise, mate!"

"Well, I think we sound like the Cockney Rejects, that's why I joined the band," said Whiff, grinning at the amused Skinhead.

Andy appeared by the side of me, "Yeah, we're The Ware Rejects."

Mark laughed, nodding knowingly, "You're the singer, aren't you?"

Andy nodded, watching the massive skinhead.

"You must be Stinky Turner, then?"

"Stinky Townsend," corrected Whiff, warming to the theme.

"He does do a bit of boxing too, don't you, Andy?" I said.

Mark grinned at him. "Ooh, I had better watch myself, I don't want to get upped," he said, laughing, picking up his pint.

Whiff surveyed another group of black clad students coming in through the doors, bopping his head up, down, side to side, trying to get a better look. "I was hoping Steph might be coming tonight," he said.

"Who's that then?" Mark asked, putting his pint down, his thirst quenched.

"The Woman," Whiff announced, proudly.

I cackled, "Whoa. The Woman? Fucking hell mate. Steady on, it's early days, isn't it?"

Andy quipped, "Is she like a man?"

Mark and Steve Bartlett - who had just tuned into the conversation - absolutely creased up laughing.

"Is she like a man!!!???" Repeated Steve.

Whiff spun around, glaring at Andy, incandescent with rage, then threw his arms up in disbelief.

Mark wiped the tears of laughter from his eyes, scrutinising Whiff, "Oh my, has she got a bit of hair on the old Georgie Best, has she?" He said, falling about.

Steve joked, "Whiff… Has she got a muff, plus one?"

Mark rolled back onto the bar, eyes streaming, "She's got an extra leg, has she?"

Steve stifled a laugh, and broke into song, "She's Steph the peg, diddle-iddle-iddle-um, with the extra leg diddle-iddle-iddle-um." Sloshing his now, wayward pint onto his Fred Perry.

Mark exploded into laughter, "She's brave going out with you, mate, she's got some bollocks."

"She has, a big fucking, pair like beach balls," said Steve, wiping a froth of larger from his shirt.

Whiff had heard enough now, "No, no, it's no... It's nothing like that, it's an in-joke we have."

Steve and Mark weren't listening anymore; they were too busy laughing, lost in the hilarity of it all. They were holding onto each other, trying not to fall off their bar stools.

Whiff had had enough by now. He turned on Andy and spat, "Cheers for that, Andy, where's your girlfriend then? ...You thalidomide."

Steve heard that alright, he grimaced, "Ooooh... Fucking hell, you're not going to break up, are you? I was looking forward to this... I'll want my pound back as well."

Mark and Steve's mates sitting around the bar were all watching the show now. Sipping their pints, laughing disparagingly, enjoying themselves, as the drama unfolded in front of them.

Dave had, had enough, too, so he stepped forward, trying to defuse the growing situation, "Nah, they love each other, really, don't you lads?" He implored.

Andy grinned lopsidedly, put his arm around Whiff's shoulders, and said "I do," like they were getting married, and the whole bar exploded into laughter,

"Whiffy thinks he gets all the girls, don't you, Whiffy?" He said to the mirthful faces around the bar.

Whiff was absolutely seething now, tersely, he pulled away from him, gave him a, not-so-playful, slap on the cheek, hoping it might shut him up. The expression on his face told me he wasn't going too, though; he was nowhere near finished. The bar had warmed to him; he was here to entertain people, and he was getting some good laughs now. Please, Andy, I thought, whatever you do, do not, and I mean DO NOT, sing that song we made up about him when he first joined the band.

Andy gazed at his captivated audience. "Whiffy gets all the girls. That's what he thinks. But he doesn't, because he's got big feet, and they stink," he sang, laughing manically.

Silence, total silence, the whole bar just gawped at us. Mark analysed Andy for a long moment, then finally, he snorted, broke off, and surveyed the rest of us with a contemptuous look on his face.

I shrugged my shoulders.

Mark asked, "Oh, is that another in-joke?"

"Er… Yeah, I don't know, I suppose it must be mate," I said, nodding slowly, trying to brazen it out.

I scowled at Andy, shook my head, and he gaped back at me, looking bewildered.

"Oh, I see. That really is sad, boys," Mark sighed.

"OK, we better get on now mate, we better get ready, we are… We are going to blow you away, we're going to do the business, y…you'll see" I said, floundering under the skinhead's gaze.

Mark nodded evenly, "I saw you lot at Bowes Lyon house back in January, so I know what to expect, I enjoyed it. You're good, but you're nothing like the Cockney Rejects, though, Skinner… Shame really," he said, pointedly looking at Whiff, "You could have played 'Bad Man' for us."

Whiff furrowed his brow, looking all at sea.

Mark crooned "Mr. She's like a Bad Man," paraphrasing the Reject's track, sending all the skinheads around the bar back into fits of laughing.

Whiff smiled thinly, dropped his head, turned away from the braying pack, and he was off at a march. I followed close behind him as he weaved his way through the rapidly growing audience over to the stage area, and when we got there, I put a placating hand on his shoulder.

"You OK, mate?" I asked.

Whiff almost smiled, "Yeah… Yeah, course I am."

"It's only a bit of a laugh, mate."

"It is for him… Now you know why I don't hang around with him outside of the band anymore. I know these people, that was embarrassing!"

"Oh, leave it out, Whiff, he's alright, I don't think he even knew he was doing it."

Whiff snapped, "Huh! Yeah, well, everyone else did, didn't they…? I mean fucking hell!"

"OK, OK, come on man, we haven't got time for this now, we've got a gig to play," I encouraged him, seeing Dave and Andy approaching us through the audience.

Whiff hesitated, sighed, nodded minutely, and made his way over to his amp, switched it on, plugged his bass in, and started making adjustments to his sound. I looked from Dave to Andy, who had been watching our conversation, with more than a little interest.

"A bit of his own medicine, eh Skin?" Dave grinned.

"Nah mate, come on, that was pretty embarrassing for all of us," I sighed.

Andy looked at me enquiringly.

I asked, "What's up with you two?" impatiently.

"Nothing," Andy dismissed.

"OK, so everything's alright then? Let's get ready for the gig," I said, tetchily.

Dave and Andy nodded, dispersed to their areas of the stage, where they began to make their last-minute checks too. I plugged my guitar into my Laney amp and tuned up, getting ready myself. It's nothing, I thought, just a bit of pre-gig nerves, whatever it is, we are mates, we can sort it out later. In the meantime, let's go out there, have a laugh, cause some proper mayhem.

Once we were ready, we left the stage and sat in silence around the back, Whiff preferring to sit on his own, away from the rest of us, puffing away on a roll-up while we were waiting to be called. He barely had time to finish it before a long-haired hippy, with a face like Worzel Gummidge, came backstage.

"Hi fellows… Come and do your thing now," he said, sounding like Worzel Gummidge.

Andy, Whiff, Dave and me all exchanged a glance, grinned at each other.

"I'll be bum swizzled," I said, using one of the hapless scarecrow's catchphrases.

Dave replied, "A cup o' tea an' a slice o' cake," using the other one, which sent all of us into fits of laughter. I thought we're fine, and we followed the Aunt Sally botherer out into the lights.

Onto the stage we went, out into the blinding lights; a swell of raucous applause greeted us from the audience. In front of us, huge monitors hummed maliciously, telling us of the awesome racket that we would be throwing out for everyone tonight. The stage was quite literally set.

I pulled my guitar strap over my head, looked out into the hall, and saw Mark, who flashed a huge grin, gave me the thumbs, so I grinned back at him, strumming my guitar aggressively.

Andy drew the mic up, "OK, good evening, we are Virus V1, and you are our audience!"

"Eeeeaaaaaahhhhhh," came back.

15

"Hi, Mum," said Andy, pulling an amused face at some of his mates down in the front row. "OK, for the people who don't know, this one's called 'Everybody's Boy'."

Dave smashed into the all too familiar intro, and we were away. The whole place came alive as our sound blasted out of the P.A. system and into every corner of the hall, squeezing the silence out. I was buzzing at our last practice, after all the bullshit that I had gone through, but that was nothing compared to this - compared to playing live, doing it in front of a decent sized crowd. It was on a higher plane altogether; my guitar felt like it was plugged directly into me; my body a mad effects box, processing the sound, throwing it out through my senses into the faces of the audience. I looked at the now all too familiar scene and saw the others were enjoying it too. Andy was prowling the stage, dropping to his knees, belting it out. Whiff confident and upright, legs splayed apart, clawing at his bass strings, the notes shaking the floor, and Dave lambasting the skins, solid as a rock as usual; I saw the crowd were enjoying it too.

Mark and his mates had pushed up to the front of the stage in front of me, barging into each other, shoving, laughing, bouncing about. Andy's mates were in the middle po-going and singing our lyrics back to us. I smiled to myself, kept on scanning the mad faces in front of me, then my roaming eyes stopped abruptly when I spotted a girl near the back who looked like Cerys. It was like Cerys, but with long hair, and she was really going for it too, pumping her fist in the air. Her hair whipping from side to side, lost in the mayhem of it all. In the blaze of the lights, it was hard to see; but I squinted my eyes up tightly, and as the spotlights crossed over the crowd, I saw it was her. She was standing next to a girl I didn't recognise. Musk man, was nowhere to be seen, either. I smiled, pointed my guitar at her, weaved it up and down maniacally until she waved widely back at me. A big friendly wave and no Musk man, I thought, this night is just getting better and better. I carried on scanning the audience and saw Glyn Matthews and Stampy, the Whiff bashers with some of their mates, The Wolf Pack, standing a few rows back, in front of Whiff's side of the stage, and I came down to earth with a bump.

A big fat fucking right wing one.

Stampy pointed at Whiff making punching actions; the pack laughing, gesturing, swigging from a bottle of spirits they weren't bothering to conceal from anyone. Whiff, head down, was concentrating on his fretboard, lost in music, completely unaware of what was going on. Mark, Steve and his group of mates weren't, though, they were steadily eyeing them up, nodding to one another knowingly.

'Christ Fuckers' was next up - even before my guitar had faded at the end of 'Everybody's Boy' and the crowd had a chance to show their appreciation - Dave hit the intro and Andy began the chant, 'Symbol of religion, a man in pain, your Jesus died, well, what a shame'. Andy's mates at the front were chanting along and when Whiff and me came in, the whole place exploded in a mass of hands and I felt that rush of adrenaline in my veins. 'Protest', came next, then 'Public Enemy', and we were going down a storm; even Stampy, Matthews and their mates had stopped trying to bait Whiff and were getting into it, leaping about. It's true, I thought, music really is the medicine that brings us all together. I moved away from our monitors during our next number 'Private War', leant out over the stage, to get a better look at the audience, and heard that the sound coming out of the PA, being thrown into the faces of the audience, wasn't the same as what we were hearing on stage. It was a lot more bass-driven, rhythmic, thumping; our normally guitar-led tracks were rumbling and shaking the foundations of the building.

"Cheers," said Andy, at the end of 'Private War' and the crowd showed their appreciation by clapping and cheering. He ran his hand through his spiked hair and continued, "OK, cheers, right, we're not doing 'SSPG' tonight, they've been disbanded, which is a bit of a pain as we'll have to write some more songs now," chortling to himself, "So this next one's dedicated to the NF, it's called 'No more genocide.'"

"Seig Hiel, Seig Hiel, Seig Hiel," came back.

Andy surveyed the audience, searching for the source, "Oh yeah, we've got some real macho men in tonight, yeah, real tough guys."

"Seig Hiel, Seig Hiel, Seig Hiel,"

I knew straight away where that was coming from, and sure enough, it was Stampy and his mates. Some of whom were chanting, their right arms skyward; others leaning over one of the monitors onto the stage, smirking and giving Whiff the wankers sign. Whiff watched them steadily, shaking his head slowly, and then a couple of half-empty cans hit him on the chest spewing lager onto his T-shirt.

Whiff rocked backwards, "Yeah, good one, fuck off!"

Andy, Dave and me moved to help our mate, then from nowhere Mark appeared behind Stampy. He grabbed him with his left hand, pulled him backwards and as he spun around, he smashed him hard in the face with his right fist, and he fell backwards, onto the speaker stack. Mark saw his chance to inflict more pain and moved in to finish him off. Clearly panicked now, Stampy looked to his mates for support. Glyn, Matthews and the rest of them moved in, thinking Mark was on his own, only to find, he wasn't.

Steve and his mates were right behind them; they flew at them, barging in, splitting the pack up, throwing volleys of punches and viciously kicking out at them. Now the odds had evened up. The Wolf Pack turned tail, ran for the doors, pushing and shouting abuse at anyone who got in their way, and then with one final shout of, "Fucking Jew loving wankers," they were gone.

An eerie silence settled over the hall; it was just the steady hum from the monitors in front of us.
Andy drew his mic up, "It looks like we've just had another genocide here tonight, and it went the right way this time!" He said, cutting through the silence.

A cheer rose up from the centre of the crowd, a ripple of applause turned into a torrent, and the hall came back to life again. On the other side of the stage, Whiff leant forward, shook hands with Mark, Steve and the other skinheads, thanking them, making actions like he was going to buy them all a drink later.

"OK, come on now, there'll be plenty of time for snogging later," Andy smirked.

I winced and shouted, "No More Genocide!"

Whiff's bass thumped out the intro and when Dave and me came in two bars later, people bounced, pushed, po-goed, and chucked their drinks high into the air. It was like, all the tension, all the aggro that we had witnessed, had made them even more determined to enjoy themselves tonight. It felt like the whole roof was going to lift off at any moment in the maelstrom, as once again our sound smashed into them, doing the damage, making them move. I watched beaming, as Andy jumped down off the stage, passing the mic around into the crowd. A crowd that only a few moments ago had

19

contained N.F. scum, and they screamed, "No more genocide!" back to us on the chorus. It really felt like, that together, tonight, we had all made a difference, with our music and our message being the catalyst.

'Suffer Little Children' was up next, and when Andy announced it, someone in the audience shouted back, "Is that dedicated to those wankers who ran off?"

Andy creased up laughing, "Those little children are suffering now."

Mark grinned back at us from the bar, where he and his mates were refueling.

"Stampy got stamped!" Shouted a laughing Mark, raising his fresh glass aloft.

I couldn't believe what I was seeing, thinking, this is turning out to be a better night than Bowes; this next track is going to finish them off completely. I waited for it to begin. It didn't, then I remembered it was me that starts this track, so chuckling to myself, I began the scraping intro, and on the second bar, when we all came in. It was lift off again, as the ominous P.A. system sent our shockwaves out into the hall.

Whiff gave his bass a proper hammering. Dave pounded the drums, and I laid down the glorious bar E's onto the frets, while Andy sang, "Suffer little children to come unto me; death and pestilence is there for all to see. Babies, the victims, on their christening day, we're all born in guilt, now it's time to pay…"

Once again, the mic went back around the audience. Andy's mates knew this one; they screamed, shouted and sang 'suffer little children' back at us, with everything they had, and we in turn fed off that, playing even harder. Next in the set was the blistering 'Auschwitz 84' and just like the first time we played live in our set, at Bowes Lyon House, when Whiff came to his solo bars after the second chorus, a girl in the crowd began screaming widely like she was watching the Beatles. I smiled to myself, thinking Whiffy Barmy Army, glanced back at a smiling Dave, who'd seen it too, and when he came back in with the beat, instead of hitting the snare drum, he playfully hit his head a couple of times on the downbeat, cackling manically at me. One minute and thirty-five seconds later 'Auschwitz 84' was done. Whiff, then began his grinding build-up intro to 'Horrors of Belsen', and as we all came in. A chill came over the hall and the crowd rocked slowly backwards, forwards, side to side, watching us intently and listening. It felt all the more poignant, after what had just happened with the NF skinheads as we sang, "Horrors of Belsen, never again, don't let six million Jews die in vain." A real connection had been made.

I felt knackered when Andy signed off with, "Cheers Mum, this is our last track, it's called V1 Bomb," through the fading applause at the end 'Horror of Belsen'.

Dave lashed into the snare drum, teeth gritted, arms almost invisible. If he can do it one more time, I thought, then so can I, and as we all came in at the end of his full kit roll it looked like the crowd had the same idea too. In front of us, the hall was a mass of energy and excitement. People jumped, people shouted, people fell, people at the front grabbed furiously for Andy's mic, so they could shout out 'V1 bomb' back to us on the choruses. On the last chorus, Andy abandoned the stage, dived into the crowd on top of his mates, and we all descended into chaos. I held my guitar high up above my head, ripping at the strings, pushing myself up against my amp, forcing the feedback to come. Whiff was off on the other side of the stage, spinning around in circles, thrashing at his bass strings, grinning like a man possessed. Dave, behind us, had found even more energy from somewhere and was doing one full kit roll after another. Andy leapt back on stage, stood imperious, arms folded, watching the crowd knowingly, nodding his head, and then with one final wail of feedback, our chaotic discord faded, and I began to hear the crowd clapping and cheering. It would have been great to have done an encore or two. The crowd certainly wanted it, but a determined shake of the head from Worzel Gummidge put an end to that idea. So, we left the stage, collapsing into the beaten-up sofas and chairs in the backstage area.

Andy, Dave, Whiff and me, sat back, sinking into our seats, relaxing, talking about the gig; how good the venue was, the crowd's reaction to us, and of course the running of the NF skinhead wankers. It had been good to see, especially for me, after the incident on the bus, where my death certificate had been signed. It looked like it had been rescinded now. Punks not dead, and nor is this Punk, I thought, grinning to myself, they've been taught a lesson, a lesson they'll never forget; that's the end of them.

Mark and Steve soon joined us, kindly offering to help us ferry our gear back to Dave's van, so with a couple of extra pairs of hands at our disposal we quickly packed our gear away safely and retired to the packed-out student union bar to quench our thirst. I sat my aching body down on a bar stool next to Dave, who had already made himself comfortable, and was trying to attract the Beki Bondage lookalike, behind the bar, so he could quench his enormous thirst.

"Cheers for all your help, lads." I said, leaning forward, massaging one of my solid calves.

Mark looked at his mates, at their empty pint glasses, and then back at me expectantly. I laughed, "Jesus, it would have been cheaper to have hired security," and they all grinned back.

I sighed, took a tenner, smoothed it flat on the bar, ordered six pints of lager, a couple of snakebites for Dave and me. As I waited for our refreshment to arrive, Dave nudged me, turning my attention to Whiff and Andy, who were in conference near the exit door.

"Uh- oh Chongo," said Dave, snatching his pint off the bar.

I cracked up laughing, "Oh what, don't worry about it, Dave, they'll be fine, they're always taking the piss out of each other."

Dave took a sip. "Who'd you reckon would win in a punch-up between those two? I know Whiff's big, but Andy's a boxer; my money's on Andy," he said, studying them.

"Nah, no way man, Whiff would gas him with his big stinky feet," I said, handing over my last tenner and watching it disappear in the cash register.

"Er Skin," said Dave, nudging me again, "Look…"

"What's up?" I said, turning.

Whiff threw his hands up, abruptly turned, and pounded off towards the toilets, while Andy stood gawking, watching his broad retreating frame.

"ANDY" I shouted, "Come and have a drink, mate?"

Andy shook his head, exaggeratedly pointed at his watch, then waving happily to both of us, he walked out of the venue, with a couple of his mates following close behind.

Dave shot me a look, "I wonder what that was about?"

Steve laughed, from down the bar, "You are going to split up, aren't you?"

"Bollocks… Piss off Steve, of course we're not," I said, watching Whiff coming over, grinning.

Whiff sat down hard on a bar stool. His face fell, "Oi, where's mine then?" He asked.

"Sorry mate, I can't, I just bought a round."

"Oh what, you didn't get me one, you tight git," he playfully, protested.

I smirked maliciously, "I thought you were OK mate… You've already had a couple of cans tonight."

"What?" Whiff asked.

"Courtesy of Stampy and his mates."

He laughed, "I didn't get to drink those, did I?"

"You could have sucked on your T-shirt," Dave reasoned.

Whiff smiled, shook his head, looked at everyone's full glasses, and said, "OK, I'll get this round in then, you can get the next one," ordering one pint for himself.

I snorted, "Yeah, good one. What was that with Andy, then?" I asked, getting to it.

Whiff shook his head dismissively, "You don't want to know, mate," he said, watching his pint glass filling up under the silver taps.

I countered, "Yes, I do want to know, mate," sharply.

"OK, I said he should tone it down a bit when there are other people about."

I nodded in agreement, "Yeah, that's right…What did he say…? And YES, Whiff, I do want to know."

Whiff grabbed his foaming snakebite, "Are you sure?" He asked, looking doubtful.

"Fucking hell, Whiff!"

"OK, I did warn you… He said, 'What's up? Can't you take it, Whiffy?"

I slapped my forehead, thinking, that's well out of order.

Dave said, "What's up? What happened?"

I was just about to say, 'you don't want to know' and stopped myself. It was too late, though. Whiff had already seen it, opened his arms like he told me so.

"OK Whiff, I get it, look, whatever it is, you two need to talk it through, sort it out. If you can't take the piss out of each other for a laugh, then you should both rein it in. Do it for the sake of the band mate, if nothing else. We're in good position at the moment… We can't let some petty bullshit fuck it up."

Dave placed his empty pint glass down, "Yeah, well said, Skin, it's supposed to be a laugh, isn't it?"

"I wouldn't be doing it if it wasn't, that's for sure, but we've got something to say too, and to get our message across, we need people to know that we're OK. OK as people; if we come out with embarrassing stuff…"

"And that's exactly what I'm talking about it," Whiff cut in.

"Whiff, listen man, you two have got to sit down and talk, sort it out, there's no other way," I insisted, staring deep into him. "Is there?" I said, quietly, "Come on man."

"OK Skin, look, I'll try again," Whiff agreed.

I thought 'again' fucking hell; how long has this been going on for? They were a bit niggly at Bowes, but surely, that was just another bout of nerves before the gig.

Mark who had been tuning in, listening to all of this, tutted exaggeratedly, "I never thought it could be so complicated being in a band. Buy an instrument, learn a few chords, write songs, play a gig, fuck a groupie, drink beer, fucking hell, it couldn't be simpler!"

"Yeah, well, that's what I thought, up until about an hour ago, Mark," I said, rolling my eyes.

"You don't fancy joining us, do you, Mark?" Whiff asked, messing around.

Mark looked at me, "No, I don't think so… I would have done, if you'd have sounded like the Cockney Rejects like someone had told me you did," his voice full of amusement.

I cracked up, "Oh well, it's all chaos though, isn't it, eh?"

Mark smiled, "Yeah, I'll drink to that!"

"To the chaos!" He shouted, raising up his glass.

"And wherever it takes us!" Shouted Whiff, standing up.

"To the chaos and wherever it takes us!!!" The bar responded glasses high, and we all drank deeply, nodding, appreciating the taste of the amber liquid, appreciating the moment, appreciating life.

Chapter Two

Pernod and Black and a Dry Slap

A few weeks after the Ware college gig, a fresh Giro arrived in the post. I cashed it, put it together with my earnings from a couple of gardening stints at Mrs. Gruber's house, and I was ready for a night in the pub. Dave, and me, hadn't been in The Anchor for a while. Dave had been finding that drinking every night had started to affect his performance playing for Thundridge FC and I had been skint, but with me being flush, and Steph out with her mates, we decided it had been way too long.

Inside the pub, we found it to be as it always was, on a Friday night; warm, welcoming, and packed out with villagers looking to forget their boring week's work and get the weekend started. 'You only live once, after all' or so Dicky Page, the oldest customer in the pub at 72, had told us on many occasions. Dicky or 'The nowhere near six-million-dollar man' as some older regulars called him, had been under the knife, for a triple heart by-pass, two new hips, two new knees, and a liver transplant, so I wasn't sure if I believed him. In his case, it seemed more likely, that you lived maybe three or four times. One thing I did know was, there's nothing like a few snakebites on a night to make the world a better place.

Dicky waved a shaky hand in our direction as we walked in, and we reciprocated by giving him the thumbs up, judging by the empty glasses on the table in front of him it looked like once again old Dicky had a march on everyone else in the pub. Dave and me weaved our way through the throng of revellers to the solid wood bar, saying hello to everyone as we went.

Dave turned, pulled out a crisp brand-new fifty-pound note, and waved it extravagantly in my face, "Whey, hey, I'll get them in."

"Bloody hell, Dave, AD must be paying well these days."

"Yeah, the company's doing well, we're always busy, got a lot on at the moment, if you wanted a couple of days, you could…" he said, trailing off, seeing the look on my face, "What's up with you?"

In one of the snugs, sitting with Lee and Glyn playing cards, was Ronnie the whispering grass, and my thirst for a drink was replaced by a thirst for revenge.

"Wanker, fucking wanker."

I shouldered passed Dave, and his crisp fifty, went straight up to him, smashed my hand onto the back of his head, and slammed his cheek down onto the table, putting my body weight on.

"You stupid little cunt, you fucking cunt… The old bill came round your house and said 'we know what you did, tell us about it' and you told them everything… You fucking grassed everyone up."

"I couldn't help it; they knew everything," he cried, tears welling up in his eyes.

"Bollocks, you fucking prick," I said, putting more weight on.

Dave came up behind me, hands on my shoulders, pulling me back, "Jesus Christ, Skinner, leave it out."

"You know the shit we've been through? All because of you, you fucking wanker!" I said, ignoring Dave, cuffing the back of the grass' head.

"Skin, for fuck's sake," Dave said, looking over his shoulder, to see if anyone else was watching. "It's not worth it," he told me.

"Oh, come on, Dave, you know the shit we've been through!" I said, easing off a bit.

Dave sighed. "I know, but this won't change anything, and we sort of got away with it… In the end… You know what the police are like, twisting the truth… Mr. T.U.R.D. here, just couldn't take it," he said, palms up.

One more push down, then I eased off, let go of him, and slowly moved back, dossing him steadily; hoping he would give me a reason. Nothing could have been further from his mind, though, he wasn't interested, just kept his head down, hoping it would be all over soon; I saw he was crying. I couldn't believe it, then I remembered Ronnie used to be called The Onion, when he was a little kid, he cried so much. Sitting in front of me now, it looked like The Onion had returned, returned in buckets.

Dave patted me on the shoulder. I sniffed, turned. He smiled, he nodded. Yeah, maybe you're right, mate, I thought, those slimy bastards will try anything; from what Danny had told me, he's been in hiding since the booze blag, shitting himself. He hasn't been out for weeks; maybe he's suffered enough already. OK, I've made my point; it's Friday night, time for a laugh, time for a couple of pints; time to let it go now.

"Ronnie, was it Cannon who came around?" I asked, my voice softening.

He whispered, "Yes," barely audibly, through the streams.

"Ah come on mate," I sighed, "You're alright. That fucking wanker, Cannon, he was loving every minute of it, wasn't he?"

Ronnie slowly raised his head, saw me half-smiling down on him.

"Yes, he was, he was a bastard," he said, grizzling, wiping at his eyes.

"What was it your sister Jennifer said? Can, can, oink, oink."

Ronnie slowly sat up, laughed way too loudly, relieved that it was over; everything was back to normal.

I patted him on the shoulder, gave him a spirited shove, "OK, go on then, get them in, and don't talk to any policemen on the way, alright?"

Ronnie brayed loudly, obligingly, got up, and headed for the bar.

"And Dave too, you owe one… In fact, you owe him a few, mate," I told his retreating frame.

Dave grinned at me. I shook my head, and we sat down to wait for some reparations.

I sighed, "Sorry about that mate, but since he grassed, it's been fucking bad news up at my place."

"Well, like I said, smashing the little twats face in won't help, even though, he probably deserves it."

"One good thing, at least your fifty will stay intact for a few more rounds," I reasoned.

Ronnie bought a round and I must say, the taste of atonement was good. It refreshed. It loosened us up, and as the night went on, and while he kept the drinks coming, Dave and me sat back talking about the band. The decent crowd at the college, the skinheads, and of course the bust up between Andy and Whiff. Dave told me it wouldn't be a problem; he reckoned, they spent most of their time taking the piss out of each other anyway, so one of them was bound to go too far sometime. I thought it was possible, but something told me, that it was different this time. A red line had been crossed. It was public, out in the open for all to see; there was pride at stake. A possible loss of face. It could be an issue, a big issue. I was worried about it, so I told Dave that I would give them both a bell, to see what was what, before our coming practice, next Saturday week, just to make sure, and he told me to stop worrying so much.

"Oh what, well, well, look," I said, seeing Diane and Cerys entering the pub, over Dave's shoulder.

Dave subtly took a peek, grinned, picked up his pint, and sunk it.

"I've got a good feeling about tonight," I said, grinning.

Dave thumped his pint glass back onto the table. "Yeah, me too," he said, looking at Ronnie, who sighed, and scurried off to the bar.

"And she definitely said she was bored with Pepe le Pew?"

Dave nodded, beckoning the girls over, and once Ronnie had brought him his pint, a relieved, and now skint, Ronnie, disappeared with Lee and Glyn to play darts, leaving us to get comfortable with the girls.

I was right about Cerys' hair, not only had she grown it long, she'd also grown out the dye, and it was now back to its original lush dark chestnut brown colour. She still looked Punk, though, in her capped-sleeved Siouxsie t-shirt, tight black skirt, and high boots. In fact, she looked amazing. It's time to put things right, I thought, do what I should have done years ago; make her mine.

"I like your hair, it suits you," I said, pairing off with her, straight away.

She smiled, "Oh, thanks, yeah. I fancied a change," running a manicured hand through it.

"I saw you at the Ware college gig, I thought there was something different about you… You looked like you were enjoying yourself; you were really going for it."

"Yeah, it was great, the band's really coming on now, isn't it?"

"Cheers, thank you, we must be improving. I remember when someone said, watching Virus V1 live was a hard watch sometimes."

Cerys smiled self-consciously, "Oh yeah, I did say that, didn't I? Ooops, well, to be fair it was only your first gig, anyway, you're a lot better now, I like V1 Bomb."

I smiled, "Yeah? That's the band's favourite, too." I took a quick swig of the last of Ronnie's rounds and continued, "Did you like our stage act?"

Cerys cracked a knowing smile, "Hmm… What the battling skinheads?"

I cackled back at her knowledge of my warped sense of humour, "Yeah, the battling skinheads," and we both laughed, gazing at each.

"I'm… Look, Cerys, about the practice at the pavilion… I don't… " I floundered, trying to find the words to apologise for flashing my knob at her, when I was drunk on whiskey.

"Hey everyone, it's time for drinks, what about drinks? Come on, we'll get them in," Diane said, taking Cerys lightly by the arm, leading her to the bar, and the moment was gone, for now, anyway, I thought.

A few minutes later, they came back struggling through the heaving pub with a couple of snakebites and two Pernod and Blacks. They set them down, and we got stuck in.

Cerys took a sip, "Aaaahh, that's nice," and placed it back on the table. I saw it had left her full red lips even redder, even fuller, if possible, as the blackcurrant in the Pernod left its sweet trace upon them.

"I like that stuff, sometimes, Hayley drinks it," Dave said, disturbing me from my carnal thoughts, and he grabbed Diane's glass, took a sip for himself, "Ah, that's lovely, that is, it tastes like aniseed."

"It gets you drunk, too, I love iiiiittt," chimed Diane, chortling, good naturedly, "Now, if you don't mind darling… Please, can I have my drink back?"

She smiled broadly, took a decent slug for herself, and placed it back onto the table, "David, so, how's AD? I've seen your signs up all over the village, it looks amazing."

Dave smiled. "Yeah, it's going OK, thanks," he replied, modestly.

"You'll be young businessman of the year, next," Diane trilled, excitedly.

"Ha… It's nothing like that," Dave dismissed.

"Where are you working next?"

"We're doing an extension at Mrs. Gruber's next week, you do a bit in her garden, don't you, Skin?"

I laughed, "I do… I wouldn't have used those exact words, though, but yeah," and grimaced.

Diane cackled lecherously, her big eyes darting around the table.

Dave chuckled. "Oh yeah, the old lady garden," he said, eyeing her back.

"She's alright, she is, Mrs. Gruber; she wants to talk most of the time, I think she's a bit lonely to be honest… I spend more time leaning on shovels, than actually using them to dig," I explained.

35

Dave nodded, picking up his pint, "Poor old dear, her husband died last year."

"Oh, that's sad, how old was he?" Cerys asked.

"I'm not sure, late sixties, I think, he left her a load of money, or so I heard," Dave raised his eyebrows.

"Oh, now I get it, that makes sense, we were talking yesterday…" I started.

Dave interjected, "While you were leaning on a shovel?"

I sniggered, sloshing my drink around in its glass, "Yeah, well, you won't believe this, but she only wanted to bequeath me some money in her will… I don't even know her."

"Oooh Skinner," Diane grinned, "Are you sure you're only talking to her?"

"Maybe she wants to lean on your tool?" She said, getting into her stride. "Maybe she wants to put your tool, in her lady garden," she finished, shrieking with laughter.

Dave screwed up his face, "Urrrrgh, have you seen her? That would be necrophilia."

I snorted, peeped at Diane, a malicious smile on my face. "You know, I used to be into necrophilia, but I had to give it up… Some rotten cunt split on me," I said, looking for the level, and finding it, Diane absolutely fell about laughing.

Cerys grimaced, "Oh ha, ha… Look, that's horrible, she's an old woman."

"A rich old woman," Diane corrected, "What did you say, Skinner? …About the money, that is?"

I smiled, scratched at my bristly chin, "I said, no, it's your money, I don't want it."

Diane countered, "Oh no, really? Why? You should have it, someone will. Why not you?"

I shook my head, looked down, feeling like I shouldn't have said anything, "Nah it's her money, I've got more than I need, it's not my thing anyway… Maybe she's got another relative, Diane?"

Diane didn't answer, so wondering what had happened, I looked up again, seeing she was now bolt upright in her chair, pushing out her ample boobs, eyes wide, looking over my head towards the bar.

"Oh, for god's sake, Diane, who's looking at you now?" Cerys sighed.

I thought, oh no, here she goes again, and leant into Dave, whispered, "I don't know why she doesn't just get up on the table, open her legs, and pull her piss flaps apart for them," crudely.

Dave clasped his hands together, rocked backwards and forward in fits of laughter, and he wasn't the only one. Cerys choked on her drink behind me, and so I spun around in my seat.

Cerys shook her head. "Oh my, you are a bad man, Skinner," she proclaimed, through tears of laughter.

I nodded happily, "Yeah, funny though."

She examined me for a moment, "Hmm… Sometimes," not convinced.

"Don, hello Don," Diane said, brightly.

I slowly looked around, fearing the worst; saw Don Ruddock, Craig's old man, drunk, bleary-eyed, swaying in front of our snug, and my bravado drained away like piss down a drainpipe. I had seen 'The Don' sitting at the far end of the bar with his son, Don Junior, when we had first come in, and hoped that I wouldn't have any contact with them. Once The Two Dons, or The Two Donnies, as some of the braver villagers called them, got drunk, there would always be a punch-up: a dry slap at the very least.

Don, smirking at his newly found audience, pointed at the empty seat to the left of Diane, and stated aggressively, "Is this chair taken then?" Even before Diane had said, "No, no, help yourself, Don." He thumped his heavy frame down into the seat and let out a huge sigh.

Don's head swivelled around, scrutinising us all individually, then his eyes settled on Diane's massive, big tits, and stayed there, "Cor, you're a decent looking bird ain't ya?"

Diane threw her head back, laughing, loving the attention, engorged by the flattery, "Oh, thank you, Don, that's sweet of you… How are you today?"

"I couldn't be happier, my love… Sitting next to you," he slurred, his red eyes focusing, then re-focusing, trying to remove her yellow blouse, trying to get a glimpse of her charms.

It was all to no avail though, his eyes could hardly see the blouse, let alone the treasure that lay within, so his head swivelled machine-like, to my snakebite. It was my turn now.

"Urgh, what's that, then? That looks disgusting, what's in that then?"

"It's a snakebite, isn't it." I replied, bluntly.

His eyes blinked furiously as he tried to focus again, "Oh, is it now?" He said, condescendingly.

Don looked around at the others like he was talking to some kind of idiot, and then back at me, raising his head in anticipation, waiting for an answer.

I sighed. "It's made with cider and lager… If you don't drink it quickly, it goes solid, and you have to eat it with a dessert spoon," I said, finally.

Don cracked up laughing, then quickly reeling it in, his smile vanished, "You're a Punk Rocker, aren't you? You're a PunK!" With the accent on the 'K' he said, to everyone, sniggering to himself.

"I'm into Punk Rock, yeah," I replied casually, not rising to it.

"Oh yeah, and you arc Skinner, aren't you?" He accused me, clicking his fingers a couple of times, like he was trying to summon up a lost memory.

"Yeah," I admitted.

He leant forward, viewing me through his bloodshot eyes. I could almost see the cogs in his brain turning over, and I thought, please don't remember the fight I had with Craig up at the gravel pit.

Don put his index finger up, "Yeah, Skinner," he said, like that was the answer he had been searching for, and satisfied, once again, that he was boss, and he knew all there was to know. He nodded and thankfully his head swivelled away from me, and he began to take Dave in.

"Why are your lips red? Are you wearing lipstick?" He asked, through narrow red eyes.

Dave spat, "No."

Don leant forward to get a better look, his massive arms joining his expansive beer gut rubbing on the table. He declared, "You are, you're wearing lipstick. Why you wearing lipstick?"

"Oh, for god's sake, he's not wearing lipstick. It's Pernod and Black, it's from the blackcurrant," said Cerys witheringly, now clearly fed up by this unwanted intrusion.

Don's head swivelled aggressively to Cerys, "Excuse me, I wasn't talking to you."

Cerys held his stare for a moment. He shrugged his shoulders at her, clearly enjoying himself now, then he swivelled back to Dave, "What are you, a poofter or something?" Smirking at the whole table, like he'd found what he was looking for. Oh no, I thought, here he goes again; it must be our turn tonight.

Dave looked at me, reading my mind. "A poofter! No, it's off the drink, it's the blackcurrant in the drink… Oh dear, oh dear, oh dear," rolling his eyes, trying to laugh it off.

To no avail, though. The Don was on a roll now, "It's what poofs wear, are you queer?"

Dave stopped laughing, looked him dead in the eye, and snapped, "No… No, I'm not. Donald."

Don took him again for a while; a long while, considering his options. He really was enjoying himself now, he wanted a few more minutes of this before he showed these little twerps what was what.

Cerys stood up, pointed at the drunk. "Why don't you piss off, we're having a nice time here, and you want to ruin it, you're just a bully, nobody wants you here… Piss off!" She spat.

Don held his hands up, theatrically, surrendering to the cheeky bint. "Whoa, calm down, I'm only having a laugh, love," he smirked, at the cheeky mare. He would never hit a tart, even a filthy one; he was a gentleman, after all.

"I'm not your love… Just get lost, you arsehole," Cerys told him, with fire in her eyes.

"OK, OK, oooh, don't get your knickers in a twist, LOVE… I know when I'm not wanted, I need a slash anyway," he shrugged and lifted his big frame unsteadily back up onto its feet. "I'll see you later… Skinner!!!" He hissed, butting his head forcefully in my direction.

"Ooooh bye, bye then ladies," his parting shot.

41

Don weaved his way through the regulars, leaning on some of them to keep himself upright, back towards the end of the bar to where Don Junior was sitting.

I thought, a butterfly could knock you down right now, you bastard, but The Don wasn't the problem. It was his twenty-five-year-old son, Don Junior, the ex-county boxing champion, who was the problem. I had seen him in action before in this very pub, and he was absolutely lethal. A hostile punching machine that felt nothing, dished out beatings for nothing, anything, just for the fun of it. If that silly old twat tells him we hassled him, we are dead. So, I let out a long sigh of relief, as I watched him stagger past Don Junior, using the wall for balance, and sway onwards, towards the toilets, and out of harm's way; for now.

"Bloody hell Cerys, you were brave there, I never knew you had it in you," I said.

"No not really," she laughed, "He would never hit a woman, would he, Diane?"

"No, he certainly wouldn't, his wife Maureen's, South African, and she's a lot tougher than he is. She would turf him out," said Diane, grinning at the very thought of it.

A couple of drinks later, our unwelcome visitor forgotten, I was chatting with Cerys again. I told her about my up-and-coming driving lessons and asked her if she was interested in learning.

She rolled her eyes, "I've had two tests so far, Skinner, the first one I took was after six lessons, I was nowhere near ready. I failed that one, and the second one, the buffoon of a driving instructor, showed up on the day of the test in a different car. I didn't know what I was doing, so I failed that one too."

"What? I said incredulously, "He showed up in a different car? I've heard it all now, it's hard enough driving in a car you're familiar with."

She nodded in agreement, and then drained half her glass, like she was trying to drown the memory.

I smiled mischievously, "I'll say this, though, I'd rather have a Pernod and Black with old man Ruddock than have another driving lesson with my old man, believe me, anything is better than that!"

Cerys snickered, put her glass down, "What happened with your dad then?" She asked, sitting back making herself comfortable, knowing it was going to be a long story.

I recounted the whole horrible episode, from the early lecturing to the so-called 'almost car crash' and as I ended the saga, the pub door swung open and in walked Del Walden, a big scaffolder, and his shapely wife Joyce, a legal secretary, who had just moved out from Plaistow in London to live in the village.

Del gave me a big smile, and after handing Joyce a thick wad of cash to go to the bar with, he coolly strolled over to our snug, "You alright Mick? You OK for drinks? And your mates, of course."

I looked around at the others, saw we were OK, "Cheers Del, I think we're alright at the moment."

Del smiled, nodding happily, "OK, well, let me know, I'll be at the bar," he said, and went to go, and then as an afterthought, "Oh yeah, what's worse than sweat on Olivia Newton-John?"

I smirked, "I don't know, Del, what is worse than sweat on Olivia Newton-John?"

He opened his hands like it was simple, "Cum on Eileen," and our table exploded into laughter.

Del grinned pleased with our reaction, and walked over to Joyce, who had got their drinks in, and had settled in at the far end of the bar and was now chatting quite amicably with The Two Dons.

"Dave, have you seen that? He's not on his own, it's The Two fucking Donnies."

Dave nodded sourly, "I know, I saw them… It's goodnight from me, and it's goodnight from him, BAM, lights out."

I cracked up laughing, saw that maybe, the drinks were getting a bit low after all, and just to confirm it, Diane and Dave gave me a nod. It was time to get them in again. So, with us all being in debt to Cerys for getting rid of The Don, I volunteered to get them; taking a handful of the empties with me, I made my way to the bar. It was busy, really busy. Stewart was rushing from customer to customer, and my waving five-pound note was being ignored totally. I heard a shout, glanced over the scrum, to see Del, behind him. The Two Dons were looking over his shoulder at me, like I was a punch bag with a poof's face on.

"Oi, Mick!" He said, raising his voice over the hubbub.

"Mick!!!!" He repeated, louder this time.

"OI MICK!" He shouted.

"Oh, alright Del?" I said, pretending to have just noticed him.

Del grinned from ear to ear, beckoning me over, so head down, I trudged over to meet my fate.

Del chided, "I thought I told you, I was getting them in."

"Cheers Del, that's really nice of you mate, cheers."

Don Junior looked me up and down, sizing me up. I turned away, pretending to look for the overworked Stewart, so he carried on with his routine, a routine everyone in the village was all too familiar with.

"Where was I now? Oh yeah, I'm not a troublemaker, I'm not into violence, I can look after myself though and if anyone messes with me, or my family I'll smack them one, smack them one good, and I know how to hurt people, hurt people bad," said Don Junior to Del, who grinned back.

Don Senior nodded proudly, Don Junior laughed to himself, "If I saw a Paki, or a Sooty, I'd smack them anyway, even if they didn't say anything, I don't like Paki's or Sootys."

Don senior conceded, "Who does?" Cracking up at his own joke.

Del smiled at them both indulgently, "I'm not a troublemaker either, I can fight, look after myself, in London you have to, you learn quick, or you're in trouble, aren't you?"

Don Junior, sensing resistance, moved in closer on Del. "I don't like Londoners," he stated.

Don Senior grinned, eyeing Del provocatively, watching for any hint of a reaction, waiting for the scrap to begin. He was pissed, but he'd back his boy up if need be.

Del picked up his drink, taking it all in his stride with an amused look on his face.

"Huh, all Londoners think they're tough, don't they? But they're not, they'll all get fucking laid out if they want to start… That's a promise. Not that I'm starting anything, I'm not into fighting," said Don Junior, his eyes boring into Del, getting ready, watching every twitch, waiting to block any pre-emptive strikes.

Del was finding all of this hilarious, cracking up laughing, good-humouredly.

Oh no, don't laugh Del, I thought… Please don't laugh, Del, nervously, sweeping my hand back through my peroxide spikes.

"Yeah, I know mate, there are some right wankers in London, I've had a few of them myself," said Del, casually picking up his pint.

He took a huge draft, enjoying it, then placed the half empty glass back on the bar, wiped the froth from his mouth, and gave Joyce a pleasant smile as the larger hit the mark.

Don was confused, either the bloke was thick, or he was fucking winding him up. One way or the other he was going to find out which, so the wind-up intensified. He smirked, "I'm a Londoner myself, so I know how to fight Londoners. I could do any of them, they'll all get fucking upped."

Don stood up menacingly, fists balled, ready to ruck, scrutinising the still smiling Del, then, seeing no come back, he spat belligerently, "Huh… I'm going for a piss."

"Yeah, me too, come on, let's go water the old horse, make room for another pint or three," said Don Senior, chuckling to himself, getting up unsteadily.

I watched them go; as soon as they were out of earshot, I leant into Del, "Del… Don't, mate."

He looked confused for a moment, and then, understanding what I was going on about, he laughed loudly and said, "I'll be alright, Mick."

I shook my head, "No seriously, I wouldn't."

Joyce piped up, "I wouldn't worry about him Michael, he can handle himself, can't you Del?"

"I do alright," Del replied modestly.

"Seriously don't, he's a county championship boxer," I warned.

Joyce countered, "Oh yeah… And Del's a street fighter," resolutely.

Del smiled at his wife's support, put a calming hand on her knee, "It's fine, you worry too much Mick, now what do you want to drink, how many are there of you?"

I thought, OK, I hope you're right mate.

"Nine," I replied, putting my worries aside with a mischievous grin on my face.

Del peered at me for a moment, "Bollocks," he said, and we both cracked up laughing.

"Nah it's only four mate, a pint of lager, a snakebite, and two Pernod and Black's."

Del flourished a bulging wallet from his back pocket, "No problem, you can carry them all over though, I'm not going anywhere. I'm happy standing right here."

I nodded, "OK, cheers, that sounds fair, Del, I'll get you two, one later."

Joyce smiled graciously, "Well, that's very kind of you Michael."

Once a totally stressed-out Stewart had served us, I balanced the wavering drinks precariously in my arms, and thanked Del again, who gave me a pitying look. He didn't want to see me struggling, or, worse still, spill any of the precious liquid; so, he grabbed a tray from behind the bar, and we carefully switched the sloshing drinks over, just in time for me to see The Two Dons returning.

"Cheers Del thanks, I'll see you later mate," I told him.

Del grinned and gave me the thumbs up, and I dodged my way back to our snug, bringing forth a cheer from my mates, as I placed the brimming tray onto our table.

One round followed another, and by the time the bell rang for
chucking out time, the four of us had lost track of how many we had
had. One thing I did know was, I didn't want to say goodbye to
Cerys just yet; I had plenty more I wanted to say to her, so I asked
her if I could walk her home.

Cerys smiled broadly, threw her chestnut brown locks back, "Yes,
I'd like that," she told me, and then without any hesitation, she stood
up and picked up her leather jacket from off the back of her chair.

Dave and Diane, were still chatting away, laughing, fooling about,
enjoying the effects of the alcohol; they weren't going anywhere, not
until Stewart got shirty with them anyway. So, Cerys and me told
them, we'd see them later, and made our way to the door. I opened
it, felt the cold bite of the air outside. Then we turned, waved a big
goodbye to our new friends Del and Joyce, who waved back to us,
with lopsided drunken smiles on their faces. Behind them, just
visible, The Two Dons, dossed us out sourly, like they were
observing two cockroaches fighting over a dead dung beetle in a
field of dog turds. I shut the door on them, and their random,
unwarranted hatred, and we walked up the pub's steps onto the main
road.

In the orange glow of the street lights, we found it chilly, chilly away
from the warmth of the pub's hearth, and the throng of bodies. On
the pavement beneath us, an early trace of frost was beginning to
cast intricate glinting patterns onto its dark surface. Icy fresh air
surrounded us, turning our exhaled breath into small cloud-like
plumes, that vanished almost immediately into the orange glow from
above. Cerys zipped up her jacket to keep the cold at bay, and pulled
me closer to her, as we walked unsteadily across the main road. I had
a slight feeling of Déjà Vu, crossing the A10, but this wasn't Clare,
though, this was Cerys. This was something different, something that

might be lasting; something more than a sexual urge. She was with someone else, though. I thought it was time to find out where I stood.

"I've really enjoyed tonight, well, most of it, anyway," I said, laughing.

Cerys nodded her long, flowing locks, "It's been lovely catching up."

I nodded back, playfully, and blew out a huge plume of iced breath. Inflated by the alcohol circulating within me, I ventured, "Cerys? What's happening with you and Mark? Are you still together?"

"Hmm… I wonder who's been talking?" She replied, keeping her eyes straight ahead. Not waiting for my answer, which wasn't forth coming anyway, she continued, "Yeah, well, sort of."

I smiled at the contradiction, said as gently as I could, "Well, either you are or you're not?"

Cerys hesitated, thinking about it for a while, then, choosing her words very carefully, she said, "I really like him, he's a really nice bloke, but we are more like friends now."

"What does that mean?" I said, pushing a bit harder.

"Well… We're not doing anything… If you know what I mean," she laughed, self-consciously.

I thought, that sounds unlikely, as the Cerys I used to know was well naughty. "No way, really? I don't believe you," I intoned, light-heartedly.

Cerys laughed, "Oi cheeky," tilting her head to one side, like she was trying to see around a problem. "No, you're right, it is weird, though," she conceded, drifting off into thought.

I nodded, hoping that she would say more, say what was on her mind, tell me she was going to finish with Mark, but I only got a thoughtful silence. I let the silence hang, thinking, if they had a problem, then it was down to them to sort it out between them. If that problem was so big, that they couldn't deal with it, then good, all the better for me, but there was no way I was going to impose myself upon her, not right now. If we were going to get together, then she would have to want me, want me enough to dump Mark. It had to be a fresh start for both of us. I wasn't going to try and do the dirty on him, be a sneaky bastard, and steam in when she's off her nut, on Pernod and Black. I had learned a lot tonight, certainly more than I had expected. It made me believe that maybe, someday, someday in the not-too-distant future, we would be together. In the meantime, instead of talking, and maybe saying the wrong things and pushing her too far, I pulled her in close, feeling her warmth. It was a beautiful night, there didn't seem to be any reason to talk, to take away from this uncomplicated beauty; in the sky above us, a galaxy of stars sparkled, like diamonds showing us the way, and arm in arm, locked together, like the lovers I dreamt we would be one day, we walked up her street in our companionable silence, taking in the heavenly lights.

One step at a time, I thought, if it's the only way that I'm going to be with her, then that's the way I'm going to take it. I've already shown her, the stupid drunken me, dropping my guitar, dropping my trousers. Now it's time to show her I can be OK, hold my booze, and be someone she could spend more time with, without her worrying about what I might do next. It won't be easy knowing that she's still with Mark, even after her disclosure, but I'm glad she told me. It showed me just how close we really were, trusting me with something like that, something so personal. It would only be a matter of time now, and I would give her that time, knowing deep down inside of me, that she would be worth the wait.

"It's been great, Cerys, let's do it again soon," I said, as we strolled up to her garden gate.

Cerys eyes twinkled back at me, in the majestic starlight, "Yes, let's, it's been really nice, Mike."

I didn't think a try for a kiss would be appropriate, so I said, "OK, see you Cerys, take care."

"Yes… See you soon, Mike, and you take care too… Really," said Cerys, smiling at this new Skinner, Skinner the gentleman.

Cerys turned on her high heels, opened her gate, and with one final wave she was gone.

Chapter Three

Sandringham Road

In the hall downstairs, the phone rang, disturbing me from my thoughts of Cerys the night before – it had been a brilliant night, despite the bullshit from The Two Donnies, and I was looking forward to seeing her again. On and on the phone rang, insistently, demanding attention; then finally Mum answered it with a cautious, 'hello'. It was Martin, my older brother. I snorted to myself; he would phone every now and again, hoping the old man or me might talk to him, but there was no chance of that. He never gave up, though, even after all the years that had passed. I knew why I had stopped talking to him. It was simple. The bloke was a bastard, a bastard, who broke hearts and minds, sometimes even bodies, in the pursuit of his happiness. As for the old man, I wasn't sure, Martin had upset him by leaving the R.A.F. before his five years were up, and he was upset about his divorce later on. I doubted whether those two events would have been enough, though; there was something else, something nastier, or the old man would never have closed him down like that. I didn't really care, not when it really got down to it, for me, big brother Martin was the past; a living nightmare that faded with every passing day, but for some reason, I found myself slipping out of bed, softly, opening my door, and creeping out onto the landing to listen in. It was completely silent, nothing, so I hesitantly started down the stairs, one by one, being careful to keep off the creaky third step, still nothing – silence. I leant forward, craning my neck, trying to see what was going on, and saw that the phone was off the hook, lying on the phone chair, taking in the dead air, then Mum appeared from the lounge, with a sad look scrawled on her face.

"I'm sorry. Pudge… No, I'm not going to, and that's that," I heard the old man say from behind her.

"Mike, oh hello, Mike, come and talk to Martin," she whispered, conspiratorially.

"No, Mum. No."

"Please, Mike… Please, he's sorry… He's changed," she almost begged.

"I don't want to, please Mum… He's changed? I doubt it."

"Mike!!!" She actually begged, her eyes welling up, her hand shaking, as she passed me the phone.

"Alright. Martin?" I said, for the first time in three years.

"Hi Mick, how are you?"

"Yeah, not bad, cheers."

"I've seen your band in the N.M.E., it's going well, isn't it?"

"Nah, that's not us, that's a different Virus, we're Virus V1."

"Oh… Right… I thought it was you… Hey, I tell you what. I'm working for a company called Church's Engineering. We do a lot of welding for the R.A.F., big company it is, big workforce…"

I thought, here he goes, I wonder where this is going, it might be a while till I find out, though, so I turned; zoned out on the fisheye mirror in the hallway. It was weird if I pulled my face to one side, the bowed mirror made it look like a sort of crescent moon version of the scream by Edvard Munch.

"We've got this massive contract over fifty million a… We've got…"

Edvard Munch. Munch!!! …I've got the Munchies; I'm fucking starving, I wonder how long he's going to take to get to the angle; Martin always had an angle, was always looking for something.

"We've been having a dispute with the managers, everyone hates the boss, Howard Church, so at our last union meeting, I put on your track, 'Church War'."

"What? How?" I enquired.

"Mum sent me a tape, I asked her for some of your music. But listen to this. When I put it on The Tannoy system on the factory floor, everyone started cheering and singing along… 'Church War, Church War'… You should have heard them Mick, brilliant, it was… And get this, when the boss Howard Church came in, even he started laughing – it was brilliant Mick, you should have seen it."

I was beginning to wonder when he was going to get to it, tell me what he was after, and sure enough.

"Brilliant, brilliant it was… So… How's Dad, Mick?" He asked.

"Yeah, he's alright," I said, guardedly; I knew the angle now.

"You couldn't have a word with him, could you? Tell him I'm sorry. I need to talk to him about something, something important it is, it could change the family!"

55

I exhaled, "Nah, I can't."

"Listen, Mick, I've changed, I'm not the same person I used to be."

"I don't know… If Mum can't persuade him, I'm not going to be able too, am I?"

"Come on Mick, I've always helped you, we've always helped each other."

I sat down, listening, thinking.

"I've always stood up for you," he said.

No, you didn't.

"I've always helped you out," he said.

No, you haven't.

"I supported you when you were getting into Punk," he said.

Yes, you did; now that much is true, then using the old divide and rule method, you told the old man that he should fight me all the way, causing a lot of unnecessary aggro, aggro, which has only just gone.

"I'm your brother Mick, we are blood, you could give it a go, I'd do it for you."

I sighed, "I can't, just leave him alone, everything's good here at the minute."

"Yeah, good for you. Cheers for that, Mick. Huh, after all I've done for you over the years, I've stuck up for you, put my neck on the line for you, time, and time again, now, you listen to me, you are…"

I placed the receiver down gently in its cradle, ending the stream of abuse that I knew was coming, and straight away, Mum popped her head out of the kitchen, smiling, happy now.

"Thanks for that Mike, he misses us so, how was he?" She chimed, cheerily.

"Yeah… Yeah. He was fine, Mum, he had to go, he was just off to work at Church's, I think, he said."

Mum frowned, "Oh… No. No, he works at British Aerospace."

I smiled to myself, thinking, no, you haven't changed, Martin, but I have. I don't listen to bullshitting fantasists anymore, and with one more lopsided look into the fisheye mirror in the hall, I went and made myself some breakfast; got back to thinking about something important, something about me and my life. Cerys and me. It may also have been a fantasy, but at least it wasn't hurting anyone; not yet, anyway. If I did get back with Cerys. It was down to Mark, she was Mark's to lose, as far as I was concerned.

Once I had got Martin out of my mind, which took less time these days, I spent the rest of the morning watching an old film with the old man - The Cruel Sea. He loved it, it was his favourite film, he told me it just about summed up his late teenage years. It was a grim spectacle, to say the least, and I began to think I was lucky to have been born at all, as he could have gone down with his ship, like so many of his friends did. In the kitchen afterwards, we sat down, had a bit of lunch together where, I managed to drag a few more old war stories out of him; he showed me the scars on his arms where he had been hit by shrapnel. It was good talking to him man to man, he was alright really, really funny sometimes, especially when he talked about what he and his mates got up to, on shore leave. I couldn't believe how much he had opened up to me, he told me things that he would never have done only a few weeks earlier. He was happy, but I still wanted to know what Martin had done to upset him, in fact, I had to know, it was now or never.

"Dad… What happened, with you and Martin?" I asked.

"That's none of your business, Mike," he said, getting up, swiftly making for the door.

"Yeah, but it is though, I've just had him on the phone, asking me to get you to talk to him."

Mum looked up from her book. "Mike!?" She admonished.

"It's alright, Mum," I said, pursuing the old man out of the room.

Into the lounge, he strode, dropped into his rocking chair, picked the paper up, pulled it up like the portcullis in a castle, his usual signal that the conversation had ended.

"Come on Dad, I've had him on the phone abusing me, what happened?"

"Oh, was he now, well, that doesn't surprise me."

"Please, Dad, you told me all that stuff about your navy days… Surely this isn't any worse… Is it?"

"Hah, it's a lot bloody worse, the bastard…"

"What? What, did he do?" I asked, frustratedly, pushing on.

He shook his head, wearily.

I sighed, "You can't just leave it like that, if I know what it is, then if he wants me to ask you, to get you to talk to him again, then I'll know why you won't… I know he's out of order, but I don't know why you think he is… Why is he a bastard? What happened?"

"Just tell me, Dad. Please."

It was my turn to beg now, I thought at some point, everyone had demeaned themselves when Martin was involved - he loved it, thrived on it; it was the food for his fragile ego.

"OK, OK, but you better not tell anyone. Not till I'm long dead."

"I won't, why would I? Even then, I can't think of any reason why I would."

"OK, sit down," he said. I sat, and he began Martin's, sorry, story.

"You know he joined the R.A.F.? Well… He was dishonourably discharged for dangerous driving; he got blind drunk and crashed his car head on into another car coming the other way. It had a young family inside; it really shook them up. He ran off to save his own yellow hide, just left them to it. Of course, the police caught him, the stupid bastard, and after spending time in R.A.F. nick, they kicked him out……"

59

I nodded; it was a familiar story. I knew most of this from Mum, and just like when Mum had recounted it, the old man was finding it difficult; his mouth spitting out the words like each and every one of them hurt him deep inside, rocking him to his core. I began to feel bad, and not just a little bit guilty. It was me that had made these festering revelations come to the surface again, and I had done it by chatting with him about his life and things that were important to him; getting him to open up; and then once he had, I had pushed ahead with my own agenda, my own angle; was I any better than Martin? I thought yes, yes, I am. Sometimes in life, when seeking out a bastard, you have to be one yourself.

"Once he left prison, no one would touch him, he found himself homeless on the streets, found a shelter run by a local charity - Help for Swindon - where Tracy, you know, his ex-wife worked. She helped him get back on his feet again, and in the process, she fell in love with him, the poor girl, and they got married as you know, then they had the little girl Nadia, my granddaughter, you remember her? Lovely little thing, pretty as a picture…" he hesitated, the colour draining from him.

I shouldn't have asked him, I thought, he was happy, and now, well, Jesus Christ. Fuck being a bastard, even if it was temporary. I don't need to know that badly. I put up a hand to stop him, tell him it was OK, forget it, but it was too late, the wound was open again, the memory bled out of him.

"…And when that bastard was supposed to be looking after Nadia, while Tracy was working at the shelter, helping people, he would leave her alone to go and visit some tart he'd picked up in a club, the poor little mite would lie in her cot for hours, wet, while he was…"

60

"OK, I understand now, dad…" I said, making sure he saw my hand, I wanted this conversation, the conversation that I had started, to end now; no wonder he didn't want to tell me, it was terrible.

"Oh no. No, no, no, that's not all of it. You asked for it, and you're going to get it… Tracy discovered what was going on, and from what she said, it had been going on for a long time, a very long time - she couldn't understand why little Nadia had nappy rash all the time. She thought she might be allergic to the nappies. She had it out with him, and he punched her, almost broke her jaw… The bastard."

"Jesus Christ Dad, really? I know he could be a bit nasty sometimes, but I didn't think he could do something like that."

The old man, drooped in his seat like an old rag doll, looking down, wrestling with it all over again, but then, something else.

"Hmmm, you did deep down Mike, he gave you nothing but trouble growing up, he laid into you, I should have seen it, but I was up to my neck in work, trying to put food on the table."

"Oh what, it was just Martin, Dad… It's what he does, it's not your fault."

"I'm sorry…"

"What……?" I said, my mind rushing.

One word, 'sorry'. A small word with huge connotations. It could mean everything; maybe, the old man was worried, worried for me, always had been, worried that I would follow in Martin's footsteps into homelessness and out onto the streets, maybe, that's what all that stuff about Hungerford Bridge was. He worried about how I would look after myself after he and Mum had gone.

"I'm sorry… Sorry for everything."

One word 'sorry'; maybe, it was never about trying to control me, or telling me what to do, just for the sake of it; maybe, he wanted to help me, always did, wanted to help me make my way in life. I just couldn't see it though, because the trouble with the old man was, he was a doer, not a teacher, and to teach is a very special talent of its own - a talent he sadly did not possess, in any shape or form.

"I'm sorry I didn't protect you… I'm sorry for what happened when Mum was in hospital…"

One word 'sorry', sometimes, it's the only thing we can have…

"Oh what. Don't worry about it Dad, it's fine," I said, smiling, trying to lighten his load.

I didn't want to see my Dad cry - Dads didn't cry, especially my one. I watched him grappling with it all - the mind-to-mind combat. The guilt, the anger, the frustration, the missed opportunities, and was relieved to see that he was still fighting it out, making his claim, doing it the right way. He'd done it before, he could do it again.

"I've known for a long time, since he was young… There is something rotten inside of Martin," he said, inhaling deeply, "I don't know what it is. Something rotten."

I've done this, I thought, over the years, he must have reasoned it away, or just buried it, forgotten it; and now I've come along in my big size tens and dug it all up again. It's time to make it right again, what can I say to put things right? I had a brainwave.

"I know what his problem is, Dad."

"Go on then…" he said, looking up sceptically.

"He's a dildo."

A moment passed, as the old man considered my summing up of his firstborn. I thought, thanks a lot brain, sarcastically; you really have surpassed yourself this time, and then thankfully he rocked back in his chair, tossed his head back, and broke out into raucous laughter.

"Yes, a dildo," he concluded, laughing, rocking forward, reaching for the zapper, drawing a line under this for once and for all.

"A white ribbed knobbler," I told him.

"I won't ask what that is, but I can imagine," He guffawed, pushing the red button on the remote, making the pixels dance and take shape on the TV.

In the corner of the room, out of the cathode ray tube, blasted the theme tune to the one o'clock news, warning me of incoming bullshit. So, I jumped up, made my way out of the room, still laughing, still not quite believing how that one turned out. 'He's a dildo' nice one brain, I thought, I never doubted you, and opened the door, almost ploughing into Mum, who had been doing a bit of eavesdropping herself.

Mum looked worried, then confused, when she heard the old man sniggering, from his rocker.

"He's a dildo," the old man repeated to himself, chuckling.

Mum gave me a questioning look. I shrugged my shoulders.

"Right, let's turn this crap off, hey Pudge," said the old man, "There's a repeat of The Last of the Summer Wine on, shall we watch it?"

"Now? …OK, yes, lets," she said, beaming at me.

I thought, well, that was simple enough, laughing to myself sarcastically. I fancy a drink after that and with Sunday lunchtime being a busy time in The Anchor, it was irresistible. I set off out the front door, passing our intact number three, to the sound of Mum and the old man splitting their sides at Compo, Foggy and Clegg, getting up to mischief in their village, and wondered how they would fare in ours.

Compo would be called a tramp by most, and the younger kids of the village would roll up dog shit in newspapers, light it, ring his doorbell and scarper off into the night, laughing their heads off.

Foggy wouldn't fare much better, every time he took a stroll out, people would shout 'knobend' in his general direction, and as for Clegg, he would fit in perfectly, he's a top bloke I concluded.

*

Once I had sorted The Last of the Summer Wine's cast out, I started getting back to reality, thought about Cerys again, wondering whether she would be in the pub right now. The truth was, I couldn't wait to see her again after last night; it felt just like the old

64

days when we had our little puppy love thing going on, back when we were kids, when things were simple, and life straight forward.

Dave was seeing Steph at her place, so instead of vaulting the wall into the churchyard, I carried on down the Pickel, onto Ermine Street and down to The Anchor for a couple of nice, easy lunchtime pints. On entering the crowded main bar, I saw Danny sitting in one of the snugs, with Phil, and a couple of the older regulars with their heads together, speaking rapidly. I nodded a hello in their direction, got myself a nice cool pint from Stewart, and then pint in hand, I went over, took a place in the snug next to Danny.

Danny asked gravely, "Skinner, have you seen Del?"

I picked up my glass to take my first swig of the afternoon, "Yeah, I saw him last night, why?"

"Oh my god, you should see him. He's a right mess, he can only see out of one eye."

"Shit, really? What happened?"

"Don beat him up last night."

"Yeah? Jesus, where is he?" I asked, forgetting my pint, placing it back on the table.

Danny pointed towards our bar, "He's through there, with Joyce."

I forgot my drink, hurriedly got up, made my way into our bar, and there he was sitting over near the dart board with Joyce, nursing a short in his hands. I couldn't believe what I was seeing, poor Del. He was almost unrecognisable; his face was so smashed up. It was just a bloated mass of reds, purples, blues, and some areas were beginning to turn black as the pulverized skin and splintered cartilage, died.

"Del? …Jesus Christ, are you alright, Del?" I asked, coming over to the bloke.

One blood-red eye scrutinised me, then he warned, "Shut up, don't say anything."

"OK," I nodded gloomily, and carried on through our bar to the toilets. I squeezed out a piss that I didn't really need, thinking I knew it, I fucking knew it, The Two fucking Donnies, what a couple of bastards; I'll give him a bit of space, I won't look at him on the way back out, the poor sod.

I couldn't help it, though. Del slowly looked up at my shocked face, "Oi Mick, are you OK for a pint?" He asked, in a conciliatory tone, pulling a painful smile onto his battered lips.

"I'm OK at the moment Del, maybe later, cheers mate."

Joyce put a protective arm around him, "OK, see you later then, Michael."

When I got back to the snug, I took a long draft of my snakebite, then thumped it back down again.

"I can't believe it, he looks like he's been hit by a fucking wrecking ball," I shook my head in dismay.

Danny grinned, "Yeah, a fucking big one…"

"You were here, weren't you, Skinner?"

"Yeah, I was earlier on, I saw them winding each other up, and then I walked Cerys home."

"And she's not happy either…" Danny stated.

A whole swarm of butterflies flew into my stomach, spreading panic.

"Why?" I asked, tentatively.

"Taddy got headbutted," Danny explained.

"You're fucking joking, aren't you? Why would anyone hit Taddy?" I asked, rubbing at my brow furiously.

Danny shook his head sadly, "I don't know… Apparently, when Don started on Del, Taddy stepped in between them and said, 'Oh come on Don, leave it mate'."

I exhaled loudly, "Jesus, the bloke must be suicidal."

Danny countered, "Well, he hangs out with Craig all the time, doesn't he? He probably sees Don when he goes around his house, probably thinks of him as a mate."

I ran a hand through my spikes, flattening them on my bonce. "I tried to warn him," I said, despondently.

Danny nodded, I shook my head, we picked up our pints, quaffing them back, both mystified that someone would actually want to hurt somebody, anyone, anything, just for fun.

Phil piped up, "I don't understand, Del's a really nice bloke."

"Yeah, he is, and that Don Ruddock is a fucking cunt," I said, loud enough to make, Ski Sunday, Coops, and Mal a' La Tete, spin around in their adjoining snug, and gawk back at me.

"Well, he is," I told, their dumb pervert faces. "Don Ruddock, what a CUNT!"

BANG, BANG, BANG, the window shook behind me, making me jump in my seat, letting everyone know I was about to shit myself; Suddenly, dumb pervert faces were smirking at me, waiting for the smell of shit, to join the smell of alcohol and mass-produced Sunday lunches coming from the kitchens.

I froze. It was no good though, I would have to look some time, so slowly turning, trying to delay the inevitable, the moment that would be the precursor for me getting a proper fucking hiding. I saw my gypsy mate Ashley, his face warped, flattened, against the window, grinning insanely back at me.

I sighed a huge sigh of relief, felt my bowels firm up again, "Hey wanker!" I said, even more happy to see the herbaceous rogue, even more than I normally was.

Ashley unstuck his face from the window, "You alright, Skinner? Danny? I'm going up The Frontline, you coming?"

"Yeah, sounds good to me, let's get out of here, I've had enough of this place," I looked at Danny, told him, "Are you coming or what?"

Danny didn't hesitate, he nodded enthusiastically.

I sank my pint quickly, smirked at the pervs, then Danny and me followed Ashley out to his transit van, where we piled into the front, onto the bench seat, and set off for London, Hackney and The Frontline.

*

Ashley Bolsworth and me met for the first time, when I was walking back from the pub one night with Danny. Ashley slowly drove past us in his bright orange transit van, dossing us out, and then pulled into a side street up the road, waiting for us. I thought this could mean trouble, as in the early days of Punk, I had taken a lot of abuse from people driving by, just wankers normally, with nothing better to do. None of them had actually stopped before, so I tensed up, steeling myself, making myself look bigger as we walked unsteadily up to this unknown person waiting in his van. I need not have worried though, as we came up to the idling van, Ashley casually got out, smiling broadly, introducing himself and started talking to us like he'd known us all of our lives, and my tension soon evaporated.

Ashley told us he had just moved to the static caravan site in High Cross, just up the A10. He also told us that his dad had to leave London as some gangsters who were something to do with the old Kray firm were after him, and they needed to lie low for a while. I stifled a laugh, thinking yes, mate, I'm sure he did. I didn't say anything, though, as he was such a funny guy to listen to, that I didn't want to break his rhythm. Once he had finished his funny flight of fancy, he asked us what we got up to in the village. I told him 'not a lot' and seeing the disappointed look on his face, I mentioned the band and our gigs.

He seemed really impressed, like he thought, that bands didn't exist outside the sphere of London and the big cities, and he said, "If you're into music, you must smoke dope then?" Grinning from ear to ear.

"Yeah, when I can get any, there's not much around here," I replied, honestly.

Danny said no, he hadn't even smoked a cigarette before and seeing Ashley's amused face, he said he used to be into glue-sniffing, like that was the same thing, which cracked Ashley up even more.

Once he had stopped cackling away at the Pritt Stick Warrior, he shook his head and asked us if we wanted to smoke some sensi right here, right now, and we didn't hesitate. Danny led us to a quiet spot, out the way, and Ashley sparked up a spliff and as it went around, he told us about The Frontline in Hackney. I thought he was bullshitting to start with, like he had been with his old man and the Kray firm, but the more he told us, the more plausible it all sounded, and the more the spliff hit its mark, the more intrigued I was by the sound of it. Yeah, I thought, this sounds amazing, man, I've got to see this for myself, so the next time we saw Ashley, he drove us up and showed us Hackney Frontline.

I had enjoyed The Frontline experience, and since the first time we had been up there, we had been back, maybe, eight or nine times. It was pretty much the same scenario every time, we would drive nearly all the way down the A10 from the village to where it begins in London; then when we came to Stoke Newington High Street, we would turn off, head down Amhurst Road, then turn right into Sandringham Road, which was The Frontline. Once we were there, we would see a couple of Rastas out in the street waiting and watching, and as soon as we gave them the nod, they would signal to the dealers who were waiting in the basements or around the back of the houses to come out. A swarm of them would appear from nowhere, and as we pulled up, they would all come running up to the van, leaning in through the windows with their little bags of sensi, insisting that we 'buy mine, buy mine'. Whoever was riding shotgun, normally me, as we couldn't trust Danny, would take a couple of bags, check the goods, and if we were happy, I would hand over the money and we'd be off in a matter of minutes. It was quick, it was simple, and the sensi, or flowering heads we were getting served up with, was of the highest quality - or straight out of the Caribbean, as Ash liked to say, through clouds of aromatic blue smoke.

Hackney Frontline sensi was light, bubbly, smooth, and sometimes it made us giggle so much that it actually hurt, we were laughing so much. On other occasions, if we were feeling knackered after a hard day of being a Punk in the satellites and just wanted to relax, we would sit back, put some music on, and let it wash over us, dissipate the stress, the negativity, and talk about quite literally anything.

On a session, normal barriers came down, boundaries were crossed, people opened up, let their thoughts be heard, no matter how daft they sounded. It made people come out of themselves in a way that I had never seen before; it never ceased to amaze me how deep some of my mates could be after a smoke, and in amongst all the laughs we had some incredibly poignant conversations - or so we thought.

In the weeks that followed our first few trips to Hackney, it started to go wrong; the dealers started to recognise us, thinking, quite rightly, that this was the one and only place we knew where to score, so they started playing their little tricks. I thought, it was a bit of a laugh to start with, and although someone trying to rip you off was never good, outwitting them was not only fun. It was always satisfying. I learned quickly that it was about a combination of two main elements; sleight of hand, which came in a variety of movements - the idea being to show you some decent sensi and then

71

switch it and serve you up with something 'off the spice rack', as we called it. Sleight of hand worked well in conjunction with the second element, which was preying on our fears that the old bill might show up at any moment and bust us all; it worked a treat for them on our last journey up. It had been going smoothly, then someone yelled, 'it's the police! It's the police!' And while we were distracted, panicking, looking for the blue flashing lights, the dealers chucked some 'spice rack' into my lap, scooped up the cash, and were gone before we realised what had happened. I felt like a right idiot sitting in Ashley's van, heading back to Thundridge, with what was essentially twenty pounds worth of oregano, with a little bit of sensi chucked in, on my lap. I was not only disappointed in myself for falling for it in the first place, at being ripped off so easily, I was getting a couple of bags for my mates too, and they had already paid me in advance. When we got back, I knew that when I laid down the bags of 'spice rack' in front of them, no matter what I told them, their faces would say it all. It would look like I was the one who was trying to rip them off and stitching up your mates wasn't what it was all about. It was supposed to be about comradery and helping each other out.

Ashley was particularly pissed off as he originally came from that area and felt like he was part of the scene and therefore, shouldn't be ripped off. On his next trip up to Hackney to meet his girlfriend Shari at a Blues he tried to scout out somebody who dealt out of Sandringham Road and after a couple of conversations with some friends of Shari's he was introduced to a guy called, Solomon. Solomon told Ashley, he could sort him out on the regular, or be 'his regular man' as he called it and gave him a house number on Sandringham Road. It couldn't be simpler; it was him that we were on our way to see tonight.

One after another, the street lights flickered on above us as dusk settled on the A10. It was as if they were guiding us, guiding us on our quest, towards Hackney Frontline and the golden fleece. Once we got up to The Frontline, Ashley found a parking space between a burnt-out Morris Minor and a dilapidated old Ford Escort with a smashed windscreen, and we slid out, keeping our eyes wide open, looking for dealers, looking for the police, looking for the SPG. Danny, Ashley and me cautiously walked up Sandringham Road, passing the three-story town houses with their steep steps leading up to their ornate front doors, still watching out for any movement in the shadows. A couple of watchers greeted us as we ventured down the road, saw us approaching, gave us the nod, and Ashley shook his head; we had a regular, and they melted away. Ashley strode on, then ducked through a bush and keeping close behind, we followed him down a steep flight of steps leading to a basement door, with a huge lion's head, gold knocker on it. Ashley let it fall twice, then the door opened a crack, two eyes appearing, regarding us suspiciously.

"Is Solomon about?" Ashley asked, confidently, and immediately the door slammed shut.

Danny shrugged his shoulders. Ashley waved him away and the door opened to reveal a massive bald-headed black guy, sporting a goatee beard, with a plough harness of gold chains around his neck.

I suppressed the urge to laugh. Fucking hell, it's Mr. T. I thought, I pity the fool who messes with this guy - he is enormous - his biceps are about the same width as my thighs. Danny glanced at me, I could tell he was thinking exactly the same thing, and we both looked down, concealing our grinning faces.

Solomon and Ashley came together, bumping fists.

Then smiling broadly, showing a couple of golden teeth, Solomon said, "Ash, how's it going brother?" Indicating that we should follow him inside.

Solomon marched ahead of us, leading us down a small, dingy lit corridor, and then out into a sparsely furnished kitchen, where almost everything had been ripped out. On the far side of the room, someone had knocked a hole in the wall to make a serving hatch, and through it, I could see there was another room, a lounge area, with a pool table, and a massive sound system standing next to a curtained window.

Danny gave me a nudge, nodded his head towards a table in the middle of the room where a Sainsbury's shopping bag full of sensi sat brimming, filling the room with a sweet aroma.

Solomon saw us eyeing it up, "Yeah man, special delivery last night," smiling a golden smile back at us.

Ashley feasted his eyes on it, too, "It's not from Sainsbury's, either, is it Sol?" He joked.

Solomon creased up, "No man, you don't get this in any shop, so how much you want Ash?"

"I'll take six, Sol," Ashley said.

Solomon grinned, "What you having a party, Ash?" He asked, lifting up the Sainsbury's bag.

Ashley answered, "No, I'm sorting these two and their mates out."

Solomon glanced over at me as he began filling the bags, "Ay, Punk Rocker!"

I nodded my head, not knowing what to say to this mountain of a man.

Solomon was used to it, had seen it before, especially with white kids; unperturbed he went on, "I used to go to The Roxy up West, you been up there man?"

I shook my head, "Nah, I missed all of that, I was too young for The Roxy."

He chuckled, "Oh!"

"I've been up the 100 club a few times, though, that's good," I said, relaxing at the bloke's easy way, and his knowledge of music.

Solomon smiled, threw his head back, nodding enthusiastically, "I know the 100 club, yeah man, that is a good club, my mate DJ's up there sometimes."

"Oh, nice one, sounds good mate," I said, smiling up at the friendly giant.

He nodded, "Had me some big nights up there, I tell you."

"Yeah, me too," I said, smiling at a memory.

Once the bags were filled up. He handed them to Ashley, who gave them a cursory glance, before folding them into his jacket pocket for safe keeping, and then he handed Solomon a bunch of rolled up notes.

"Ash, trust me man, that is the proper sensi," he said, unfolding the notes.

Ashley beamed back, said to Danny and me, "It looks like good herb… Come on, let's go," and then turning back to Solomon like he'd almost forgotten, "Oh yeah, you got something to go with this, Sol?"

Solomon hid the flattened notes in a coffee jar, smiled knowingly, and produced three cans of red stripe from the cupboard above him, "What you mean, something like this?" He smiled, his golden smile.

Ashley smiled back. "Yeah, for real, cheers," said Ashley, taking the three tins, and began walking towards the door.

Solomon walked us back through the basement to the door, bumped fists with Ashley, and then as we left the basement, he said to me, "See you at the 100 club Punk Rocker!"

I smiled, gave him the thumbs up, and the three of us walked back up the sheer steps, back out onto Sandringham Road, into the now fully fallen darkness. Danny and me followed in Ashley's wake, moving quickly, dodging around the disappointed dealers and waiting watchers to his van. One more elated glance at the stretched green bags, and we left Hackney, drove north, back up the now completely illuminated A10 towards home. It was strange to think that this road went through the village; it was so different down here, so far removed from my life, but whatever the differences were, the fact remained that The Frontline is a couple of roads away from where I live, I thought, laughing to myself.

Sandringham Road > right on the A10 > right on Woodlands Cottages > right on Ducketts Wood.

On the way back through Tottenham, Ashley turned off the A10, drove to a park that he was familiar with, where he pulled up under some trees, where it was quiet and away from anyone.

Ashley pulled out one of the fresh bags of herb from his pocket, waved it in front of us, laughing madly, "Oh my, look at that, look at that… That's the proper one!"

Danny took it in his hand, nodding, clearly impressed by what he was seeing, "It looks good, Skinner."

I nodded, opened one of the tins of Red Stripe, thirstily drinking it down, while Ashley skinned up. As soon as he'd finished building, his 'masterpiece'. He sparked it up, took a couple of long hard pulls on it, took the rich white smoke down, and then with a huge grin on his face, he passed it over to me.

"Yeah… Whoa, that's some good shit," he told me, through a cloud of smoke.

I took it between my thumb and forefinger, put it to my lips; had a decent toke on it. It felt good, as the rich incense made its way into my system, gently caressing, and curing; then I passed it on to Danny and watched in amusement as he took his first awkward toke of the evening.

Danny smoking was hilarious; he didn't smoke normally, he had this weird way of screwing his face up as he pulled on a spliff, which made him look like a Gibbon licking its own arsehole. I smirked at the gurning Danny, picked up the Red Stripe, took another long swig, to head off the approaching cotton mouth, and passed the can over to Ashley.

His already misty eyes searched me. "It's good, isn't it?" He asked.

I was definitely getting something, but it was definitely time for a wind-up. I looked him dead in the eye, "Nah that's cabbage mate, straight off the spice rack," I told him, totally straight-faced.

Ashley gapped at me disbelievingly, then his face cracked into a smile, "Bollocksssss."

Danny mewed, "No, no Skinner, it's good, it's good."

"What are you stoned, then, Danny?" I asked.

He took another ugly toke, "Yeah… Yeah… It's…" and trailed off, dreamily, drifting away on the smoke.

I scoffed, "Oi Danny… You're a one spliff, Cliff!"

Ashley cackled, repeated, "One, spliff, Cliff!"

"Oh, fuck off, don't hassle me man," Danny grinned, gurning through a massive nimbus cloud of white smoke, and we all creased up laughing.

Danny flicked some built-up ash out of the window, and passed the spliff back to Ashley, "Seriously, though, it's good isn't it, Skinner?"

"Yeah, it's a creeper," I agreed, nodding my head thoughtfully, feeling my toes tingle.

Ashley puffed out another gigantic aromatic plume, "I had better stuff last week, though, it was the strongest I've ever had, one puff, and you were on your back."

Danny smirked, looked at me, rolling his eyes expansively.

I snorted, "Is that right, Ashley? One puff, eh?"

"One puff and you're on your back? What's your name? Cliff - one spliff - Richard?" Danny taunted.

Ashley protested, "No straight up, I'm not joking. One puff, just one, and you're on your back. Solomon got it for me. It was a special limited-edition type of sensi from Cuba."

On the verge of the giggles now, we let the classic Ashley bullshit hang in the air, where it drifted up there with the smoke for a while; the verge was approaching.

I snorted, "It was from Cuba, yeah? ...Was it from Fidel Castro's personal stash?" I said, descending into fits of laughter, taking the other two down with me.

"Or was it Che Guevara's?" enquired Danny, grabbing the spliff from his hand.

"Oi… Oi. Nah seriously, I'm not joking, just one puff, and you were on your back, it was grown on one of those communist collective farms," said Ashley, eyeing Danny theatrically.

"I've seen that stuff; it's red and the leaves are shaped like hammers and sickles," said Danny, watching the smoke snaking out, from the burning essence.

"Yeah, maaaaann, power to the people, every man is equally stoned, but some are more stoned than others," I said, plucking the rapidly burning spliff, from Danny before it got to his lips. "Stick to Pritt Stick, the Pritt Stick kid," I cackled.

"Oi Skinner, no, no, no," he protested, still laughing.

"The man from Pritt Stick, he say no," said Ashley, making his claim, grabbing at my hand.

"Ha, ha, too slow mate," I laughed, pulling it away.

On and on the hassle went. It went backwards and forwards, as the spliff went backwards and forwards, then with one final toke on the sweet spliff, saying goodbye to it like a lost friend. I chucked the roach out of the window, grabbed my three bags from Ashley, put a couple of them safely in my pocket for Whiff and his mate with the Fostex four-track, and began to build another best friend.

A few moments later, with the building completed, I lit our new pal, took a couple of good lungfuls, before passing it around to my mates, and we sat back, carried on where we left off, speaking of its delights and the possibility that Fidel Castro could have been Bob Marley's dealer. I began to feel ultra-relaxed and more perceptive to our surroundings, so I left Danny behind as he blathered on about something or other and began to zone out. A multitude of lights shone around us, street lights, lights from houses, from businesses in an array of glowing oranges, cheeky raspberry reds, and lotus whites, all spreading their warmth out into the world. I took them all in, saw they weren't having it all their own way, at the edge of the park; the skeletal trees of late winter cast their long, formidable shadows in amongst them like accusing fingers. It was like a battle between light and dark. Inside the twisting fingers I could see people walking their dogs, and I thought is this the park where I slept after I missed the last train home on the way back from my first gig? I nodded inwardly, it certainly felt like I had been here before, it was about the same size, and the blocks of flats that lay across the park from us looked very familiar to me. One man and his dog, wandered out of the shadows towards us, his dog trotting at his feet, and I wondered if that was Toby, the same dog that woke me up on that cold morning by sniffing my leg?

I smiled to myself, thinking nah, don't be stupid, "I reckon I've been here before," I said, cutting through the now silence in the van.

"What, you mean like, stoned?" Ashley asked, returning from his own thoughts.

I laughed, "Yeah," I said, dozily.

"Oh yeah," Ashley said, stretching, perking up, "I meant to tell, you know that Blues I went to where I met Solomon?"

Ha, ha, I thought, is there another Ashley classic coming here? He said, "There was a Rasta there who had three ears!"

I smiled at the image of a Rasta, with the superfluous ear, and shook my head.

"What three ears…? Fuck off," said Danny, coming back from wherever he had been.

"Oh yeah, I read about him in Sounds, he's the deaf, sound engineer, isn't he?" I said, hoping to keep it going.

Ashley sniggered, maintained, "No, no, seriously, he's got an illness, it's called, Otexia."

I repeated, "Otexia, what you mean like Otex, like the ear drops?"

A found-out, Ashley laughed heartily, getting back into his stride now, "He's known as The Three Eared Rasta, he's in a band, does a bit of toasting, when he goes up on stage, he says, 'now, ear, me, now'."

I creased up laughing.

"Yeah, sure he is, so where is this 'extra' ear then?" said Danny, watching him intently.

Ashley grinned lopsidedly, "…It's on the back of his head!"

I laughed, "You don't do yourself any favours, do you Ash? If you said it was under one of his other ears, it would be more believable, mate… On the back of his head though. Otexia… Nah, no way."

"I tell you what, he would make a brilliant dealer, wouldn't he? The old bill would never be able to sneak up on him," said Danny, evenly, and that was it, we all dissolved into fits of laughter again.

Inside the van, the laughter was as thick as the smoke, but as the weightiness of the proper sensi took hold of us once more, a more peaceful vibe circulated. I was laughed out, we were laughed out, stoned serine. It was time to go, time to head for home. Ashley started the van up, and as it hummed into life beneath us, he pulled a cassette tape from the glove compartment, and rammed it home into the player.

"You've got to listen to this, Skinner, if you like good music, you'll love this," Ashley insisted.

"What is it?" I asked, smiling.

"It's dub reggae," he said, a big grin cracking his face.

"Sorry, it doesn't sound like my thing at all, mate," I said, regretfully.

Ashley smiled confidently, "Trust me," he said, turning the bass right up.

A sound of trumpets blasted out like a call to arms, then echoed off into the distance, and as it fell away it was followed by a charging beat erupting from the speaker in front of me. I didn't know what was going on. It sounded like everything was being put through an echo chamber, then the bass dropped in, and suddenly everything seemed to fall into place, it thundered, rocking the van right down to its axles.

I started nodding my head, this is brilliant, I thought. Ashley took his eyes off the road ahead, glanced over at me, knowingly, nodding back, "I told you, I told you," he said, grinning.

I had heard some reggae over the years. Bob Marley, Steele Pulse and UB40, and I thought it was OK, a lot better than some of the music I had heard on the radio or in the charts. None of it didn't touch me like this though, this dub reggae, sounded like it had been recorded in outer space, and then beamed down for us to enjoy. It was reggae that was stripped down to its bare bones, the bass and drums being the main elements; everything else, from the guitars to keyboards and snippets of vocals, seemed to be going through an echo chamber. I loved the way those separate elements were utilized, the way the music built up using the snippets of vocals, splashes of melody from the guitars and keyboards to create a massive crescendo of sound, only for it all to slowly echo away, decaying through analogue delays, taking you down on a journey deep into the pulsating rhythm of the drums.

"Who is it, Ash? It's fucking brilliant," I said, incredulously.

Ashley smiled, nodding like he was introducing me to the secret of eternal life. He said, "It's an album by Prince Jammy, called, 'Prince Jammy Destroys the Space Invaders', Jammy's like a Dub chemist, he works with a group of session musicians called, The Roots Radics; I got it at Dub Vendor in Battersea."

"Whoa… OK… You know your stuff, don't you, mate? …This is brilliant!"

"Yeah, no doubt," he laughed again.

In the streets of Tottenham, I disappeared into the rhythm, into the bass, and flew off majestically as the splashes of colour sent my mind soaring high into the sky, only to drop me back into the rhythm once again. It was amazing, even Danny had stopped talking, which was a miracle in itself; he too was nodding his head methodically to the infection rhythms.

Ashley's bright orange van left Tottenham rocking to the sounds of dub reggae, continuing north on The A10 on to Green Lanes, and as we approached The North Circular Roundabout, I took the last swig of Red Stripe, dropped the can on the floor, and suddenly realised I needed a piss; needed a piss badly.

"Ash, I need a piss mate… Can we turn off somewhere?" I mewled, wriggling in my seat.

Ashley gestured at the long line of traffic snaking up towards the roundabout, so I sat back and held on.

One by one the cars slowly made their way up to the roundabout stopping as the traffic streamed by, waiting, watching, waiting as my full bladder pushed, pulsated, swelled up; even The Dub couldn't take away the fact that any moment now, for the first time in about seventeen years I was about to piss in my trousers, and once I started there would be no stopping it. A couple of minutes later, we still weren't any closer to the roundabout, and I was leaning forward, doubled up with the pain of it. I felt like my bladder was about to burst open inside me, at any moment, so taking the problem into my own hands, quite literally. I dropped into the van's footwell, grabbed the empty Red Stripe tin from the floor, put it between my legs, unzipped my bondage trousers, and haphazardly started pissing into the can.

"Ahhhhhhhhhh," I said, as relief swept over me. "Oh my god, that is so good… ahhhhhhh."

"Oh… Fucking hell," I purred happily, not realising that the traffic had opened up in front of us.

Ashley cackled maniacally, and seeing his chance, he floored it and began to spin the steering wheel around, swerving the van widely from side to side, sending the flowing piss down the side of the can.

I creased up, gave him a withering look, "I don't care, it's your van mate!"

Ashley and Danny descended into fits of laughter as I tried to control my geyser of piss in the swerving van, bouncing backwards and forwards between the console and the bench seat, piss dripping, splashing in all directions, I thought must stop pissing now, or I'm going to be covered. I couldn't, though, it was impossible, it hurt, even to try. So, getting up, I wedged myself between the seat and the console to keep balance; but still, most of the piss wasn't hitting its mark, dripping down the side of the can onto the floor. I snorted, and absently went to hand the dripping can over to Danny.

"Urgh you dirty bastard," he shouted, pulling himself away from me, barging into Ashley, who was on the verge of losing control altogether, swerving hazardously towards another car, both in hysterics.

A couple of shakes, and I was finished, so I did up my bondage trousers, and then thought fuck it, and placed the sopping wet can in between Danny's knees and dissolved into fits of laughter.

Danny's eyes widen in horror. "Err fuck off, fuck off, FUCK OFF!" he shouted, snatching the can up between his thumb and forefinger, splashing piss onto his jeans.

"Nooooo," he screamed, dropping it onto the floor, then flattened himself against Ashley again, who let go of the steering wheel completely.

"Oi watch it Danny, fucking hell!" He yelled, and inadvertently slammed the brakes on, bringing an angry blast from a car behind us.

"Come on, leave it out," cried Danny.

"Oi Danny mate, you fancy a tin of yellow stripe?" I said, picking it up from the footwell, waving it in his direction, splashing some more of the yellow viscous liquid towards him.

Danny shouted, "Dirty bastard… Dirty bastard," and then threw himself commando like over the bench seat into the back for safety and creased up laughing along with Ashley and me.

I was laughing so much, my ribs ached. Ashley was the same; he had one hand on his ribs and the other on the steering wheel, trying to keep the van on the road, tears running down his cheeks.

"OK look, Danny mate, come back in front, it's fine I won't do it again… I promise," I reassured him, between heaving breaths.

"Bollocks," Danny called from the back, howling with laughter.

"OK look, check it out," I said, winding down the window. I chucked the offending can of yellow stripe out and watched in the side mirror as it twisted and rolled, spilling its inky yellow fluid onto the road, sending the car behind us swerving right to avoid it and, it blasted its horn at us again.

"Ash, I think we might have some trouble here mate," Danny warned, looking at the car through the back window, rapidly flashing its lights at us.

"Oh what, do you think we might have pissed them off," I quipped.

Danny cackled from the back.

"I don't give a fuck, I'll take anyone on, let's see what they've got to say," said Ashley, staring into his side mirror.

A couple of grinning London Punks shot passed in a red mini giving us the wankers signs, and we reciprocated, cracking up laughing, watching them, as their car careered off the main road and up Southbury Road, the mini's wheels screaming on the tarmac trying to find purchase.

"Oh… Are they your mates, Skinner?" Asked Ashley, looking a bit disappointed.

"All Punks are mates," I told him.

Ashley nodded thoughtfully. "OK Danny, come on, you get in front mate, it's safe now… It's a piss-free zone," Ashley encouraged.

"Mind the puddle though mate," I said, grinning down into the footwell.

Danny snorted, gave me a reproachful look, and jumped back into the front next to me, wiping the tears of laughter from his red eyes. I patted him on the back; he laughed again, and finally we settled down. It had been another good night, I thought, it was over for now, but that's the thing about being free, you could always have another one, the following night - if you were free. I felt the bags of sensi in my pocket. I had tons left, there was one for Whiff, and one for Whiff's mate with the four-track, which I would give to Whiff at the next practice with his, and then we could start thinking about making that demo tape.

Ashley viewed Danny and me through slitty eyes, smiled dopily and banged up the cassette player, and we sat back together, mates, listening to the deep space drums and seismic bass of the dub, watching as the bright lights of the city slowly blinked out, and became the home fires of the countryside.

Chapter Four

Peace In Our Time?

Inside the relative warmth of the pavilion, Dave and me set up, talking away about Crucifix's new album, Dehumanisation, while outside an early morning mist filled the valley, covering it like a soft blanket. In the sky above, an orange sun shone down, warming it, turning the blanket a bright gold.

Whiff loomed large out of the mist, like the sasquatch trying to avoid David Attenborough, head down, jacket done up to his neck. He marched into the pavilion, gave us a peace sign as a hello, and went straight over to his amp, plugged his bass into our tuner and began turning the keys, tuning up.

"Yeah… Woodstock… Far out maaaaaan… So where's Andy?" I asked, flatly, watching him.

"What the Thalidomide?" He replied, breaking into The Pack's song. "Thalidomiiiiiiiide," he sang.

Dave and me watched him straight-faced, waiting for an answer.

"No, he's alright, he's at some boxing tournament or something," Whiff replied, which I knew to be true, as I had phoned him a couple of days earlier.

I eyed Whiff for a while, waiting for more information; nothing was forthcoming.

"Well… Have you talked to him then?" Which I didn't know, I had phoned Andy before him.

"Yeah," Whiff answered, distractedly, watching the needle on the tuner bounce left then right.

I exhaled, "So how is he? What did he say? Whiff?" More firmly.

Whiff looked up, smiled lopsidedly, "Oh he's fine, he reckons he's sorting us out a gig in Hoddesdon."

"Ooh, that's a London Postcode. Well just…," said Dave.

I raised my eyebrows, "Sounds good, anything else?"

Whiff's head dropped back to his bouncing needle, ignoring the intent in my voice, like it was just a normal day in the band. It wasn't, I needed to know that they were OK again.

"Whiff… Fucking hell, mate, are you two OK now?"

Whiff started, looked up at me for a moment, surprised at my persistence, surprised by my tone, surprised I was even bothering to ask such a stupid question.

"Yeah, yeah, of course we are, we're fine," he said, like there never had been a problem in the first place and twisted one of the keys on his bass to allay the dancing needle.

I whispered, "OK, good, well thank fuck for that," wiping my brow theatrically, looking at Dave.

Dave grinned back at me, "You know, you worry too much, Skin."

"Well… Some bugger has too," I replied, concisely.

"Is that one of your old man's?" Dave asked.

I nodded and Whiff said, joining in, "Is he still talking to the TV?"

I chuckled, "Yeah, he is, last night he was having a debate with Dennis Healey. Well, it wasn't really much of a debate. He just kept saying, 'oh shut up, you stupid bastard'," and we all creased up laughing.

"Oh, by the way, man," I said to Whiff, "I went up The Frontline. I'll sort you out later."

Whiff forgot the errant needle, grinned over at me, "Yesssss, nice one."

I smiled back at his love of the herb, "I got some for your mate too, for the four-track."

Whiff shook his head sadly, "What for Paranoid John? Nah, he hasn't got it anymore; he had a party and some Punk with a Mohican nicked it. He said his name was Larry… Larry? No, no Barry, yeah that's it. Barry."

I creased up laughing, "Oh what… You mean Basher?"

Whiff shrugged his broad shoulders.

"I bet it was, he'd nick anything, that bloke. You know what? This could work out well for us; I see him around in Hertford all the time; if he has got it, I'll buy it off him, we could probably get it for twenty quid."

Dave and Whiff nodded, looking suitably impressed.

"Oh no… What about the other bag Whiff?" I said, thinking there is no way I could afford to keep hold of that and carry on drinking in The Anchor over the next week.

"What about Mark, he puffs, doesn't he?" I asked, putting my plectrum between my lips.

"Bloody does he… He's on it all the while, yeah, OK, maybe it'll stop him going on about Georgie Best's hairy chest all the time."

Dave laughed; Whiff shot him an angry look, turning Dave's laugh into a cough, while I watched my plectrum shoot across the floor as I tried to control the hysterics that were rising up inside me.

"Nah, nah, nah, it's out of order. Every time I bump into him when I'm with Steph, he's got this look on his face. I know he's going to say something, and then what am I going to do?"

I couldn't help myself, "Tell him to watch it or Steph will 'aaave him saaaannnn," I said, standing up, dipping and weaving, throwing out a few jabs.

Dave's cough suddenly cured itself, turned back into full-on laughing, and I joined him, our laughs echoing around the pavilion.

Whiff sulkily plucked at a couple of his strings and re-adjusted the volume setting on his amp, "Oh yeah ha, ha," he said to the children, and got back to business, "Anyway, look, I've got some good news, looks like there could be a couple more gigs coming too."

"Yeah?" I asked, "That's brilliant news mate, it sounds like Andy's been busy."

Whiff shook his head dismissively, looking a bit miffed, "Nah it's not Andy, I saw Dirty Den in The Tap a few nights ago; he reckons there's a C.N.D. benefit on Hartham Common, and one for Rock Against Racism in Barclay Park in Hoddesdon. I've told him to give them my phone number."

"Oh what… Come on man, I know you get us gigs too," I said, trying to placate the bloke.

"No, no, it's not that… It's… Well, the N.F. have said they'll be 'attending both events in numbers to put across the other side of the argument'," he replied.

I scoffed, "What the argument that they're racist cunts?"

Dave nodded wholeheartedly.

Whiff smiled, "Yeah probably, but we'll still do them?"

"I wouldn't miss them for the world, mate, of course we'll be doing them!" I assured him.

"Yeah, definitely," said Dave, stretching his arms, making ready to let loose.

Whiff made one final adjustment to his sound, gave me a nod, and we both looked to Dave, who did a couple of full kit rolls, letting us know he was ready to.

"OK gentleman… Shall we make some noise?" I asked, feeling the adrenaline coming.

"Yeah, definitely. I reckon Reg wants some more," Dave replied, pointing a drum stick out of the window at the silhouette of Reg Cooper in the mist, pushing his line marker, marking the pitch out for this afternoon's match.

Whiff jumped up and punched the air, "Yeah, yeah, yeah… It's fucking Reg Cooper time," laying into his strings, making the floor beneath us shake.

Whiff wasn't going to stop anytime soon, so Dave and me joined in with the cacophony, laying into our instruments.

Reg Cooper laboriously paced the line marker up and down the football pitch, totally oblivious to our impromptu homage to him, and a full minute of chaotic discord later. I held my hand up for us to stop, and the maelstrom faded, to be replaced with the sound of us cracking up laughing.

I thought it would be a complete waste of time going through the full set without Andy and would be a good opportunity to try something new. So, I asked Dave and Whiff if they wanted to have a go at the new track, 'Church War' and they both nodded back at me enthusiastically. 'Church War' was not only a great track; it would be a step forward for us as a band, with its intro, proper guitar solo/middle eight and end sequence lifted from a piece of classical music. It had appeared on our last couple of Test Tapes in various forms, and Dave, Whiff and Andy had thought it was a beast of a track; Whiff in particular, who was always enthusiastic about the music I wrote, which encouraged me to write more. Whiff already knew the root notes, so I asked Dave to use the beat to 'Dutchmen' by Rudimentary Peni, until he could come up with his own beat, and without any hesitation, Dave launched effortlessly into 'Dutchmen' to show me he knew what I was on about - we were ready to go. It was surprising how quickly it all came together, and after an hour or so we had the embryo of 'Church War'. Now that we had the basics, Dave and Whiff relaxed, and began adding their own licks and riffs to make it smoother and flow better, between its multitude of parts. I loved their input; it was what we needed - I had written all the tracks in our set apart from Andy's 'Horrors of Belsen' and the band had pretty much played them exactly as I had envisaged them. 'Church War' was turning out to be totally different, though - with both Dave and Whiff contributing. It was so much better working together as a band - we could bounce ideas off each other, take parts of the track off in a completely different direction. If someone had an idea, they would stop playing, and say, 'hold up, hold up, I've got an idea, let's try this', and we would stop, go back over the part again; see if it worked, and if it did, it became part of the track.

On a couple of occasions, I found that a new part being put forward by the other two, wouldn't work with the original guitar riff. It wasn't a problem, though; I would adjust what I was playing to incorporate the new and better part, and as we refined the track, all of our little alterations made it tighter, heavier, and more varied than our tracks that had gone before. 'Church War' had a proper solo on it, and as we came to the middle eight, and I began to play it; we soon realised that it just wasn't working. In fact, what I had written in my bedroom at home was pure dross. Dave and Whiff played the middle eight over and over again, to give me a chance of finding something better, but it was all to no avail. I just couldn't do it. So, I stopped, pulled out a couple of readymade roll-ups, chucked one over to Whiff, sparked mine up, took a huge pull on it to ease the frustration, and give myself time to work out something else.

"Alright, alright! I know I can't play guitar solos!" I whined, glancing at their amused faces.

"You should do a Doggy and pretend you're a cat on stage doing a big lead," suggested Whiff, striking a pose with his bass, gurning Van Halen like.

Dave laughed and said, "Meeewoooow, meeeewow, meeewow," and then checking himself, he added, "Oh dear, oh dear, that was sad… How is your best mate these days, Skin?"

I shook my head, smiling, scratching the bristles on my chin.

Whiff cockney Doggy-Ed, "I'm gonna make you saaaannndd," Then posh Doggy- Ed, "Absolutely spiffing old chap," sending us into fits of laughter.

"Sorry about this, but can we do the middle eight again?" I asked.

"OK… You know, I like your usual solos, the three note wonders," Whiff shrugged.

Dave smiled, "Three note wonders? That's a little bit harsh, isn't it, Whiff?"

"Harsh realities of life, my friend," I conceded.

Once Whiff and me had finished off our roll-ups, and Whiff had been a cat on stage, doing a big lead again, we got back to it, and this time, knowing I had nothing else. I started off with my favoured three-note wonder lead, and just added another couple of notes, making it a five-note wonder. It was good enough for me, for the moment, anyway; I could work on it later. I reasoned that it was never going to be easy writing guitar solos for Virus V1 tracks, as none of the riffs we used were in the same key, so holding down the same few notes and bending the strings was probably about the best I could do. I was happy to have it out of the way, and the amused faces disappeared with the early morning mist outside. It was all about tightening, polishing the track up now, and as we played it for the last time that day, the one thing that became apparent was, we were right about 'Church War', it was a beast of a track.

Reg Cooper had finished with the line marker and was now on his sit-on-mower, slowly going up and down the football pitch. So, we knew we had at least another hour before we would have to pack our gear up, and as 'Church War' had gone down so well, I thought that we should try something else, something even more challenging. I asked Dave and Whiff if they would like to have a go at another new track called, 'Exhibition', a track that was heavily influenced by the new Punk Metal crossover movement that was rising out of the ashes of the third wave of Punk and Black Metal.

Dave and Whiff both liked Slayer, Motörhead, Metallica and Venom, who I particularly liked, and they said they were well up for another challenge, so we got straight to it. On our early tracks, the drums would stay at the same tempo all the way through, with rolls at the end of every four bars, the usual change from rider cymbal to high hat during the vocal parts and then getting busier with more rolls on the chorus' and the few instrumental parts. 'Exhibition' was totally different; in fact, it was a whole new world for us, with its many stops, starts and tempo changes, we would all have to concentrate, particularly Dave, as the different tempos would all have to be set by the drummer. It was hard going, to start with and as we suspected, it was a real challenge for Dave, who I had to signal a tempo change, or stop was approaching. It was hard work for me, too; after an hour of bopping my head up and down like a nodding dog on the back rack of a car, my neck began to ache like I'd been head-banging at a Motörhead gig. In the end, to simplify matters, we broke the track down into lots of little mini tracks, practising them all in the right order. Once we had learned them all, we played them like a mini set, putting them all back together to make 'Exhibition'. Dave was still finding it difficult, and I thought he must have felt the same kind of helplessness I did, when I was stuck on my guitar solo. He was never going to give up, though, because when it came down to it, Dave was not only an excellent drummer, full of energy, and technically gifted - he always relished a challenge, no matter what it was.

An hour or so later, we had the embryo of 'Exhibition'. It was shaky, but we could go all the way through it without it all falling apart, and there was minimal head-nodding involved. I looked out of the window and saw Reg Cooper had finished cutting the grass and was now pushing the corner flags into the soft soil, which was our cue to pack up. I made a mental note to lend Dave some of my American hardcore albums, Bad Brains, MDC and one of our favourites 'Plastic Surgery Disasters', by The Dead Kennedys, which was full of the kind of stops, starts and tempo changes that he was now facing on 'Exhibition'.

Dave, Whiff and me humped our gear out to Dave's van, parked up on the beautifully quaffed grass, and we talked passionately about 'Church War' and 'Exhibition' our new tracks. I told them I had a whole batch of Punk/Metal crossover tracks in the pipeline, and as usual they were full of encouragement. Whiff, was particularly animated as ever, talking about a possible change in the band's direction, and maybe we would be on the crest of the rising wave instead of following in other's footsteps. I was made up with their compliments and thought, I'm going to see what else I can come up with.

Once the van was loaded, we left the pavilion behind, bumping up the stony track through the last vestiges of the early morning mist, towards the allotments, feeling good, like we had stretched ourselves not only as musicians, but as a band. I couldn't wait to see how they would sound with Andy's vocals.

*

On the way down to the pub that evening, with a fresh twenty-pound note from Whiff in my pocket, and a smile on my face, I went around for Dave as usual and, as soon as I walked into the kitchen and saw him, I knew something was up, he was in a right state, his eyes red, puffy, his face ashen, and drawn.

"You OK Dave? What's up?" I asked.

Dave held his hand up. "Hold on, come outside," he said, and made his way out of the kitchen, under the carport, with me following close behind, wondering what was going on.

"I've broken up with Steph, Skin," he told me, his voice dour, cold; he was broken up.

"What! Really?"

He forced a smile, "Yeah, really. She chucked me; can you believe that?"

Steph wasn't popular with me, nor Whiff or Andy and that was really saying something if Andy didn't like somebody, as he seemed to like everyone. Steph never had time for us, right from when they had first started going out with each other, so my first thought was -

good. Dave was my best mate though, had been for years, would always come through for me; I hated seeing him cut up, like this.

"Oh no, fucking hell Dave, that's bad man, and she chucked you! …Why? What happened? You seemed alright to me!"

Dave smiled, patiently, "No, not really, it hasn't been good for a long-time mate. You've seen it, Skin."

I shrugged my shoulders, producing a strained smile for my mate; he was really suffering.

Dave paused for a moment, reliving the moment, the heavy words so lightly thrown, trying to digest it all, take it in, still not believing it; then laughed hollowly, "You remember I told you about that bloke she plays badminton with? …Well, she reckons she's fallen in love with him."

I scratched my head, "No way, you're fucking joking, aren't you?"

"Nooo. I wish I was, mate. She chucked me…" He sniffed, totally lost.

Now I felt angry for my mate, "What a bastard, we should do him, I'll help you out!"

"No, I've already thought of that, after she told me I waited down the road from hers, and he showed up. I couldn't do it. It's just not me. It wouldn't bring her back anyway; she'd just hate me."

"Yeah, I suppose so… Fucking hell, Dave."

Dave said, exasperated, "I wouldn't need your help anyway, I could have him easily, the short arsed little twat…" He trailed off, staring into nothing.

Silence crept in around us, like frost. He was destroyed, totally done; eventually, he said wearily, "I should have known… I should have fucking known… All the clues were there. How could I have not seen it?" Remonstrating with himself, taking the blame, he let out a long-wounded sigh, and sniffed loudly.

"Ah Dave, it's not your fault mate. You said it yourself, you couldn't have kept her locked up."

"I know, I know, but I feel like a right bloody idiot, I should have seen it coming. I knew something was up with her."

Dave shook his head and repeated the mantra, his penance, "I should have known. I should have known, huh, fucking hell. I've been so stupid; how can I not have seen that coming Skin?"

"Look Skin!!!" He said, catching himself before he completely broke down in front of his mate, and clapped his hands together, "I'm staying in tonight, I can't face anyone tonight, sorry about this."

I nodded, fully understanding, "Yeah of course Dave, you're going to be alright though, yeah?"

Dave grimaced, "Yeah, yeah," forcing a laugh. "…I'll be alright," he said, walking quickly out from under the carport.

"OK mate, look, I'll see you tomorrow then?" I called out.

I wasn't sure whether he was going to answer me or not, then just before the kitchen door slammed home, he said, "Yeah OK… Cheers Skin, thanks mate."

I thought, no way did Dave deserve that, he had always done right by Steph; always put her first when he could. He had also taken a lot of crap from her over the years too, sometimes in public, which was not only embarrassing for him, but for everyone else who saw it. I doubted anyone who really knew Dave would be sorry to see the back of her. Once he had got over her, which knowing him wouldn't be too long, as he could be strong mentally when it came down to it, it would be better for him. In fact, the short-arsed, little badminton playing twat, had probably done him a favour in the long run; a big one.

Chapter Five

Cerys

Virus V1 had another three-piece band practice and a normal one over the following weeks after our first tentative steps into Punk Metal. I was happy with the progress we were making on the new tracks; both were coming together nicely, particularly 'Church War', which seemed to get better and better every time the three of us played it. Andy liked them too, and although he hadn't sung on 'Church War' or the, as yet unfinished, 'Exhibition', I had given him the lyrics, along with a test tape with me singing on them, so he could get the diction right; and a few days later, Andy told me confidently, he was ready when we were. It felt like everything was getting back to normal in the band, and we were all going in the same direction, and once again, I began to think about our ultimate goal of getting a record out; surely it wouldn't be long now. It was just about keeping at it, practising, gigging, practising, gigging, we were in a good place. It got even better when Andy phoned me one afternoon, to tell me he'd got us that gig in Hoddesdon. I thought, yes, maybe this will be the one that gets us noticed outside of Hertfordshire - gets us closer.

"Oh, nice one, sounds good Andy," I said, beaming, "It seems like a long time since the last one."

"It's all part of being in a high-flying Punk rock band!" Replied Andy.

"Yeah, that's us alright, high-flying. High-flying straight into a fucking brick wall," I said, sarcastically.

Andy sniggered, then sang, "Step forward now, no need to hide, we can't lose with Whiffy on our side, oh bring the walls down, bring the walls down," paraphrasing the Bad Brains track.

I creased up. "Is he on our side, though, Andy?" I asked, pouncing on the opportunity, now it was just the two of us.

Andy laughed a little too loudly,

"Well… We are all part of the Whiffy barmy army," he said, parrying it away.

"Yeah, we are, for better or worse," I said, nodding to the fisheye mirror in agreement, which immediately acquiesced.

I wasn't quite done yet, though, "Did you two walk up from Ware, the last practice?"

"No, Whiffy got a lift with his old man, I came up on my own."

"Oh, right OK… He came up with Bad Brians, did he?"

"Why?" Asked Andy, ignoring my joke, cottoning on to my obvious investigations.

"Oh… It's nothing Andy, I just wondered how you two are getting on. These days…"

"We're fine," said Andy, in the same dismissive tone Whiff had used when I had asked him, and when I looked into the fisheye mirror, it viewed me like, not only, was I a twat. It viewed me, like I was King Twat, King Twat of Twatsville, and the occupied territories that surrounded The Kingdom of Twat.

"OK man… Er… Brilliant. That's good to know… Anyway look," I said, keen to change the subject, "Great news about the gig Andy, I phoned Bowes, not such good news mate, they usually only let the first bands play once, it wasn't a complete no, though, they said we went down so well for a first band, that we might be able to play again later in the year."

"Maybe, we should change our name to The Ware Rejects, after all," said Andy, as normal service was resumed.

I snorted, "Hmmm, not sure mate… How about Bad Brians, in homage to Whiff's old man?"

Andy cracked up, "Or how Ham 69, like a posh version of Sham 69."

I cackled back at him, "Yeah, I like it, we'd have to get Doggy in on vocals, though." I sang, "If the children are unified, they will never be divisible."

Andy crooned back, "Richmond boys, Richmond boys, lace-up brogues and corduroys."

"No, maybe not," I said, through tears of laughter.

"Definitely not," said Andy,

"How about Ducks of Pink Indians?" He suggested.

I fell about laughing, "Ducks of Pink Indians!!! …Now that is classic… Hold up. Hold up. I've got their album. 'Fucking punts treat us like chicks'."

Once we had both stopped laughing, I said, "Oh, talking of Flux, they got a gig in Hartham coming up." Bringing us back to planet earth.

"Yeah, I know, and there's a Rock Against Racism gig at Barclay Park in Hoddesdon a few weeks after that. Whiffy and one of his druggy mates in Ware are trying to get us to play."

"Dirty Den, The Shake or Vac man… What's this Hoddesdon gig then, Andy, is anyone else playing?"

"Not at the moment, I heard my old band Necro might, not sure though."

"So, not Ducks of Pink Indians then?"

Andy sniggered, said "No, sadly not," and went on to tell me the details of the Hoddesdon gig.

Virus V1's next gig was to be in a hall at the top of Lord Street on the coming Sunday night, so we arranged a full band practice on the Friday night before, to sharpen us up before the gig. Andy would let Whiff know and I in turn would tell Dave, and after saying our goodbyes I hung up, feeling even more positive about the band. I had heard it from both of them now; Andy was fine with Whiff and Whiff was fine with Andy, so whatever had happened was in the past, we were back to normal now. It was time to start thinking about the most important thing - the next gig. I sat back in the telephone chair, trying to make myself comfortable, thought this could work out well for us, not only is Hoddesdon a big town with a decent Punk scene, it would be easy for both the North London Punks and our mates in Ware and Hertford to get to as well. Sunday night wasn't ideal, though, but I was confident a lot of people would make the effort to come and see us as Andy had a lot of mates who lived over there, so I was sure that the word would get around. I smiled, remembering what Dave had said about the London postcode, and yes, it would be good to get our first London gig under our belts, even if it was the second last post code of the sprawling city before it turned into the green fields of Hertfordshire.

Brriiinnnnnnggggggg brrriiiiinnnnnnggggg the phone blared beside me, disturbing me from my thoughts.

I wondered, who that could be? Maybe it's Andy with some more info on the gig? Maybe, he can't make it now? Maybe, he needs something? Maybe, you should just pick the fucking phone up.

"Hello," I said, enquiringly.

"Hi Mick," said Martin, "Mick, look, I'm sorry I got shirty with you last time; I just need to talk to Dad alright?"

Oh, fucking hell, I thought, I can't be bothered with this now, "No Martin, you look, it's simple… I asked the old man, and he told me what you did leaving Nadia, he won't talk to you, end of story. I can't help you."

"It's not simple Mick, I didn't leave her, I would never do that… I only went out to get some fags. That's all, I only went to the corner shop!"

"Yeah? …Really!!?? Where was the corner shop? …In fucking Alaska?" I said and hung up.

*

On the Friday evening of the practice, I was sitting back in the lounge watching Nationwide on TV with Mum and the old man. It was surprising; the old man didn't want to watch the news, but then, after Frank Bough's piece on the perils of drug use, he announced the show's special guest for this evening, Esther Rantzen; it all made sense. Esther walked out from the wings beaming, sat down, all business like, and after smoothing down her light blue smock with soft manicured hands, she began her story about a dog that could say 'sausages'. I looked at the old man; he was totally enchanted. Mum rolled her eyes expansively at me, but George, curled up in a ball on Mum's knee, couldn't have cared less.

"Oi, stop that Pudge," she said, playfully.

"What? What?" He returned, all big-eyed, and innocent.

"Esther…" she said, pointing at the cathode ray tube.

"I'm watching the dog saying, 'sausages'," he grinned.

"Hmmmmm… I bet," said Mum, totally unconvinced.

"I am, I am," he still protested, open-palmed, "I'll say this, though, I'd be more impressed if they had a sausage that could say, 'dog'."

Mum and me cracked up laughing.

"Anyway, you can talk, you're always drooling over Leonard Nimoy," he told Mum in his defence.

"Oh well, yes, he is rather gorgeous."

109

I snorted; it was funny listening to them sometimes, sometimes you could actually believe that they had been young themselves once. George raised his sleepy head, gave me a double wink like he agreed with me, and sank back into his sleep; one of many of his daytime naps, while I continued to study the two old teenagers, as they discussed the merits of their TV beaus.

A few minutes later, with Esther still in full swing, we were disturbed by the sound of the doorbell ringing. I knew who it would be, so leaving the teens, to their Esthers and Leonards I made my way out and opened our front door to find Whiff and Andy, grinning back at me on my doorstep. Andy, smiled, laughed, gave me a huge grin, while Whiff's eyes bored into him, like he'd had enough.

"You ready then, Skin?" Asked Whiff, sourly.

I nodded, shouted goodbye back into the house to anyone who was listening, grabbed my guitar, bags of leads, effects pedals, lofted my amp onto my shoulder, and we set out for Dave's. It was hard carrying all of my gear, so I stopped outside the Harrington's oak tree for a breather, thought, sod this, and handed my amp to Whiff, who grinned mischievously. Immediately passing it onto Andy, who in turn, sighed, gave me a withering look, and uncomplainingly hoisted it up onto his shoulders, and we carried on.

Andy, Whiff and me strolled down my road, passing the pampas grass at the front of Doggy's and stopped outside the reverend Hilary Charman's tip of a house, where we saw a crucified Action Man, complete with red paint for blood at its stigmata. It looked like the plastic Palitoy man really had suffered for our sins, as during his crucifixion; he had not only lost an arm, he had lost his head, too.

On through the twin white fences we strolled, finally coming to the wall at the edge of the churchyard, where again, we stopped for another breather. I took in the view while Andy and me got our breath back. It was a beautiful evening, clear and vivid, essential, and life-affirming, despite the rows of the sleeping dead that lay in front of us. In the sky to the west a low evening sun emitted its warm pleasant rays onto the gravestones, which in turn cast their long shadows onto the short grass, beneath them.

Andy was keen to get on, get the job done, so he moved to the wall lifting my amp up high, the strain clearly showing on his face.

"Whoa, hold up Andy, you need a hand, mate?" I offered.

Andy nodded appreciatively, shooting the empty-handed Whiff, a look, who ignored him, walking on ahead, pulling out a roll-up. I put my shoulder under the amp, and together we lofted it over the wall.

"Cheers," said Andy, through the essence of Whiff's roll-up.

On the other side of the wall, Andy took the strain, and heaved the amp back up onto his shoulder again, then we carried on through the long shadows of the all-so final grey stones.

A crow emitted a series of loud caws from the high branches of the first of the cypress trees at the top of the hill, that lead down to the All-Night-Garage and Dave's place.

"I said, "I hope Dave's alright now, he was really cut up about Steph," looking for the crow in the tree.

Whiff stopped, letting me and the struggling Andy catch up. "Yeah, me to mate, bad news, wasn't it?" He said, offering me a readymade rollie.

"Cheers mate," I said, taking it, sparking it up, "What about you? How's your Steph getting on?"

Whiff smiled contentedly, puffing on his rollie, smoke billowing, "Yeah... It's going really well, Skin, she's a lovely lady... But there's this other cutie I like too," he said, chuckling mischievously to himself.

Andy snorted from under the amp, like he'd had enough now, "You think all the girls love you, don't you, Whiffy? You think you're Punk's answer to Casanova, don't you, Whiffy?"

Whiff span around, dossing out Andy, who cracked up laughing manically, under his scrutiny; I could almost see the cogs working in Andy's head as he prepared his riposte to Whiff's scowl.

I thought oh no, not the song, please don't sing the song, not now when everything's going alright.

Andy sang, "All the girls love Whiffy, that's what he thinks, but they don't because he's got big feet, and they think that he stinks," striding off in front of us, cackling wildly.

Oh, here we go again, I thought, he isn't going to like it, and sure enough, when I looked to Whiff. He was absolutely furious, teeth gritted, almost snarling, eyes steadily burning into the back of Andy's head, as he marched on, still cackling.

112

Whiff chucked his smoke onto the ground, crushing it into the grave of someone's dearly departed, slowly shaking his head, and the three of us carried on in an ominous silence, dodging through the gravestones to the top of the hill and down onto the shingle track that led to Dave's.

Dave appeared, jumping out from behind one of the huge cypress trees that lined the track, greeting us with a friendly, "Boooo. Alright lads?"

I nodded a hello back, and out of the corner of my eye, I saw Whiff's hand sweep up, and scrape across Andy's face, making him jolt backwards, recoiling, and he began to cough, rubbing furiously at his face.

Dave pointed at Whiff, laughing hysterically.

"What? What's so funny?" I asked.

"Uuuuurrrrghhh," said Dave, tears of laughter welling up in his eyes.

"What happened?" I asked, still clueless.

"Oh my god, didn't you see that? …He just put his hand in his sweaty arse crack and rubbed it on Andy's face," said Dave, sending the three of us into hysterics.

Andy spat on the back of his hand, frantically swiping at his face, trying to wipe the residue of Whiff's arse crack off. "Oh, nice one, Whiffy, good going, well done Whiffy, brilliant, really funny, Whiffy." He snapped furiously.

113

In all the years I had known him, I had never seen Andy get angry
before; no matter what happened, he usually took it in his stride, so I
tried to stop laughing, reign it in. I couldn't though. It was
impossible with the other two, rolling around on the grass in
hysterics. I just couldn't help it, and soon I was laughing so much
that I began to think that my ribs were actually going to split open. It
took us ages for us to calm down; we laughed until it hurt, and then
greedily sucked the air in to spare our aching sides, and then we
would look at each other and that would be it - we would be off
again. A while later, we finally got ourselves under some sort of
control, and by that time Andy had composed himself too, so we
picked up our gear and crunched on down the shingle track towards
the pavilion. Andy pounded on ahead of us in complete silence, still
straining under my amp. I knew it had gone too far, way too far, so I
tried to make conversation with him, make it better, and finding I
only got monosyllabic replies, I gave up - feeling like the three of us
were a right bunch of cunts - and the ominous silence continued.

Once we had set up and started playing, though, everything seemed
to be forgotten; it felt normal again. In fact, it was better than
normal, Whiff was lashing viciously at his bass and Andy was belting
out our lyrics like he was already at the gig as they both vented their
anger through our music. I thought, anger really is an amazing
catalyst when it comes to music, and I hoped they would keep up
this level of intensity at our gig on Sunday. I had planned to give
'Church War' a full band run through after we had finished our set,
but I doubted whether Andy and Whiff could be trusted to work
together. So, with a nice uncomplicated Friday night drinking session
in the pub beckoning me, I decided to call it a day, and we started
packing up. It was weird. If you didn't know us, everything looked
perfectly normal, like everyone was getting on; we weren't, though. I
noticed straight away that when Andy was talking, he would be
talking to Dave and me and not talking to Whiff, and by the same

measure if Whiff was talking, he would be talking to Dave and me and not talking to Andy. It was odd, puzzling, childish, and funny all at the same time. Dave picked up on it too and after a couple of exchanged glances, followed by a quick word out of earshot, we competed to see which one of us could trap them into talking to each other.

A few solid attempts later, we found it was futile; they were determined not to talk to each other, at least not today anyway.

I admitted defeat by whispering to Dave. "Couple of bloody, Thatchers… These ladies aren't for turning," and he creased up laughing, which ironically got them to exchange a glance.

Once the gear was secured in Dave's van, this time with all of us doing our share, including Whiff. Dave and me were surprised to see the two of them walking out of the pavilion door together. It didn't last though, that surprise soon evaporated as Whiff stopped halfway across the cricket pitch to make a roll-up, leaving Andy to carry on walking on his own. Andy got about half up the hill. Whiff lit his roll-up, checked to see how far Andy had got, and seeing it was far enough for him, he set off again.

I felt Dave nudge me at my side, "I thought they were alright now?"

I nodded sadly, "Yeah… Me too, Dave."

Dave snorted. "Jesuuuussss, look at them, they're like an old married couple. Ooohh, I shan't walk with you any more Albert, so there," he intoned, in a doddering old women's voice.

I chuckled, "The whole thing's weird, isn't it? Unless something happens, I don't think it's going to turn out well… For anyone."

"What? You reckon they'll have a punch-up?" He asked, balling his fists, throwing a couple of punches.

I shook my head, "I don't know, maybe… Both of them are so mellow, it's hard to tell. If they do, it could take them years to wind each other up enough."

"Who do you think would win? …Seriously," said Dave, still ducking, and weaving.

"Andy," I said, not even thinking about it.

Dave nodded, smiled broadly, "I thought Andy was definitely going to smack him one after he rubbed his arse crack juice onto his lips."

I cracked up. "Oh what, nooo, not on his mouth? Urrrgh Jesus," pulling a disgusted face,

"Yeah… he must have tasted it," he said, rocking forward.

"Seriously though, Dave, we shouldn't have laughed so much, it was like we were ganging up on him; it was well out of order."

Dave straightened up, held back the schadenfreude grin playing at the corner of his lips. "I know, but I couldn't help it; it was fucking hilarious… And did you see Andy during practice? He kept rubbing his face, like he was still trying to get the ming of Whiff's sweaty bum juice off," and burst out laughing.

I shook my head imagining it all over again and cracked up laughing, "I reckon it would take more than a couple of swipes of your hand to get the essence of Whiff's arse crack off your face. You'd need a bottle of Domestos, and a pumice stone."

Dave sighed, puffed out his lips, "Oh dear, oh dear… Anyway, I fancy a pint, what do you reckon?" He said, trying to pull the curtain down on the whole sorry saga.

I nodded, "Yeah, definitely…"

"A pint would certainly taste better than Whiff's arse crack ordure, that's for sure," I said, returning to it like a moth drawn to feast on that curtain, and in the process lifting it all over again, "I'll have a pint of Whiffy's olde English arse sweat please, barman."

Dave cracked up, "Skin mate, stop, stop, I can't take it anymore," clutching his destroyed sides in vain.

"OK mate… Yeah, let's get a pint. Oh, hold up… Are you sure you still want to go in there, mate?" I cautioned, remembering Steph.

"What? Yeah, it's fine Skin, I had a word with Jill, and she told me Steph won't be using The Anchor anymore," he said, catching my drift.

I thought, hey, hey, at last some good news today.

"Cerys might be in there, though," he said, grinning from ear to ear.

"Oh, yeah?" I asked, trying to sound casual.

Dave grinned some more, "I've got some good news for you, Skinner, me old mate… I meant to tell you earlier, but with them two going on, well…" letting it hang in the air.

"Yeah, go on then."

"You ready?"

"Yes Dave, bloody hell mate, have a heart," I Alan-ed testily, searching his face for clues.

"OK, you're not going to believe this, but Hayley was chatting with her in The Anchor last night, and she said, if you asked her out, she would probably say yes," he said, his face beaming, happy for his mate.

I thought bloody hell!!! It's amazing how quickly life can change around; one minute you're watching your band disintegrate around you, then the next you're… hold on…

"Probably?" I enquired.

Dave smiled broadly, palms up, "Well, yeah, that's women for you."

Yeah, that is women for you, I thought, bless them, bless their little cotton frocks.

On Saturday night, I dropped into Dave's to see Hayley, as I wanted to find out exactly what had passed between her and Cerys. I wanted to know, no, needed to know everything before I asked her out, as there was a real possibility that she could have been drunk; she could have just had a row with Mark, or she could have been messing around, anything. I didn't like the word probably, either; there was no certainty in a probability. As far as I was concerned, possibilities presented themselves frequently, and in most cases that's all they turned out to be. I needed certainty, as I would only ask her once. It wouldn't be right, otherwise; I wasn't a stalker. I didn't want to be the weirdo chasing someone else's girlfriend, especially Mark's; even if he did use more perfume than Pepé le Pew, he wasn't such a bad bloke.

In the light being thrown out of Anne's kitchen, under the carport, Dave told me that Hayley was out with Aaron, and hearing those few words, my dream of certainty disappeared like a yuppy at a Crass gig. I thought well, thank you very much, Aaron the Ted, you could have left the building a bit later, you stupid throwback fuckhead. On the plus side, he also told me that he had had another word with her, and her message to me had been plain and simple.

"Just go for it, Skinner."

I nodded my head at the messenger, thinking there was something different about Dave today, he looked a lot more content with the world. In fact, he was positively beaming. I was sure he was happy with being the harbinger of good news, especially for me with all the hassle I had with girls over the years, but no, there was something else here, something big, I took the plunge.

"You look happy mate, has that slimy badminton playing twat choked on a rogue shuttlecock or something?" I joked.

Dave laughed, "No, it's better than that… I'm buying a house."

"Oh what…… Really?" I exclaimed, totally horrified.

"Yeah, I'm buying a house in the village, it's near The Anchor," he replied, excitedly.

Oh no mate, what are you doing that for? I thought, you're eighteen years old, and you're buying a house? Why do that? You haven't lived yet mate, who wants to be tied to a mortgage at your age? You're way too young. Too little, too young: I actually pitied the bloke - he looked so happy, though.

"Whoa that's great news mate, sounds really good, near the pub too. Brilliant," I lied through my back teeth, I had to, he was a mate. It was what he wanted, so who was I to rubbish it?

Dave smiled back, swallowing the lie, lost in his dream, loving it. He would have a house of his very own, what could be better than that? He proceeded to tell me all about it.

I nodded in all the right places, and then when he was finished, with a few more 'that's great news mate', I thanked him for Hayley's inside information on Cerys, and made my way to the door.

Dave smiled broadly, wishing me good luck.

"Cheers mate… I'm confident it'll happen this time," I said, lying through those teeth again, and I was off down the road towards Cery's house, to whatever her answer would be.

One step at a time, is all it takes to get anywhere, whether it be Ware or Glasgow, so I had read somewhere. I was only going down the village, so it couldn't have been simpler, or so I thought. On any other day, this walk was relaxing, especially in the ambient glows of twilight. Not today though. It was anything but, my heart was racing, my mouth dry, my palms wet. I felt open, edgy, vulnerable and a whole load of other emotions I didn't know I had, or even existed; my mind was in chaos, a chaos I wasn't enjoying. It seemed to be taking ages too, like I was walking backwards up an escalator, and when I made it to the final straight of her street. It didn't help my juddery nerves when Don Ruddock drove past me in his Merc, dossing me out, with a look that said, I'm going to rip your head off, and shit down your neck.

One step at a time was all it took to walk down her path, and up to the front door, where I knocked and braced myself. Immediately it swung open, almost like she was waiting for me.

"You alright Cerys? I need to talk to you, you coming out?"

"Oh, hi Skinner, that sounds a bit ominous," she said coolly, giving me a quizzical look.

Oh shit, I thought, 'ominous' that doesn't sound good. I should have waited, talked to Hayley, found out exactly what she said to her. Oh Jesus, maybe she didn't say anything to her at all - my mind raced out of control into a chicane – maybe, this is Hayley's way of getting me back for telling Dave about our kiss.

Cerys smiled into my insecure face, "OK, wait a minute, I'll just get my jacket, looks cold out there."

I told my stupid paranoid brain to give it a rest, averting the first corner pile-up.

"Good idea, it is a bit."

A few minutes later, Cerys reappeared, wrapped up in a warm coat. She gave me a massive life-affirming smile, shouted a goodbye back into the house, and we set off up her garden path and onto her street, striding out for the centre of the village. It felt good to be walking out with her again, we were only going into the village, but it felt like we were going to go so much further than that. Cerys and me, slipped into step easily, and as we walked, we talked. I hadn't talked to her when I was sober for a long time, and I began to wonder why, as it was so easy and unforced. It seemed like we could talk about anything, so we did, anything, everything and nothing in particular, and soon my frayed nerves began to abate.

In the descending darkness of the evening, the lights on the A10 above us began to flicker into life, and I took the opportunity to give her, a probably, not-so-subtle once over. She looked really cute, all wrapped up and warm in her winter wear, but it was her long hair that really got to me. It was even longer than the last time I had seen her; it cascaded down her long neck and onto her shoulders in a sleek chestnut brown rainbow. It was not only beautiful, it was part of someone I wanted to spend my time with, someone I wanted to talk to, someone I wanted to get to know even more, which made it all the more alluring.

"I haven't seen Taddy for a while, how is he these days?" I asked.

Cerys smiled, "Oh, he's OK, still bruised, he's on the mend now."

"Good, he didn't deserve that, did he. I heard he was trying to play peacemaker."

"Yes, he was, fat lot of good it did him,"

"He was up Craig's a few days ago, and Don apologised to him."

I puffed my cheeks out, breathed out, "Oh, that's big of him, like that changes anything, he's a right bastard he is… I saw him a minute ago in his motor and he looked at me like I'd just pissed in his pork scratchings."

Cerys smiled, "Urgh, pork scratchings, I doubt anyone would notice."

"Yeah true... What is it about pub snacks? You know those scampi fries that Stewart sells; they smell like... Well, I won't say what they smell like..." I said, trailing off, grinning suggestively.

"Yes, thank you, I can well imagine... I suppose if you're pissed, it doesn't matter if you are eating pig's guts or essence of a bad mini moo," she said, giggling.

"Mini moo," I repeated, creasing up laughing.

I thought this is going well, don't know what I was worried about, it's Cerys after all.

Cerys and me strolled up the A10 together, gently bumping off each other, and I pointed to a terraced house across the road, "I think that's the house Dave's buying over there."

"Oh yes, Hayley told me he was looking to buy somewhere," said Cerys, looking over at the pretty little two up two down cottage, "I like it... It's a lovely house but he's only eighteen, and he's going to have a mortgage?"

I pulled a sour face, "Yeah, that's what I thought... You know what mortgage means? Death pledge!!! Sounds ominous, doesn't it?"

Cerys repeated. "Death pledge... Ooooh, sounds horrible," she said, shivering melodramatically inside her snug jacket.

I smiled broadly, "You will payyyyy… Or you will dieeee," I Boris Karloff-ed.

"Oh, come on, it's not that bad," said Cerys, laughing at my silly Transylvanian accent.

"Nah, I suppose not… On the bright side, at least Steph won't be moving in, that would have been a real horror film. No one would see him again, ever; poor Dave would have been locked up like number six on that TV show The Prisoner. He wouldn't be a free man, that's for sure. Steph was like some kind of nympho-version of that weird bubble that used to chase Number 6 when he tried to escape."

Cerys creased up, "Yes, I remember what she was like with Taddy. She drove his nuts, and him, nuts."

"Yeah, you said, so what are you doing with your life now Cerys? You at college yet?" I asked, beginning to feel bad about talking behind my mate's back.

"Yes, back in class again, it's different this time though, it's not like school, you can wear your own clothes, college is more relaxed, if you want to work, you do, if not, you don't, it's all down to you, it's all about responsibility. I'm still shit at Maths, though," she said, laughing.

"Why are you doing it then?"

"I need it to go into nursing, I need a C.S.E., which I should get, even a grade 3 would do it, that's like an C at O level standard, even thick people like me can manage that."

"No, no, you're not thick. It's really good, Cerys," I said, looking her in the eye, "I'm really sorry what I said about nursing, you know, about them… Well, being, shit shovellers."

Cerys snorted, "You're probably right, but I want to help people, make a difference. Oh, and it'll get me out of the village too, if I get the qualifications that is, which is important. I'm applying to be an R.G.N. at Chase Farm Hospital in Enfield… It's London, but close enough to home to come back for the weekends."

"Nice one Cerys, you've got it all sussed out, haven't you?"

"I'm not a Clash City Rocker for nothing, you know, there's more than one way to be a Punk Rocker, it's about doing what you want to do, and luckily I know what I want to do," she said, moving in closer to me, some of her rainbow chestnut hair falling onto my shoulder.

"Oh, I see, you're trying to smash the system from within?"

Cerys laughed, "Something like that Skinner."

"If you go to Enfield, do you reckon you'll be coming back much?" I asked, trying to see where I stood in her plans. If I was in her plans…

Cerys smiled under the orange street lights, "Yes of course, I'll be coming back to see mum, Taddy… And, Mark."

I snorted, thinking that I had just woken up to find myself in the middle of a card game. My hand wasn't too bad, and it looked like someone in this game was bluffing, having a laugh at my expense.

"Cerys, what's going on with you and Mark, are you still mates? …I've been hearing things," I said, putting my first ace down.

"Hmmmm… I wonder who's been talking?" She said, flicking her hair back coltishly.

Oh my god, I thought Hayley wasn't lying. Of course, she wasn't. OK let's do it.

I cackled, "A little peroxide birdy told me, told me something very interesting."

"Oh yes, and what was that?" She asked happily, taking it all in her stride.

"She said, if I asked you out, you'd say 'yes'," I said, putting all my cards on the table.

"I'm going out with Mark, you know that Skinner," she told me, trumping my pathetic ace high.

"Yeah, I know you're with Mark, but you told me you're more like mates. I'm probably as close to him as you are."

"Err… I don't know about that Skinner; I do kiss him now and again."

"Yeah, well, so do I, when he puts The Pack live tape on his Brixton Blaster," I joked.

Cerys creased up, I pulled her in closer, found resistance, and she pulled away.

"OK, look Skinner, it's not about Mark, it's about you. You're not the most reliable person in the world, are you? You are a troublemaker. You upset a lot of people."

"Oh what, they're my best attributes. I've got my faults too."

Cerys didn't laugh; she looked away, up the A10 into the distance, "You see, this is what I mean. You just don't take anything seriously."

"Oh what, that's not true, I do take things seriously... If I'm into them, that is... And I'm into you Cerys... Into you in a big way, I wouldn't be here otherwise, would I?" I said, looking deep into her.

In front of us, above us, around us, the street lights blinked on/off, then one by one, like dominoes falling, they went out, and the darkness snuggled in around us. In a second the orange glow had gone, vanished into the distance, taking the two Clare's, Lucy, and Karen Corker with them. Cerys' eyes shone clear and clean back at me under high clouds that rippled the stars above. Now it was just the two of us.

"Bloody hell," said Cerys.

"Bloody hell, indeed," I said, agreeing with her. If there was ever a moment to ask someone out, I thought, this was it. It was like an ace up my sleeve, I never knew I had.

"I'm into you, Cerys. Will you go out with me, we'll do it properly this time. No messing about."

Cerys smiled. "Yeah, OK," she said, just like that.

"You won't regret it," I said, sincerely, taking her hands in mine.

I couldn't have stopped myself even if I had wanted to; moving forward, I kissed her lips with passion, her full red lips docking with mine. She tasted of peppermint and moonlight. We span, like two heavenly bodies in gentle pools, away from everything, everyone. It had been a long time coming, I had waited so long. She felt that, held me firm and kissed me back stronger still. A car shot past us in the darkness, tooted its horn at the teenagers snogging in the dark, and we parted, in fits of laughter.

Chapter Six

No Fun

On the evening of the Hoddesdon gig, I was walking down the hill from the churchyard, and saw Dave packing our gear into the back of his van.

I wandered up to him. "I thought we were supposed to be picking up Andy and Whiff on the way through?" I asked, concerned about the seating arrangements.

"Yeah, we are, but my old man loaded his transit up for a job tomorrow, so we are going to have to use mine, they can go in the back together, they'll be plenty of… Oh… Oh shit," he said, and we both grimaced. Dave laughed and continued, "Oh well, it'll be fun for them, they can squeeze up together, like they're playing sardines. Maybe they'll learn to love each other again!!"

I snorted, carefully slipping my guitar into the seat well of the passenger seat, "Yeah, sure they will," I said sarcastically, "I'll keep this up here with me, just in case."

"It's probably a good idea, there's a real lack of space in there, especially if you add Whiff's big feet."

I creased up, "Yeah, and that they stink."

Dave's eyes twinkled back at me, and we duetted, "All the girls love Whiffy, that's what he thinks, but they don't, because he's got big feet, and they think that he stinks," descending into fits of laughter.

129

I snorted at its stupidity; the trouble one little song could cause, for fuck's sake. I shook my head, picked up a side drum case, looked for a place for it in the cramped back and finding none, I handed it to Dave, who deftly moved the bass drum case to one side and slid it in with a victorious look on his face.

"What's really going on with those two?" Dave asked, lifting his box of cymbals.

"I don't know Dave, beats me mate, the first thing I knew about it was when Whiff told me they weren't seeing each other outside the band."

"What? When was that?" He asked, incredulously.

"I think it was after the Bowes gig, he just came out with it on my doorstep, I didn't know what to say, it was fucking strange."

Dave slid his box of cymbals in, keeping the area over the wheel arch clear, "I don't get it, Andy brought Whiff into the band in the first place, so they must have been mates, so what's changed?"

"I really don't know Dave, I'm hoping they'll remember that, a few more gigs, maybe the CND and RAR one, and we could be signed, and in the studio, we just need to keep doing what we're doing."

Dave nodded, thoughtfully.

I picked up the high hat, the final piece of the puzzle, and not even bothering to try, handed it to Dave, who smiled broadly, placing it perfectly in the gap between two of our amps. We then put our weight on the doors, wedged them shut, jumped in, and got underway.

Dave pulled out his new favourite album, Motörhead, 'No Sleep 'til Hammersmith', from the musty glove compartment to his side, eyed me provocatively, and shoved it into the cassette player.

"How about a bit of Lemmy, Skin?" He asked.

I smirked, "Lemmy out of here… Nah, it's your van mate, so your music."

"You like some of it, don't you?"

"They're alright," I said, as we raced passed The Sow and Pigs Pub.

I still wasn't sure about Motörhead; however, a combination of 'Ace of Spades', 'Bomber', 'Overkill,' and 'We are the Road Crew', coupled with Dave's heavy rotation and Lemmy's guttural voice, they were beginning to win me over. I nodded along to 'Iron Horse,' and 'No Class,' without too much conviction, watching the countryside whirl past my window, and then when 'Overkill' began, with its double bass drum intro, I thought yeah, that's more like it, and Dave smiled over at me, appreciatively slapping the steering wheel in time to the beat, and all too soon we were coming into Warc.

Whiff stood outside The Cannon's hotel, our first port of call, bass in his hand, roll-up in his mouth. I thought overkill, yeah, maybe a bit of overkill might be the solution to our problems. I sneered, stifled a laugh, gave him the wankers sign, and he grinned back, reciprocating, as we pulled up next to him.

"Where am I sitting?" Whiff asked, quizzically, a dark frown creasing his face.

131

"It's fine mate, we've left some room in the back for you, here, give me your guitar," I said, jumping out.

Whiff nodded, wandered around the back, and I opened the doors for him, and then it dawned on him that Andy would not only be sitting in there with him; they'd be up close and personal too.

"Oh, fucking hell Skin, is he going to be in here as well?" He cried, stalling like a spooked horse on the ramp of a horse box.

"Yeah, he fucking is mate, now sort it out… Whatever it is Whiff, it's not worth it mate, think of the band," giving him a friendly, if persuasive shove.

Whiff shot me a look of betray, sighed; and, resigned to his fate, wriggling his way inside, making himself as comfortable as he could on one of the wheel arches. I gave him a sarcastic thumbs up, leant my weight hard onto the doors, finally clicking them shut, and we were underway again.

In the centre of town, we found Andy waiting at the bottom of New Road, as he told us he would be. As we pulled over, he peered searchingly into the front of the van, and immediately understood what the seating arrangements were, his mouth gaping open at the prospect.

"You alright Andy? Follow me, mate," I said, trying to suppress the laugh that was rising in me.

Andy, realising his fate was sealed, resigned to it, as Whiff had been, also followed me to the back, squeezed in, and with the last bars of 'Overkill' fading out. I slammed the doors on them and left them to it.

Dave gave me a look, as I flopped down into the shotgun seat, I grimaced back. He gunned the accelerator, playfully raising his eyebrows, and drove straight into the usual heavy traffic on Ware High Street. We crawled along at about 5 miles an hour for a while, and then, with a mischievous grin plastered onto his face. Dave turned the music down, tilted his head to listen to what was being said in the back, and amazingly we heard Andy and Whiff chatting away quite amicably about tonight's gig.

"You know you worry too much, Dave," I said, smiling contentedly.

"Well, some bugger has too," he, my old man-ed back at me, tapping the steering wheel to 'Capricorn'.

I cracked up, then choked up. Stampy and some of The Wolf Pack were marching down Ware High Street towards our crawling van. I slowly eased myself down in my seat.

"What's up with you?" Asked Dave, watching my head sink into the footwell.

"Errr… Nothing mate… I thought I saw, an old readymade down here," I said, scrabbling around in the old chip papers, Mr. Kipling's Showboat cake boxes, and Styrofoam cups.

"Well, is there one there…?"

"Er… Yeah… No," I said, leaning further forward, burying my head.

A mass of dark Crombie jackets filled the window above me, then promptly disappeared. Blood-red D.M.'s stamping off down the high street. I thought, what a bunch of wankers, they just walked right passed us in a bright yellow van. On a clear day, I bet you could see it from the fucking moon.

"What's up with you? You're looking shaky, Skin. You still smoking dope?"

"Yeah, and now and again," I said, resurfacing.

"You should be careful; it's making you… What is it they get?"

He said, clicking his fingers, "Yeah, that's it… paranoid."

"Yeah… Paranoid, Dave. Yeah, that's it," I repeated, sitting up, taking a deep breath.

Dave shook his head, got back to The High Street tail back, which, thankfully, began to ease.

Once, we had found the venue, a little hall at the top of Lord Street near Hoddesdon Tower Centre, we parked up, and I went around the back of the van to open the door for Whiff and Andy.

"Oh, after you, old chap," Andy said, faux politely.

Whiff returned, "Oh, thanks old bean," smiling wryly at me, and got out.

"Yeah, yeah, yeah, very good, so it's peace in our time, is it?" I asked, their amused faces.

Both of them cracked up laughing.

"Nice one, Neville Chamberlain," I said, patting Whiff exaggeratedly on the back, while throwing a warm grin at Andy, who smiled back happily.

"OK, come on then, let's go and have a laugh," I said, and we all grabbed a few bits of Dave's kit each, made our way up to the venue.

Whiff pushed down on the metal bar, opening the light brown wooden double doors, and we walked in, switched the lights on. Immediately, a strange feeling of Déjà Vu, came over me, like I had been here before. A small, raised area served as a stage at the far end of the hall, and in front of the stage there were tables and chairs separated by a long walkway that ran down the middle from front to back.

"Er… Dave, do you get the feeling that you've been here before?" I asked.

"Yep," He nodded, despondently, "It's just like Flounder's Hall, isn't it?"

"For fuck's sake, all we need now is The Late, Late Breakfast Club, for wankers too busy in the morning to show up."

Dave nodded thoughtfully, like he was back there too, then behind us, the door flew open, crashed shut. I jumped, half expecting the old bag to appear shouting some hysterical bullshit at us again; only to see it was Andy and Whiff, a sea of calm still chatting away, brightly, bringing in a couple of drum cases.

I shook the gurning Flounders Hall mum's face out of my head, "Oh well, at least those two are getting on again."

"And look at that… Whiff's helping out too," Dave replied, reaching for his heart, like he was about to have a massive heart attack.

I chuckled, "Whoa, two miracles in one day, fucking hell we should be getting scared."

Dave whistled the Twilight Zone theme tune, wiggling his fingers in the air.

"Oh what, it looks like we're back to playing with no P.A. system again," I sighed, scanning the empty stage.

Dave nodded, screwing the high hat together, "Skin mate, we've already had two miracles today, and since one of our tracks is called, 'Christ Fuckers', I reckon we were lucky to get any at all."

I laughed, and he asked me how it went with Cerys the night before, and as I told him, Whiff joined us and offered me a readymade roll-up, which I took gratefully, sparked it up.

"I like Cerys, she's a classy lady," Whiff smiled.

"Yeah, she is mate. Cheers, she's nice. It took me a while to get there, but I got there in the end though. I reckon, she's a lucky girl," I pulled, a self-satisfied grin, felt some bacci come free in my mouth.

So, I exaggeratedly gobbed it out onto the floor, just to illustrate the point.

"You're a real catch, you know that Skin," Dave said, and we all dissolved into fits of laughter.

A few more trips out to the van and back, with all of us helping, we were soon set up and ready to go. It was a pain not having a P.A. system, but it made things simple – set up the drum kit, plug in the guitars, plug the mic in; let's play. It was still early, so we made our way across Lord Street, into the foreboding looking Tower Centre, on a search for some grub; anything would do, just something to fill up on.

Dave soon pointed out a grimy windowed fish and chip shop, so we made a dash through the biting wind, and dancing newspapers, within the Tower Centre's grey concrete walls, grabbed our paper-wrapped food, and made our way back, only to find five of Andy's mates in the hall.

Andy shouted, "Tim, Nicola!" And ran over to chat with them, while Whiff and me wandered back over to the low stage, and began eating our already cold fish and chips.

"Oh shit, looks like everyone's stopped in to watch Songs of Praise," I joked.

"Well, they can fuck their own Christ," Whiff replied, aggressively.

I nodded in agreement, "Yes, indeed, they can, and given half the chance they probably would."

Dave tutted, "There definitely won't be any more miracles now."

I stifled a laugh and Whiff gave Dave a quizzical look and finding no further information was forthcoming, he said, "Is anyone actually coming to see us tonight?"

On hearing the outer door slam, I put my finger up, like an explanation mark.

"Here we go, hope there's enough room for everyone."

Into the hall, walks Chris Almond, Basher, followed by Little Bash, his little brother, John Finlay, and Craggy, a couple of the Hertford Heath Skinheads, commonly known as 'The Dirty Dozen'.

I looked to Dave, "Ye of little faith… There you go, that's another er… Four people."

Dave smiled, shaking his head cynically, clearly not impressed. So, he picked up his sticks, lashed into a combination of full kit rolls. I hadn't seen Chris since the Newtown Neurotics gig at The Heath, where Basher had made off with the takings. Little Bash I hadn't seen, since his older brother had tried to nick my Crass 'Feeding of the Five Thousand' album. He looked exactly like Basher, right from his tartan bondage trousers, up to his little Mohican. I didn't really know Craggy and John Finlay, but like Mark Harper, Steve Bartlett and the Ware skinheads, The Dirty Dozen were alright, hated politics, hated the right wing. Basher was certainly a sight for sore eyes; it was time for us to get our hands on that Fostex four-track; I moved in, thinking that between the four of us, we could raise twenty quid, no problem.

"You alright Chris? Alright Basher?" I greeted them, nodding an alright to the other two.

Basher ran a tattooed hand through his spikes, "Yeah, I'm flush mate, got a lot of things on the go."

"Oh yeah? …You still helping people get rid of their wanted goods?" I asked, looking impressed, thinking here we go, that Fostex will be ours by the end of the night.

The Mohican nodded back, ready to fence some goods.

"What, you got then? …You got any Fostex four-tracks, by any chance?"

"Nah sorry Skinner… You know my dog, Stinky Terrier? He drunk some of my sister Carol's hair dye and went mental. He smashed it to bits… How do you know about that then?"

"Everyone knows about that, Bash," Chris informed him, "I saw Paranoid John in Tesco's yesterday, buying a psycho knife."

Basher cracked up, "Yeah, sure you did, Chris. I don't give a monkeys if he did. I'll stick his knife up his arse, the stupid fucking hippy, he's nothing… Nah listen Skinner, I'm selling 10ps mate."

I gawped at him, waiting for the punchline, a punchline that wasn't forth coming.

Chris smiled, sighed, explained, "You won't believe what this nutter did… He only robbed Wendy's Amusement's Arcade in Hertford town centre."

Basher and me, both creased up.

"Yeah, hid in the broom cupboard until that miserable twat Reg - you know, that wanker you worked for? Limp Dick Larry the Odor Eaters man - went home. Then I jemmied all the fruit machines open, got away with thousands of 10ps. Can't get rid of them now, so I'm selling them."

Oh no. Not Reg, I thought.

"It's a classic Skinner, he's been in every shop in Hertford buying stuff with these 10ps. Then the raid was in The Hertfordshire Mercury, and people started getting suspicious," said Chris, in fits of laughter.

Oh no… Fucking hell no, not Reg, my mind raced. He had a heart attack after we nicked his Odor Eaters shoe tree, from his shop, a few years back.

Basher nodded proudly, "Well suspicious, brought my sister Carol, a Bush digital alarm clock in Tandy's with a hundred and sixty 10p coins. They were looking at me, looking at the coins. I thought they were going to call the old bill; I was shitting it, Skinner… I'm knocking them out for a pound, for one pound, twenty's worth of 10p's."

I scratched my head, thinking…
I didn't know what to say…
In the end it, was obvious…

"I tell you what. One forty… I'll give a pound for one forty," I said, giving him a that's it look.

"OK then, if you dedicate a song to us tonight."

I smiled at the mad bastard, "Deal. Public Enemy, will be for you two, fuck it, the whole set will be yours, there's no one here. Do you know anyone else who's coming?"

Andy appeared next to us, with a couple of his mates.

"It's going to be one of those gigs again, isn't it?" Andy said, looking around the empty hall, "Hello!!! Is there anybody there?" He shouted, his voice echoing off the walls.

Basher grinned at Andy, "I saw Dirty Den with his missus Rosie, in the Tower Centre. He said, he'll be here soon, they're getting some chips."

"Oh, nice one, is Den coming?" Asked Whiff, from over my shoulder.

"Den!!! You mean Shake or Vac?" I replied, cracking a smile in the circle of Punks.

"No leave it out Skin… He's alright he is, he's getting his life back together now," Whiff said sincerely, fighting his mate's corner, moving into our circle.

I put my hand up, "Yeah, sorry mate, he's alright I suppose, we need everyone tonight, how many we got in now? …Eleven? Twelve?"

Andy snorted, at his confused mates. "One of Whiffy's druggy mates," he informed them, holding back a big laugh.

Whiff sighed at Andy, like he was a petulant kid, "Andy! …Den's alright. He's a decent bloke, just needs a chance, he's been clean all year, he's getting his life back on track again, his wife's moved back in with him with his kids. He loves his kids."

Andy scrutinised Whiff with an amused look on his face, surprised, grinning at his openness, "You would say that, wouldn't you, Whiffy? …He's probably got some drugs for you."

"Shut up, Andy, you don't know what you are talking about," Whiff said, testily.

Andy cracked up. Whiff shook his head and wandered off in the direction of the stage area.

"What's up with him?" Asked Andy, shrugging his shoulders, watching him go.

"I don't know Andy," I told him, watching him too.

The circle of Punks viewed me expectantly,

"He probably needs a fix, or something," I joked, sending them into fits of laughter.

Whiff stepped up onto the little stage in the corner of the empty hall, sat on his amp, and began to put a roll-up together. I've got to see what that was all about, I thought, so after telling Basher, I would see him later about his coin exchange venture. I strolled over to the disgruntled bass player to do my plausible impression of Henry Kissinger; it looked like it could be another busy night for the diplomat.

Henry Kissinger didn't even have a chance to make his opening gambit; Whiff saw him coming, put his palms up, like he had been vindicated, "I'm sorry Skin, but that's Andy for you… It's what I've been trying to tell you, Skin. He does my head in. Why does he have to come out with crap like that? Den's alright, he is… 'Oooh, is that where you get your drugs from Whiffy?' …He's like a little kid."

"Oh, leave it out Whiff, don't start this again. It's like, every time we have a gig, you two start. He was just messing about mate. You know? Having a laugh…" I replied, keeping my voice level.

Whiff sighed, nodded, took a pull on his rolly, calming down, and finally he acquiesced, "Yeah, well, I suppose so, he's alright… He shouldn't say stuff like that though, it pisses me off."

Dave's head popped up from behind his now set up drum kit, "What's up?" He enquired.

"Oh, nothing Dave… It looks like nobody's going to show up, that's all," I Henry Kissinger-ed him.

Dave snorted, "Wouldn't be the first time, would it? …We're still going to play, aren't we?"

I picked up my guitar, strummed the glorious bar E chord, filling the hall, "Oh what, yeah, of course we are mate, we've got too. I've dedicated the whole set to Basher. You two want to play, don't you?"

Dave nodded; he always wanted to play.

Whiff nodded too and puffed out a huge smoke ring. "Yeah, definitely, it's not so bad, I'm just going to think of it as another practice," he said, watching his smoke ring ghost off.

"Nice one Whiff, good idea… It'll be a practice in front of some mates. I tell you what… Let's leave it another half an hour, see if anyone else turns up? …Give some of the late comers a chance. Cerys said she was going to get a lift over with Craig. He'll bring a car full. Harper and his mates are bound to show up… Maybe, more of the Dirty Dozen will show up," I suggested, hoping.

Dave and Whiff nodded back at me in unison. I thought well done, Henry, another inter Andy-Whiff diplomatic incident avoided.

One second at a time, the clock above the main entrance slowly ticked off, and the door stayed firmly shut; then around eight o'clock, a grinning Den shuffled into the hall, saying hi, with his pretty wife Rosie in tow, who greeted everyone with a huge friendly smile. Whiff and Andy exchanged a glance, and I thought, even with thirteen people in the audience, we had better play now, better that, than risk another Den conversation between the two of them; it would only get worse, worse for everyone. It was time.

Virus V1 stepped up onto the low stage to a smattering of applause from the small group of people congregated, in front of us. As I looked down, I felt that Flounders Hall feeling of Déjà Vu all over again. Why are we bothering to do this, I thought, this is a complete waste of time, a step backwards after our last couple of gigs, we were making some headway; now we're back to this bullshit again.

Shut up, I told myself, calm down, concentrate, stop taking it all so seriously. If I wasn't here, what else would I be doing? Sitting in the pub probably, which is fine, I love doing that, but I would rather be playing, even if it was a Flounders Hall part two. I needed to relax, let the music do its thing, do what it always did. Smiling to myself, I wondered, if anyone was going to start running about playing chase down the middle walkway or start haranguing us for saying fuck in front of their dopey looking kids.

144

Dave bashed out the intro to 'Everybody's Boy' bringing me back to reality, so I quickly formed the bar E chord with my left hand, and we were off, up, running again. All things considered, I thought, even without a P.A. system, our sound was pretty good, so I nodded my head along with Dave's hardcore beat and as the always, all-encompassing music ran through me. I wondered if anyone else was feeling it. Checking the audience, I remembered that only thirteen people had come to see us tonight. It was sad, embarrassing, a new low, and we'd had our share of lows over the years since we first came together.

On the left of the stage, Den and Rosie were watching us in silence, but clearly enjoying it, and on the right, Andy's mates were really getting into it, as they always did - but the whole thing was ridiculous. It reminded me of something I had seen on TV called, The Comic Strip Presents 'Bad News Tour'. Bad News hadn't had many people in either, and when the band had finished playing, they were told by the promoter, that the gate was so small, there was no money for them. Den Dennis, their dozy bass player, had replied, 'I saw quite a few people in there, there was the man with a dog. You didn't let the dog in for nothing did you?'. I looked up, and for fuck's sake, we hadn't even managed to get a dog to come and see us tonight. Only thirteen humans. I suppressed a laugh, got back to doing something I could control, which was smashing the chords down onto the frets, right up until 'Everybody's Boy' ended.

Andy drew the mic up, acknowledging the applause with a low bow, "Cheers Mum and Dad, I'm glad you could make it again, and if that's not you out there. Tom and Nicola, you can be my Mummy and Daddy for tonight, but only if you return me to my real parents tomorrow in the same condition that…"

145

A massive nerve shattering screech of feedback emitted throughout the hall, drowning him out, sending the audience's fingers rushing to their ears for protection, as Whiff pushed his bass up against his amp.

Andy spun around. "Oh ha, ha, Whiffy, well done," he mouthed, in his direction, dossing him out.

Whiff dossed back at him, provocatively, hoping for what, I didn't know. Andy held his stare for a long while, shrugged, laughed, turned his attention back to his mates in the audience, drew the mic back up.

 "OK. Right, so… Er, yeah, this one's for all you Jesus freaks, it's called, 'Christ Fuckers'."

A few of his mates clapped, and made whooping noises, like they were on an American daytime TV chat show, and Andy shushed them with his hand, and finally, the whoops stopped, echoed off into silence.

Dave hit the intro and barely audibly, Andy whispered, "Whiffy fuckers," into the mic. I almost stopped the track then and there. It was unbelievable; I definitely heard it, though, but when I threw a glance, at the two of them, they were grinning at each, like it was all a big laugh. OK, I thought, maybe, they are just trying to make the best of a bad situation, lightening things up; maybe I should too.

'Christ Fuckers' ended two minutes, twenty-three seconds later, and Andy said, "Cheers, this one is called, 'Protest'. When in doubt, I always say 'Protest' and what's the best way to protest… Anyone?"

One of Andy's mates put his hand up, grinning like he was a student in class. I thought, what the fucking hell is going on now? What is he doing? Andy pointed to his grinning mate, like he was a teacher, signalling his student to answer. Inevitably, there followed, another massive shriek of feedback, as again Whiff rammed his bass up against his amp, making the audience wince and reach for their ears again.

Andy didn't say anything this time. It was like he was expecting it, so quickly, before things went any further, wandering over to Whiff, as casually as I could, when you're up on stage, I told him, "Whiff mate, come on, give it a rest, it's embarrassing."

Whiff snorted, "Yeah… It fucking is," nodding pointedly at Andy.

"OK, right, I get it. But not now man, let's just play, we can talk later."

In front of us, a few people laughed at the rapidly developing soap opera up on stage. I thought well, it's cheap, it lures people in using humanity's worst traits, and it's getting nastier by the minute. Maybe, we are on a day-time American TV chat show, after all – whoop, fucking whoop, indeed.

Whiff gave me an imploring look, "Please Skin, I've had enough, mate."

"OK mate, I'll sort it out, not now though, let's just play the set through," I said to his unconvinced face, he just stared back at me vacantly.

So, I pounded straight up to Andy, pulled him in close, whispered, "Come on mate, let's just play the tracks, you can have a laugh with your mates later," into his ear.

He pulled back, a surprised look etching itself, onto his face. I smiled thinly at him, trying to reassure him, trying to get him to stop, but I saw only confusion. Shrugging, I made my way back to my place on the far right of the stage, thinking, there is nothing more I can do right now; we'll make things better, later.

Andy silently looked down at the floor for what seemed like a very long time, so long, in fact, that I started to believe that he was going to walk off, then just as I was about to go and reassure him again, thankfully he drew the mic up and said, "I think we'll save that one for later. This is 'Protest'."

'Protest' starts with me, so I hit the intro and as I watched the bar E go up and down the fretboard. I couldn't help feeling that I probably would have been better off in the pub tonight after all, because this was turning into a nightmare, a nightmare I was only two tracks into, with a dozen or so to go.

Once we had all come in, I could see it wasn't just me either. Whiff and Dave were feeling it too. Both of them played mechanically without enthusiasm, and with that, little mistakes began to creep in.

In the middle of the stage, it was a totally different story. Andy was having a great time, exaggeratedly prowling the stage with great gusto, giving his mates a decent show, and they in return responded by grabbing at the mic, shouting our lyrics back at him. It was a strange scenario, I thought, one band as a whole, playing together, being so split, but what could I do about it? I couldn't stop; it would make us look ridiculous. What would anyone do about it? Just keep on playing, it was the only way.

One by one, Virus V1's tracks passed us by, vanishing into the nearly empty hall, along with our long-gone enthusiasm. Andy and Whiff still exchanged glances, like they were daring each other to go a stage further, ramp it up; and then when we came to 'No More Genocide' after my one note intro. Whiff powered into his bass part and Andy's mic to let out a huge nerve shattering screech.

Whiff jolted forwards, hit a bum note, his plectrum flipped up into the air spinning like a coin, and with big saucer like eyes, he watched it fall to the ground, and the audience then shifted nervously beneath us.

Andy turned to Whiff, grinning from ear to ear. "Whoops, sorry Whiffy," he said.

Whiff threw his big frame forwards, bent over, picked it up, stood back up, steadily, dossing out Andy all the way. Andy didn't even blink. He stared back, held his glare, a huge smile playing at the corner of his lips. Yeah, I was right I thought, we are now an Oprah Winfrey Punk band; any minute now, Dave and me will have to be the security and get between them; hold the two slavering guests apart.

Virus V1 was a band, not some kind of American freak show, made to satisfy the moronic masses. I was furious, so I shot both Andy and Whiff a look. Hit the intro, and this time when Whiff started his part, thankfully, there was no interruption, and we played it through to its end without any further incident.

"OK thanks," said Andy, to the silence at the end of the track, it seemed like everyone apart from Den and Rosie were now more interested in the unfolding drama between Andy and Whiff than the music.

"OK, right, this is our last track, before our last track, so the track of the last, of the last, if you know what I mean, so to get straight to it, the penultima…"

'Sreeeeeeeeeeeeeeeaaaaaa.' Shrieked Whiff's amp.

"It's called…." shouted Andy.

'Sceeeeeeeeaaaaa…Sccccccceeeeeeeeee' continued,Whiff's amp.

Whiff smirked over at the floundering Andy, who turned red-faced, "Oh well done Whiffy, right, if you can sort that out for us… Thanks, Mmmate!"

Whiff pulled away from his amp, and the noise abated.

Andy drew the mic up, "Right that's better, right, so this one's called, Suffer Little Children… It's dedicated to all the druggy parents in the audience tonight," said Andy, smirking at Whiff.

I knew what he was saying or trying to say. Den didn't, though, he was too busy studying Dave's white pearl drum kit, and from what I knew of Dirty Den, he wouldn't have cared anyway. He'd heard it all before, he had been doing smack on, and not so much off, since the sixties - it was like bong water off a duck's back.

Whiff certainly did though, so did Rosie; she'd heard it all before too, but unlike Den she did care. She cared about a man who was

addicted to a body-destroying, brain-numbing, family ripping, slow death. She looked up at Andy, like it was him that had sold him his first wrap.
I thought for fuck's sake, we have moved on from Oprah now, we are now onto Christiane F so, I quickly played the intro to the track, keen to stop this farce, get it over with, end the embarrassment.

On our last track V1 Bomb, I was counting the seconds to its end. I couldn't wait for it to be over, so we could get out of here, have a pint, and maybe, regroup. It was shit, but not in the way that I had expected it to be. It looked like my initial feelings of Déjà Vu had turned out to be incorrect; this wasn't the same as playing Founders Hall, after all. It was so much worse, we were a united band then, we had a lot of fun too, but this was no fun. No fun at all. One minute and fifty-five seconds later, thankfully, it was all over, and as my guitar faded away into the depths of the hall, an applicative applause broke out from the people watching, which surprised me, as I thought that was probably the worst we had played in years, absolute shit. It continued unabashed. I didn't know what they were thinking, and personally I didn't give a shit. All I wanted to do was get to the pub, have a few pints of the sweet, brown liquid and put this sham of a gig behind me. Andy bowed deeply, and then stepped down from off the low stage, greeting some of his mates while Whiff, Dave and me held back on stage, and started packing up the gear.

I pounded over to Whiff's side of the stage quickly; it was time to forget that wanker Henry Kissinger. Why I thought his kind of diplomacy would work in the first place I didn't know; the Vietnam War raged on for ten years. I thought this war had to end in ten minutes at the most. It had been five years since I had first picked up my guitar, I had done my tour of duty, and I wasn't going to let it all go to waste now.

"What the fuck was that all about, Whiff? …You can't do that live!"

"I'm sorry Skin, it's the things he comes out with, it's embarrassing, he's our frontman, he represents us."

Dave nodded sadly, "He's right, Skin, that was pretty embarrassing."

"OK, OK, yeah, I heard it too, it was embarrassing, it's not a big thing though, is it? He was just having a laugh with his mates; there was nobody here to hear him anyway… I'll talk to him later. OK, Whiff?"

"OK, Whiff???"

Whiff said, "Yeah, OK," begrudgingly.

Andy's laugh rang out from the huddled group of Punks near the main entrance.

I put my palms up, gesturing, "See, he's only having a laugh with his mates… He didn't do it at Bowes or The Triad, did he? …Fucking brilliant nights, they were."

Whiff pulled a thin smile, at the memory, "Yeah, well, true."

"Whiff, look mate, it wasn't the best night for all of us, was it? Let's forget about it. Think about the R.A.R. and C.N.D. benefits we've got coming up, there's sure to be more people there. Andy won't do that in front of a proper audience… And we'll be playing through a proper P.A. again. …And I'll have a word with him later… OK?" I concluded.

Whiff scratched at his stubbly chin, "Yeah, that's right, it's just a bad night."

Dave repeated, "It's just a bad night, lads."

"It's a bad night. So far," I corrected them, "Let's go and have a couple of pints in The Tap, let's make it a good night."

"Nice one, come on, let's do that," Dave agreed.

"Nah, sorry lads, I loved to, but I can't. I've got something else on," said Whiff, beaming, brightening up his mind, on the evening he had in front of him, "I've got a big bag of sensi at home, and the woman's coming around for a smoke, and when she smokes dope, she gets…," he cackled lewdly, leaving us to fill in the gap, about him filling in her gaps.

Dave and me filled in the gap, laughing heartily. Pleased to see our mate back to his normal happy self again. What is it about girls called Steph? I thought; are they all nymphomaniacs?

Whiff was on a roll now, he jumped up and started singing, 'Slip It In' by Black Flag, and pretty soon his infectious good vibes got Dave and me up and singing along too

"You say you don't want it
You don't want it,
Say you don't want it,
Then you slip it on in,

In, in, in…"

"I'm going to see the woman… It's fucking woman time," solo-ed Whiff, grabbing his bass, running his shovel like hands over the curves of its black body, "It's fucking. The Woman time." He punned.

I cackled back at the mental git, "I love that… The woman."

Whiff smiled, "Yeah, she is. The Woman, she's lovely, we really get on, she's a great laugh and there's no doctor whites, so it's going to be one of those nights…"

"Oh what… We don't want to know, man," I said, playfully.

Dave slapped his forehead, "Oh yeah, how is the old boat race?"

Whiff grinned, remembering his opening gambit to her, "Nice, well nice, and when she's had a spliff, she… Oh, those legs."

"Jeeeesuuus!!!" I shouted, quickly putting my hand up in front of his face to ward off any details.

Dave pulled a revolted face, "Yeah enough already, Mr. Hammersmith," putting the last piece of his drum kit into its box and Alan-ed, "Bloody hell, have a heart mate, I don't want to see that, do I?"

"OK mate, no problem, you go and see The Woman, and we'll have a pint another time," I said.

Whiff nodded absently, still thinking of what was waiting for him tonight.

Dave nodded towards him, shook his head, rolled his eyes, "Look at him, he's got it bad, hasn't he? She must be alright? …Have you seen her, Skin?"

"Yeah, I have, saw her on Ware High Street. You pointed her out to me, didn't you Whiff? She's well nice. She's slim with long straight black hair. It goes right down her back, doesn't it?"

Whiff smiled at the image, hopelessly lost in it.

I continued, "Her old man's Maltese, isn't he, Whiff?"

He grinned, "I think so, she's got beautiful soft dark skin… And her Mum's well horny too."

Dave sang, "Here's to you, Mrs. Robinson, Jesus loves you more than you could know, whoa, whoa. Whoaaaa, alright Andy?"

Andy drawled, "Oh no, you're not talking about your many, many, girlfriends again, are you, Whiffy?" Appearing at my side.

Whiff snorted, "Nah, not with you around, Andrew."

Andy roared with laughter.

"I'm afraid, he is mate," I said,

"I reckon she sounds alright. Black hair, dark skin, smokes dope. I'd like to meet her," I continued with my summing up of the woman.

"Hmmm. She smokes drugs? …Doesn't sound good," said Andy, stroking his chin, thoughtfully.

"Oh what, have you actually met her, Andy?" I pressed tersely, and as soon as it was out of my mouth, I knew I had made a mistake, a fucking big one. Whiff was now watching him like a hawk.

Andy paused, looked from me to Dave, and back again.

A couple of his mates drifted in with Chris, Basher, and their mates, joining Den and Rosie, who I hadn't noticed had been listening in too,

"Yeah, I've met her, she's OK," he said, smiling.

Yes, I thought, OK is good, OK is more than good enough. Nice one, Andy. Now don't say anything else, keep schtum, let's just get packed up, and maybe, we can...

"I wondered what she was doing going out with someone like you," he added.

Dave sniggered behind me, then stifled it. Oh, shit, I thought, that's not good. Not good at all.

"You be around Ware tomorrow, then Whiff?" I asked, trying to head off the rapidly escalating situation.

"Oh, leave it out Andy," interjected Whiff testily, shifting uncomfortably on the low stage.

"I'll tell you what, when you get a girlfriend, then you can have an opinion... She's better than OK. She's well nice... Better than anything you could get," he told him, with venom.

Andy's brain seemed to go into overdrive; his mates were watching, his mates in the band were watching, the druggy and his wife were watching, heck, the whole world was watching. I could almost see the cogs turning in his head, and I thought, whatever it is you're thinking of saying, please don't.

In a second, the cogs dropped into place. Andy had it, the perfect answer, he said it, "No, she's only OK, if she was 'well nice', she wouldn't be going out with you, Whiffy… Whiffy and your little stiffy," Andy laughed hysterically, and everybody apart from Whiff joined him, exploding into laughter. The hall shook with it, and it echoed straight back into Whiff's puce angry face.

Dave repeated, "Whiffy and your little stiffy… That's a little bit harsh, isn't it, Andy?"

Andy grinned, "It's the harsh realities of life, my friend," and they both creased up laughing.

Whiff scowled, looked Andy dead in the eye, "Fuck. Off. Andy!" He snapped and stomped off.

I sighed, feeling the last of my energy, ebbing away from me.

"Jesus fucking Christ." I stormed.

Andy grinned inanely, "Sooorrryyy… I thought it was funny," he then shrugged his shoulders, and disappeared in the opposite direction, with his laughing mates in tow.

On the journey back, Dave and me decided that it would be best for everyone if we separated our vocalist and our bass player. So, I had to sit in the back squashed up against Whiff, while Andy took shotgun, with Dave, as the atmosphere between the two of them was on a knife edge. It was the worst I had seen them, since the day Whiff had wiped his arse sweat onto Andy's lip in the churchyard; worse than George Best's hairy chest at Ware College, and both episodes were bad enough to break up any band.

In the dark, cramped, back of the van, I started feeling claustrophobic, like I couldn't breathe; worse still, my mind kept racing back to Andy and his 'Whiffy and his little stiffy', comment. It was stupid, it was immature, it was childish. It was fucking hilarious, my mind looped it over and over again, until I went into a coughing fit, to stop the laugh that was desperately trying to rise up inside me.

Dave banged up the volume on the cassette player right on cue, almost like he was battling the same 'Whiffy stiffy' demon, that I was. Instead of battling with our over-active imaginations, we listened to Lemmy whining about 'how he was born to lose'. Yeah, sure you were mate, I thought bitterly, with your gigs, your record deal, your legions of fans and groupies. I bet you don't have two members in your band niggling at each other all the time, embarrassing you in front of everyone, you warty-faced twat.

A short uncomfortable ride later, sandwiched between Whiff and the bass drum case. Dave pulled up outside of Tescos, and Andy hopped out, came around the back of the van to let us out and after saying 'see you later' to Dave and me, he sauntered off down Ware High Street.

Once we had untangled ourselves and Whiff's bass from the back, I said testily, "OK Whiff, I'll see you later. And sort it with Andy, will you? Phone him, go around for him, fucking, talk to him."

"I'm sorry about that Skin, he does my fucking head in," Whiff sighed.

"Yeah, yeah, yeah, talk to him, sort it out," I said, hurrying him along, and with a quick nod, he disappeared into the darkness of Church Lane, taking the short walk back to his place.

In a second, I jumped into the passenger seat, regaining shotgun, glad to be rid of them both, and stretched out my aching legs, trying to get some feeling back into them. Dave gunned the engine, and we set off back to the village. As we put some distance between us, and Ware, I regained a bit of blood flow in my legs, calmed my mind down, reached forward, turning the whining Lemmy down.

"Oh well, that was a load of fucking shit, wasn't it?" I sighed.

Dave laughed, "Yeah fucking shit… I'd say that just about sums that night up."

"I counted thirteen people in there, Dave… Thir-fucking-teen, and OK I know we'll still have to play gigs like that sometimes but fuckiiiiiinnnnngggg hell…" I said, slapping my forehead.

Dave nodded thoughtfully, focusing on the dark road before us.

"And what about those two? Bloody hell," I continued, my whining only just beginning.

"Whiffy and his little stiffy…," said Dave, his face lit up, cackling into the rearview mirror.

"Another Andy classic," I laughed back.

"We should call Steph, Whiffy's little Stephy," I said.

Dave chuckled back, "I don't want to be the harbinger of doom here Skin, but I reckon one of them is going to leave, and I think I know which one it will be too."

"Whiff?"

"Yeah. Andy would never leave the band."

"I don't know, maybe. One thing I do know is… They're both replaceable."

Dave grinned, "We're the V.I.P.s in this band," he said, nodding to himself.

"C.U.N.T.s, more like," I said, laughing,

"Nah… Seriously, if it goes the other way and Andy leaves, I know a couple of people who would be interested."

Dave smoothly changed the van up into fourth gear, "Oh yeah, like who?"

"I know Basher would."

He smiled, "What old light-fingered Larry, the kleptomaniac?"

I sniggered, "Yeah that's him, he'd be good though; looks good, he's got a good voice, and he already knows most of the early tracks, we'd just have to nail everything down if he came into our houses."

Dave laughed, "I don't know, he sounds dodgy mate, who else?"

"OK, don't laugh… He's one of Doggy's mates."

Dave laughed, "Oh dear, oh dear, let's hope it doesn't come to that, eh?"

"Nah, he's good, his name's Sulli, he's alright Dave," I protested, "He's already in a band, though."

He snorted, "Who's he with? The London Philharmonic?"

I cracked up, stretched some more blood into my legs, "No, he sings in a Cambridge Punk band called, The Sickos, trouble is, I don't see him unless I'm with Doggy, and after the last time we saw Doggy…" I trailed off.

Dave nodded again, changed down into third as the van struggled up Ware Hill, "Hmm not good, so what happens if Whiff leaves then?"

"Now that would be easier, Chris Almond, Basher's mate, the other bloke with the Mohican at the non-gig tonight plays guitar, and he's good too."

"Chris Almond! He's not Mark Almond's brother, is he? …If he is, I'm the one that's leaving," said Dave, changing up again.

I sniggered, "Nah, he's one of the Hertford Heath Punks, he's a decent guitarist."

"Er… But we'll need a bass player, Skin."

161

"I know, I know, it's fine mate, trust me, being a guitarist would give him a head start. Wouldn't take him long to pick it up. He'd love to join us too, every time I see him, he talks about the band."

"Sounds promising, anyone else?"

"Er… There is, yeah," I replied, tentatively.

He took his eyes off the rolling tarmac, gave me a quick glance, "Go on then."

"Basher plays bass, he's pretty good too."

Dave took his hand off the wheel, slapped his forehead, "Jesus, Skin!"

"What? It might work out… Anyway, look on the bright side, he could nick a P.A. system for us," and we both cracked up laughing.

"Nah, seriously, though, let's hope it doesn't come to that."

I nodded, "It'll be OK, I'll talk to Andy, tell him to stop winding him up, he's alright, he'll listen to me."

"I hope so mate, I like them both."

I nodded back, agreeing with him, then he turned the music back up, for the final part of the journey, pulling the curtain down on the conversation. I sat back, gazing out of the window, and as we passed the Thundridge Village sign, from out of the driving console, Lemmy sang, 'the chase is better than the catch' gruffly. Not for the first time that day, I thought, this bloke is talking out of his arsehole;

I'd take the catch every time. In fact, there wouldn't even be a chase without a catch, the warty tosser.

"Oh, by the way, I've got a date for my house," Dave said, disturbing my internal rant.

"Sounds good mate, when you moving in then?" I asked, feigning interest.

"It's happening, I can't believe it Skin, the solicitors came through really quickly, it's only a few weeks away now, I'm going to gut the place before I move in, and listen to this, before I rip it all out, and do it all up, I'm going to have a massive house-warming party, get everyone around," he beamed over at me.

"Now that is a good idea, man!"

He nodded proudly, "We'll have a proper piss up, invite everyone we know, fill the place up!"

I thought, maybe buying a house when you're young isn't such a bad idea after all.

Chapter Seven

Dapper Destroys the Spice Rack Dealers

Cerys and me was everything I had dreamt it would be. She was a
positive girl, intelligent, funny, and when we talked, it felt natural and
unforced, which meant we always seemed to have plenty to talk
about; sometimes I was surprised just how much we had in common
– so was she. We wiled away our time in The Anchor drinking with
Del and Joyce, who not only shared the same sense of humour as us,
they were always up for a proper session too. In fact, they were on a
different planet to us when it came to drinking, as both Del and
Joyce had worked in pubs at some point in their lives and both loved
pub culture. Del and Joyce would be in the pub most nights, and
Cerys and me would join them, which more often than not would
end up in a mammoth session, where we would drink solidly from
opening time till the last bell and then go back to their place with a
bottle of wine and a few carry-outs. If I had any sensi, or Del had
any Squidgy Black or Red Leb, Del would entertain us by building
enormous twelve-inch long spliffs, using bamboo dinner place mats
to keep the monster joints together, and then once the task was
completed, we would spark the rolling pin sized spliffs and puff
away, swigging our pints, while the girls drank their wine. I had a
decent amount of money coming in, and Del and Joyce could be
generous beyond belief, but after a while, Cerys, being a student with
only a few quid coming from her Mum, found it expensive going out
every night, and Cerys being the stand-up, independent, free-
thinking kind of girl that she was, wanted to pay her way.

Cerys' days were taken up at college, where she was re-doing her O-
levels; her plan was that once she had passed them, she was going to
follow her dream of enrolling at Chase Farm Hospital in Enfield to
train to be a Registered General Nurse. So, with her days being taken
up studying, she looked into getting a job working in the kitchen at

The Feathers Inn, where her Mum had worked when she was younger.

In The Feathers, it was a completely different world to The Anchor. It had a five-star Michelin restaurant and the clientele to match, so with the promise of higher wages and the likelihood of better tips from the richer pub users of the village, Cerys took the job doing Sunday lunchtimes and a couple of nights a week. Soon after, I started hanging out there too. I felt totally out of place the first time I entered its plush interior, and the looks I got, well; it was hilarious. I hadn't seen that kind of dumbfounded open mouth gawping since in the early days of Punk in 1977. Chris Severn, the owner, didn't look too happy either, seeing the scruff standing at his polished mahogany bar with five-inch blonde spiked up hair, wearing 16-hole D.M.'s and black bondage trousers. His attitude to me soon changed though, when Del and Joyce followed me with their huge wards of cash. Soon to be followed by Dave, and then once Dave was settled in, the rest of the lads from The Anchor came over too, packing the place out, and the cash registers didn't stop ringing. I soon found a quiet spot, similar to 'our bar' in The Anchor. It was away from the posh restaurant, away from the rich, leaving them in peace to eat their quail's eggs, and veal forestiere. I made it my second home, was in there most nights; I would have a few drinks with my mates and then when Cerys had finished her shift, she would come and join us, and sometimes her co-worker Jackie Hopcroft would come along and have a couple too.

Cery's co-worker, Jackie, was a posh girl who lived in a big stately house in Braughing, a village just north of ours, and some nights after work, her brother Richard would come and pick her up. Richard Hopcroft, or Dapper as people called him, was an estate agent, always dressed well, hence the moniker; he drove a brand-new red Alpha Romeo, and from what Cerys told me he sounded like a right wanker - the quintessential Yuppy. One night I was waiting for Cerys to finish her shift when Dapper strutted over to the bar in a dark navy Ted Baker suit, and we started talking; much to my surprise, we clicked straight away. I quickly ascertained that he liked to smoke cannabis and to drive his car, so putting two and two together, I told him about The Frontline, he sounded intrigued, so I suggested we go up there and, he quickly agreed. I was out with Cerys the next night and I wanted to get Danny to come along with us too, as he was always a laugh on a session, so we arranged to meet up later on in the week.

A few days later, Danny and me were waiting outside The Feathers, when Jill Saunders approached us, dangling an empty choke chain in her hand. Her eyes were puffy, red, like she'd been crying, crying a lot.

"Hi Jill, are you OK?" I asked, my voice full of concern.

"No… No, I'm not. It's Benson… He's… He's dead," she said, waving his empty collar in my face to show me he had gone, then she collapsed onto my shoulder, convulsing.

I snorted, and she pulled back, searching my face.

"Ohhhh noooo Jill, that's terrible news… I… Tsk, oh… Nooo," I told her solemnly, burying my rising joy. I thought, yesssssssss, Man, one. Dog, nil.

Jill buried her head back into my shoulder. "I knew you'd be upset," she said, sniffing loudly.

"Yeah… Devastated…," I said, grinning at the grinning Danny.

Jill pulled away from me, as she was hit by another tide of mourning. She wailed, "I'm going to miss him so much, he loved you, every time I mentioned your name to him, his little tail would wag."

"Did he?" I gulped.

"Yes, I would say Skinner's coming and aw…"

I felt a lump of grisly guilt rising like a shark in my guts, and as it rose menacingly towards the surface, much to my relief it was flattened by a falling nausea, as I remembered the bloody thing boaking up pools of white cud onto the pavement, which steamed like hot scotch porridge oats on cold, frosty days.

Jill struck away the fresh batch of tears from her eyes, "I came downstairs this morning and… And he was dead… Dead… Cold in his little basket, he must have been very poorly… He hadn't even drunk his milk."

Oh, for fuck's sake, I thought it's no wonder the little projectile puke machine died, his cholesterol must have been through the fucking roof; I bet it was a heart attack that sunk the Churchill-faced chump.

I was disturbed from my Quincy-like autopsy, by a toot, and turning my attention away from the inconsolable Jill, I saw Dapper in his Alpha Romeo hurtling down High Cross Hill towards us. A second later, he screeched to a halt next to us, smiled, and gestured for us to get in. I hastily patted Jill on the back, apologised, and piled into the shotgun seat, while Danny settled himself comfortably in the back.

Once we'd belted up, Dapper stamped on the accelerator, and we sped away down the A10, towards London, Hackney, and The Frontline.

Dapper, eyes ahead on the rapidly scrolling road, asked, "What was that all about?"

"Ah, nothing… Some mutt just went to the great kennel in the sky," I answered.

Danny creased up and filled Dapper in on the death of the little Puke-ahontas, the reason why it was so funny, and why I hated the little bastard so much, while I took in my new surroundings.

Inside the car it was a completely different world, a world I had never seen before; the yuppy world. It was like no expense had been spared in manufacturing this car. It was top of the range throughout, from the driving console with its numerous white-faced dials on black clocks, the small race steering wheel, right down to the light brown, brushed leather seats and full silver metal door frames, complete with silver gear stick head. I took it all in while the Bee Gees screeched 'Night Fever' unpleasantly, from a pleasant and expensive looking Blaupunkt car radio system, which sat on the centre console between me and Dapper. Into the sumptuous seats, I relaxed, enjoying the ride, while Danny nattered on unfalteringly from the back. I loved the drive into London, the way the silent empty fields slowly gave way to the bricks and mortar of the big city, with its alluring sights, sounds and smells. It was vast, vibrant, exciting, full of colour, and sometimes it felt like the centre of the earth to me. I came back from my reverie as we powered through Stamford Hill and Danny was still jabbering away in the back. He had moved on from Benson the chunder dog, to Craig and Taddy, who had been caught red-handed by Pig Man Cannon syphoning petrol from old man Dawkins car. 'They were due in court next week' he told him. Danny then began 'the booze blag' story, and as the all too familiar story fell from Danny's flapping gob, I zoned out watching the fields go by. Mary-Anne, his mum, was Irish, and she had talked my ear off on many occasions over the years; some people said that she had kissed the blarney stone. I didn't agree though, I thought it was more likely that she had been fucked by The Blarney Stone and Danny was the bi-product of that human/geological encounter. I couldn't believe anyone would have so much to say. He was like a world champion of talk, a non-stop automated teller of all the triviality you could ever, or never, need. Normally I did need, he cracked me up, but not today, I was in a more serious mood.

A few minutes of blather later, Danny finished his summing up of 'the booze blag', and I tuned back in as he briefed Dapper on the many ruses that street dealers used, to stitch people like us up. Once Danny had finally shut up, which wasn't any time soon, I warned Dapper that every time we had been up to The Frontline, the dealers had tried a new tactic to take our money in exchange for something that was more akin to the oregano you found on your spice rack than sensimelia, so to be on his guard. Dapper looked totally unconcerned, told us confidently that, 'nobody rips him off'. Good, I thought, I hope not, as without Ashley and his mate Sol around, we'll need to keep our eyes open.

In the last moments of the day, we drove into the twilight of Hackney; the shadows of the surrounding buildings grew long, deep like concrete mountains, the street lights flickering awake above us.

Dapper smoothly pulled off the A10 onto Amhurst Road, carried on past a line of old three-story town houses, and then turned the red Alpha Romeo into the business end of Sandringham Road.

On the left a large group of Rastas were standing outside The Stanley pub, enjoying an early evening drink, while further down, stood the watchers, who immediately straightened up, waiting for the signal.

I checked to see if there were any police around, and seeing none, I gave the watchers a wave, and a group of dealers came up from the basements nearby, running up to the car, and once there, they hung their little bags of sensi through my window.

Inside the bags I saw the dark green shade of sensi, so I grabbed a three, off the closest dealer.

"It's the proper sensi man. Have a look, have a look."

"Yeah, it looks alright mate," I said, peering at them in the rapidly falling darkness.

"Open a bag man, have a sniff if you can't see it, you'll know. Good weight too. OK? OK? OK?"

"I don't know, hold on," I said, weighing them up in my hands.

In a second, a dazzling light came flooding into the car from behind, making us all jump in our seats. I was momentarily blind, didn't know what was going on. I put a flailing hand up, shielding my eyes, squinted into the wing mirror, and there behind us was another car tight up, with its full beams blazing, burning into my retinas. It was impossible to see who it was or know what was going on; then a horn blasted aggressively, making us all duck down in our seats, followed by a flashing blue light. I felt panic rising inside me. Oh, fucking hell no, I thought, we are in trouble now; we're fucking trapped.

"BABYLON, BABYLON, QUICK, GO, GO, GO!" Someone shouted behind us, sending some of the pack scattering, towards the safety of the basements.

One of the dealers hanging in the window, the one whose bags I held, became agitated, "Come on hurry up, we going to get busted man, come on… COME ON," he said; then dropping three bags onto my lap, he snatched the money and the other bags from my hands and disappeared into the darkness.

"Shit, fucking hell go, Dapper… GO!" I shouted.

"I've only just got this car," he bleated, turning the engine over.

Dapper pulled out, tires screeching, and we shot off down Sandringham Road at high speed, while I held my breath, checked the wing mirror, and I was relieved to see that there was no one following us.

"It's OK, there's no police behind us… It's clear," I said, exhaling, and then the penny dropped. I felt a gnawing sense of realisation. "Oh shit. Oh, fucking hell," I said, picking up the bags.

One at a time I held the bags up, inspecting them, hoping my suspicions were unfounded. The first one looked OK, phew, I thought, but the other two… Ahh… No!!! They were straight off the spice rack.

"Fucking. Wankers… Look at this shit," I said, angrily, smashing my fist down hard onto my seat.

Dapper took his foot off the accelerator; the car slowed, "What's wrong? What happened? We haven't been ripped off, have we?"

171

I looked again, more in desperation than anything else, "Yeah, this one's OK, the other fucking two look like someone picked them off Hector's House's cabbage patch."

Dapper braked hard, throwing Danny and me forward in our seats.

"I'm not having that. Let's go back," he raged.

"I don't know," said Danny, "I don't think we should mess with them; I've heard they can get nasty, what do you think, Skinner?"

Not only did I feel angry. I felt responsible. It was my job as shotgun to make sure it all went down the right way. It hadn't - it was the worst Sandringham rip-off I had seen.

"Yeah, fuck it, let's go back. I'll do the talking, though… And Dapper mate, if things do get heavy, you'd better be ready to get us out of here quickly."

Dapper gestured to his car and said breezily, "Yes, quick, I can do."

"It won't come to that. Will it?" Danny pleaded.

"I don't know. One thing I do know is, I'm not fucking getting stitched up again, come on, let's go back," I told him.

Dapper nodded determinedly, slung his hands onto the racing steering wheel, effortlessly spun the car around, and we cruised back up Sandringham Road in total silence, watching for any sign of movement. I couldn't believe it, it was as if nothing had happened; the watchers saw us coming, gave us the signal, we nodded back, and the dealers appeared from the basements. Once again, coming over

172

to the window in groups of silhouettes. I couldn't see if it was the same group and didn't really care - it was time to sort it.

"You alright?" I spat, to the first couple of dealers, "See this? …Look, we just got stitched up. Look at this shit." I held up the spice rack bags.

One of the dealers took it, inspected it, sucked air in through his teeth, "It's not good man."

"Nah it's not, where's the guy who sold us this shit?" I asked.

Indulging me, he quickly glanced up and down the road. "I don't know man, he's gone. Look, buy mine, buy mine. It's the proper sensi. See for yourselves," he said, thrusting a handful of bags in through the window.

"Where's the old bill?" I asked, looking into him.

"They gone too…" He said, grinning at the little rich kid, sitting in his Daddy's car.

One by one, I sniffed them individually, taking my time, and pleased with the sweet smell of the incense, I laid them out on my lap, like I was playing solitaire with the great, green. Pressing them between my thumb and forefinger, I felt for the consistency of the bags - they had a good firm feel to them.

I thought, yeah, this is the stuff, this is the proper sensi, straight out of Fidel Castro's personal supply, as Ashley would say. Why couldn't we have met this bloke earlier on, before we got burnt? It's fucked up, sometimes how life could be like that, sometimes it's just about timing, a minute here, a minute there. One minute can make a massive difference in the great scheme of things. Oh, well. I sighed, looking at them on my lap; then out of the corner of my eye, I watched unbelievingly as the silver gear stick slipped smoothly into first gear. I braced myself, held on tight, and the car shot forward as Dapper floored it.

Inside the car, arms whipped back out of the window like a video on rewind; outside it was utter pandemonium, angry faces shouted, hands scraped at the fleeing vehicle, there was a huge BAAAM, as something big connected near the back wheel arch, rocking us sideways. Followed by a hail of stones cracking off the boot and back window, and then, at last. We were free, clear, and away.

Dapper changed up to second, then third, soothing the Alpha Romeo's screaming engine as we raced down Sandringham Road towards the junction with Amhurst Road. He didn't look right or left at the junction; he just spun the racing wheel aggressively, and floored it, making the Alpha Romeo's wheels scream out in protest. A few hundred yards down Amhurst Road, Dapper saw the green light on the A10 junction shining out like a homing beacon. So, he dropped the Alpha Romeo down into second, stamped on the accelerator, chucking us all backwards in our seats like rag dolls.

Danny and me, cracked up laughing.

"This doesn't half go! Bloody hell," I said, enjoying the ride.

Dapper said nothing, his eyes focused on the sweet green exit light in front of him.

One hundred yards, green, fifty yards, green go, go, go, and then at thirty yards the lights turned amber and the car coming up to the junction, braked hard, stopping. Blocking our escape.

"Noooo, don't fucking stop… There's still enough time… Oh, you bloody moron," shouted Dapper, stomping down on the brake pedal, catapulting us all forward in our seats.

Dapper knew his car, knew there was no way we were going to stop in time, so he threw his hand down, wrenched up the hand brake with everything he had, making the tyres screech, and the car fishtailed, finally skidding to a halt, a couple of feet behind the overcautious car driver's boot.

"You stupid fucking twat," I mouthed, giving the wankers sign to the fearful eyes viewing us in the stopped car's rearview mirror.

Danny shifted uncomfortably in the back.

"Er, Skinner, there's a couple of blokes coming," he informed us, his voice rising in pitch.

"Yeah, sure there is. Fuck off, Danny," I told him, laughing hollowly.

"I'm not fucking about Skinner, there is, there is, look, look!"

Oh yeah, sure there is, I thought, looking into the wing mirror, sure, that Danny was on the wind up, and saw two blokes sprinting towards us, coming up fast.

"Shiiiiit!" I cried, my head swivelling to the mirror, to the traffic lights, to Danny, to Dapper.

In front of us, the red light beamed down on us, behind me. Danny cowered down low, watching our pursuers. I looked to Dapper, our only hope. His eyes were fixed on the red light, inwardly cursing the stationary car in front of us. There was no way out for us, we were fucked. Fucked by a red bulb. I prayed for the first time since I had been at the Junior Mental Institution, willing the lights to change; they weren't changing anytime soon, the instruction was clear.

STOP. In the wing mirror, I stared beseechingly; they were close, now, really close, bearing down on us, in fact, running like the wind, like mad men. Oh, no, this is it, I thought. The central locking system clunked, we braced ourselves for the inevitable impact…

Danny, Dapper and me, watched them run straight past us.

In the car, it was silent as the three of us gaped at them running away, putting distance between us, and then finally they disappeared around the corner onto Stoke Newington High Street, out of sight, out of mind. I was fucking out of breath.

I cracked the window open, took a deep life-affirming breath, sucking it all in, thirstily, and even in the diesel-polluted streets of London it was beautiful, a thing of wonder; then from the backseat of the Alpha Romeo, I heard Danny laugh nervously. I wheeled around, saw his lopsided grinning face gawping idiotically at me. Sniggering back at him, I placed my hands over my eyes theatrically.

"Well, well, well, that was entertaining, wasn't it!?" Dapper understated, sending us all into fits of raucous laughter. Soon the car was rocking with it – it was like the whole world was laughing.

Whoa, what happened there? I thought, fucking hell, that was a whole new level of adrenaline,

"You fucking mad bastard, you fucking mad bastard!" I told the braying Dapper.

"Yes, yes, yes, yes, yes!" He repeated, nodding his head, laughing like a mad bastard.

"OK, so who wants to smoke some free sensi!" I enquired, holding the bags aloft.

"Mmmm, it wasn't free though, Skinner. I'm going to need some new boxer shorts. I think I've shat myself," said Dapper, descending into laughter.

"I know mate, me too, me too… Oi, check it out, I'm a dealer… Buy mine, buy mine, buy mine," I grinned, waving them in Dapper and Danny's faces.

A sounder of police hurried passed us - maybe six or seven of them. They turned left, disappearing onto Stoke Newington High Street, following in the direction of our, supposedly, assailants.

"Oh, my, fucking, go… D. What? …We need to get the fuck out of here," I said, from the footwell.

"I think that would be wise. Don't you?" Said Dapper, his face cracking into another smile.

"Why?" Said Danny.

"What!!? …The old bill just went passed, you dickhead," I cried.

"Bollocks…"

"I'm telling you Danny, the old bill just went passed, a whole sty's worth, didn't they Dapper?"

Dapper nodded, still, watching the errant traffic lights.

Danny fell about laughing,

"You should see your face, Skinner. Course I saw them, they must have been after those blokes."

"Oh, ha, ha, well done Scooby fucking Doo, you solved the mystery. Come on Dapper, can we get the fuck out of here, in fact, fuck it, can we leave him here," I said, heaving a thumb at Danny in the back, who cracked up laughing.

"I don't mind, give me my bags, and I'll go sell them back to the dealers," said Danny.

"You know what. I believe you would… I know how that would go," I said, handing him a couple of swelling bags, making throat cutting gestures with my other hand.

Dapper snorted, shook his head, put the Alpha Romeo into gear. "Oh, at last," he said, as the light changed to green.

The car in front of us, kangarooed forwards and stalled.

Dapper dropped his head, let out a sigh, "Do you know what guys? …I think we must be in The Hotel California, we'll never leave."

"Oh well, while we're here," said a grinning Danny, winding down the window. "Do you want to buy any sensi?" He asked an old Hasidic Jew trudging past on his walking stick.

"Is it Kosher?" Enquired the old boy, smiling back at him.

Dapper and me cracked up at the old geezer's chutzpah. Danny seemed lost for words for a moment. A strange occurrence, I thought, but not for long, though.

He grinned, "Foreskins for sale. Foreskins for sale, you want to buy a foreskin?"

"Oh what... Fucking hell, Danny, leave it out," I told him.

The old boy stopped, turned, leant forward, examined Danny over his glasses. "How can you sell me a foreskin? When you have no dick of your own?" He returned, and with that, he put his weight on his walking stick, and shuffled off down the road.

Dapper and me fell about laughing, I turned to Danny.

"He knows you, then?" I said, cackling at his floundering features,

"Seriously, Dapper, we need to go, before this knob gets us nicked."

"Yes, I see that Skinner, your mate is a nutter," he said, shaking his head.

A few minutes later, the lights changed again to green, and the overcautious driver in front of us, gingerly pulled away, turning left at the junction, following, what felt like, everybody else's destination that night. Dapper eased the Alpha Romeo into gear, kicked down on the accelerator, effortlessly spun the racing wheel right, and we raced away from them all, up the A10, leaving Hackney Frontline behind us. We headed out of the vast city towards the peace of the countryside - a place we understood so much better - while the Bee

Gees screeched, 'Staying Alive' poignantly from the Alpha Romeo's impressive stereo.

Chapter Eight

The Red Spider

I thought that would be it, as far as Dapper and The Frontline was concerned, and a few days later, he confirmed it, when he told me. 'It would be suicide to go back up there again in a bright red Alpha Romeo and expect no one to remember us'. Not only that, his Mum had noticed some 'rather nasty scratches' on the side of her son's 'new, just out of the showroom' Alpha Romeo. On the bright side, though, he also told me that, as he was now going out with one of the barmaids at The Feathers, called Jo, or Blow Jo as he called her, when Chris Severn, the owner wasn't around, he was going to drown his sorrows in free lager, and I was welcome to join him if I wanted to. OK, I thought, nice one, I'll drown with him; but for me, it wouldn't necessarily have been the end of my trips up to The Frontline, if Ashley had been about, but he hadn't been seen around the village for a long time. He had vanished, and with good reason, too, if you believed his story. Danny had been the last person to have spoken to him, and in true Ashley style, he had told Danny that during a raid on a post office in Lincolnshire, his old man had had an allergic reaction to his balaclava and thrown it off as he legged it under a security camera outside of Boots on the High Street. Ashley reckoned that a few days after the raid, a picture of his old man had appeared in the Lincolnshire Echo that made him look like Bluto from the Popeye cartoons. I had seen Ashley's old man, Mr. Swailey Bolsworth, a mountain of a man, with his tweed Gabor hat and copper tipped walking cane around the village a couple of times. He certainly reminded me of Popeye's rival for Olive's affections, as for him sticking up post offices with sawn off shotguns, I thought it was quite plausible, then again, you never knew with Ashley. One thing I did know was, without Ashley, The Frontline would be hit-and-miss again. I was sick and tired of watching every move the street dealers made, and after our last trip up there, I could see how things could so easily escalate, and get out of control, someone could get hurt. Hurt bad. It was time to start looking elsewhere, somewhere closer.

Once I had sold a bag to Coops, and another one to Del I had one left, then a few days after some decent sessions, with Phil, Mal a la Tete, and Coops, I was dry, totally out: not a good position to be in. I was chatting with Aiden, one of Den's Shake or Vac mates in The Tap, a few days into the drought. I told him of my sad predicament; told him I had plenty of money, and he gibbered, 'Dope gets you through times with no money, better than money gets you through times of no dope', which I didn't think was true, nowhere near it - but it was funny, and I thought, I'll remember that one. In amongst some other gibbering, where he said that, according to the Mayans, the world was going to end in 2012, he told me, he had a mate who knew someone, who knew someone else, who lived in Harlow, on The Bishopsfields estate, or the Kasbah, as it was known locally, who could sort us out. Aiden also told me that the guy was quite naturally paranoid about selling cannabis to strangers, so we would need to use a password, the password being 'cassettes'. He said once we had uttered the magic word, hey presto, we would be in with him, and he, in turn, would serve us up some top class sensi. Danny and me talked it over later, and thought we should give it a try. Our thinking being, it would be good to get out of the village for the night, have a look around the Essex town - what was the worst that could happen?

I had never been to The Kasbah before, and even though my old man had worked in Harlow, passing it every day on his way in and had described it to me in some detail, I was astounded as we approached it.

Bishopsfields was one of those 1960s living experiments, where people were told that this is what the future looks like, which was a lie. It was more artful deception than anything else; a way for the government of the day to build houses on the cheap for people who couldn't afford to buy their own. I didn't know where the architects had got their inspiration from, maybe, Watership Down, as it looked more like a giant rabbit warren than anything else. Inside the poured concrete, the people lived tightly packed together in identical boxes, which were corralled in, bisected, by a multitude of high walkways that seemed to go everywhere and nowhere at the same time. On top of them, high stanchions held huge floodlights, which bled out cold light onto the steep staircases that led down into the dark, rubbish-strewn underpasses. Incredibly, even under the illumination of a thousand burning lights, everything was grim. Grey, depressing. I thought, surely. This is a future that nobody wanted.

Once we entered the maze, only the wind seemed to know which way to go. It blew newspapers, yesterday's news, through the multitude of underpasses, chucking the headlines of murders, strikes, shortages, and political unrest up into our stony determined faces. I noticed that some tenants, had tried to make their little corner of the world look better, by planting shrubs in pots near their front doors. It was no good, though, they were fighting a losing battle, as some of The Kasbah kids, bored, hemmed in, sick of the sight of the place. Had taken out their frustrations on these modest islands of green inside the grey circle, by smashing them to pieces, burying them under yesterday's news.

Danny and me wasted half an hour of our lives wandering backwards and forwards through the bleak labyrinth to find the right house number, finally arriving at 335, our destination.

Danny sighed, kicked off a newspaper, which had entwined itself around his legs, stepped up to the door, and gave it a hefty bang with his fist.

A middle-aged bloke in an AC/DC T-shirt, wearing glasses, opened the door, "Yes?" He asked questioningly, looking from me to Danny.

"You alright mate? You… Er…. Got any cassettes?" Asked Danny, stepping forward with a winning smile.

AC/DC squinted over the top of his half-moon glasses at him, "Cassettes!?" he repeated, frowning.

Danny winked, "Yeah Cassettes!! Have you got any?" he asked, winking again, for good measure.

AC/DC looked at him blankly.

Danny leant in confidently, "Yeah, you know? Cass… Ettes?" He whispered, just to make sure the bloke knew what he was talking about.

"Yeah, course… I don't understand," AC/DC replied, looking up and down the walkway like he expected Jeremy Beadle might be there, cameras rolling.

Oh shit, I thought, the bloke doesn't have a clue what he's on about; something's gone wrong with that fucking stupid gibbering hippie's information. He said 335!!! It could have been anything, from 335 BC, the Mayans first prediction of the apocalypse, to the 335 millilitres he had coming on his next methadone script. It was time to go, let the headbanger get back to his 'Whole lot of Rosie', give the bloke a bit of peace; judging by the huge cock and balls with spunk shooting out from the helmet, that had been sprayed in bright yellow on his outside wall, he probably needed it.

Danny couldn't see it, though. He just ploughed on.

"Sooo, you have got some, then?" He asked, turning to me, hands open, like, now we're getting somewhere.

A shake of my head went completely unnoticed. He was nearly there now.

"Nice one, you've got some caaasssettes," he grinned magnanimously, rubbing his hands together.

AC/DC, barked back, "Yeah! Well! Yeah!" Losing his patience with this weirdo standing on his doorstep - maybe it was one of those spray-can wankers, playing another trick.

Danny smiled like he had just sold water to a school of fish. "OK good, have you got any for sale then? Not all of them, just some for us? …We've got some money… Not a lot, but some," he said, reigning in his enthusiasm, playing the cool businessman.

AC/DC snorted, ground his teeth, "What are you going on about? He shouted, "No, I'm not selling my bleeding cassettes to you. I'm not selling my cassettes to any bleeding body. What do you think this is? A bleeding record shop. Sod off," he told the little moron. And then with one sideways scowl at me, he slammed the door, hard: the bang echoing off down the long walkway.

"It's no good mate, come on, let's get out of here," I sighed, turning to leave.

Danny snorted; he wasn't giving up now. He could persuade him. It was only a matter of time, he raised his fist up to knock the door again, so I spun back, quickly grabbing his wrist.

"What the fucking hell are you doing?" I said, totally aghast.

"Skinner, didn't you hear him? He said, he's got some," Danny told me.

"Oh, for fuck's sake. He means normal cassettes… You know C60, C90, C120, you fucking plank!"

"You reckon?" said Danny, laughing.

"Yes, I reckon. Now let's get out of here, before he comes out and shoves a C120 up your arse… Jesus," I said, looking up for that Jesus in the heavens.

On the way back to the station, I remembered a conversation I had with Mark Harper; he wondered why my mates and me travelled all the way up to Hackney Frontline to buy our sensi when there were places a lot closer. It was 'a laugh' I told him, 'Good to have a reason to go up into London, have a look about', but that was before our last trip up there. Mark had shrugged and said, 'If you want to shop closer to home', try one of his mates called Kipper on the Berecroft Estate in Harlow, 'he lives at 237, just say you know me. He'll see you right'. I hoped that I had remembered it right, hadn't got a case of the screaming gibbers, like most of the hippies in The Tap. Nah, I've got it right, I thought - I only smoke cannabis.

"Come on, Danny, the quest isn't over yet, mate. I've got another contact, it's over on The Berecroft estate, I've got the house number, but we need directions to the estate," I said, pointing at an all-night garage, at the end of the long overpass we were striding along.

186

Once we had got directions, we strode out towards Berecroft; by the time we got there it was nearly eleven o'clock, and the place was dark, deserted. Inside the all-encompassing darkness, a light drizzle tickled our jackets, while blankets of mist began to form in the low ground around us. Danny and me walked one way, then the other, searching for 237. It was hopeless, like we were back in The Kasbah, but this time, instead of all the walkways being known by the same name, here, every road was called Berecroft. It just didn't make any sense, and to make matters worse as we wandered from concrete pillar to concrete post, the mist plumed, settled in around us, turning the roads into blind alleys.

On and on we trudged in the steadily thickening mist, and when we passed a kid's climbing frame that looked like a huge red spider, for the second time, I stopped, turned to Danny.

"I don't know about this, Danny, what do you reckon?"

"Have you got any cassettes?" Asked a grinning Danny, out of the mist.

 I creased up, repeated, "Cassseeettttess."

"Nah, seriously Danny, fuck this. If we're not careful, we're going to miss the last train, let's go back to the station, get out of here."

"We could do that, Skinner, but there's one problem."

"What's that?"

"Have you got any cassettes?"

"Fuck off man."

Danny and me strode back across the sodden playing field, and into the estate; something was wrong, though, I turned and, in the distance, I could just about make out the lights of the Harvey Centre.

"Oh, Fuck it… We're going the wrong way, we should be heading for the centre of town, the stations near there," I said.

"Have you got any cassettes?" Asked Danny.

I took no notice, once Danny had got his teeth into something, I knew the only way to stop him, was not to react, just say nothing. I began the walk back. The numbers on the houses went, 225, 227 and 229.

"Er… Danny, check the numbers out…"

"What? What numbers?" Danny asked, sounding confused.

I sniggered, shook my head; I couldn't be bothered, just pointed at the number 237, on a 1960s build end of terrace house, with a boarded-up downstairs window.

"We're here mate, look at that, that's a good omen, just found it without even looking."

Danny paused, turned to me, "Oh yeah. How did you do that?"

"Lemon entry, my dear Watson."

Danny smiled broadly and made his way up to the door.

"Oh no you don't, I'll handle it this time," I said, barging him aside.

I smirked at him, pushed the doorbell, heard a muffled ringing from inside the property.

"OK, young grasshopper, watch and learn from the master, this is how it's done," I told him, full of confidence, and the door opened to reveal a nice-looking middle-aged woman in a red tracksuit.

"Yes?" She enquired.

"Oh hi, yeah sorry to bother you, a mate of mine, Mark Harper said that you might be able to help us out with a bit of sensi, do you know Mark?"

"Yeah, I know Mark," she said, smiling at her visitors. "Kipper… KIPPER!" She shouted, back into the house; there was no reply.

"Hold on a mo," she said, disappearing behind the open door.

I looked at Danny with a smug look on my face, "See it's not difficult, mate."

A few moments later, deep inside the property, a door slammed viciously. There was the sound of raised voices, and then a bloke roared.

"I've got a fucking baseball bat here, and if whoever you are, don't fuck off now, I'm going to come out there and play baseball with your fucking heads… You fucking hear me!?"

Danny and me stood, eyes like saucers, watching the door. It opened to reveal the woman's face.

"Er… Sorry, we can't help you… And if I, were you, I'd, go now. Oh, and say hello to Mark for me," she said, grimacing, and swiftly closed the door.

"Oh yeah, that's the way to do it, alright, Skinner!" Danny taunted.

"OK, Danny, don't milk it mate. Let's get out of here while we've still got use of our legs," I said quick, marching towards the playing field.

"What a complete fucking waste of time. That dopey fucking hippy."

"Ooooh, it's my mate, mates, mates, mates… Fuck off," I raged, pounding onto the soaked grass of the playing field, with Danny lagging behind, hardly being able to keep up.

"And Mark… Jesus fucking Christ. He told me, just tell the Kipper Mark sent you… Yeah, and he'll smash your bonce in with a fucking baseball bat. That worked well, didn't it? Brilliant."

In front of us, out of the gloom, the shape of the red spider began to form in the deep mist.

"I thought Mark was a skinhead, not a hippy…," said a befuddled Danny.

"What the fuck are you on about now?" I seethed, picking up pace, splashing in the shallow puddles of the playing field; hoping he wouldn't answer, hoping to leave this fool behind, so I could think straight. "I'm fucking giving it up, I am."

I ranted on, "It's a joke, smoking dope is supposed to be about peace, about…"

"Skinner……SKINNER!!!!" Danny hissed, coming to a halt.

"What? No, I don't want any cassettes. It's not funny anymore, Danny," I told him, stopping, reeling around on him.

Danny looked ahead; eyes wide. I followed his look.

On the lower rungs of the red spider, a dozen figures sat; orange embers of cigarette ends, glowed through the mist. A lighter flicked a spark. A flame grew from it. Stampy's face grinned in our direction.

"Well, well, well, look who isn't? You're not going to believe this, Moley, but it's only that bumboy Virus guitarist, and look, he's got another bummer with him. Looking for somewhere quiet to bum, are we girls?" He laughed, hopping down off the climbing frame, coming over, the others falling in behind him.

Danny and me moved back, shrunk away.

Stampy advanced on me, shoulders low, fists balled. Pre-emptive strike, pre-emptive strike, my mind yelled, and I smacked left, right. The first punch, stopping him. The second sending him reeling backwards.

"You fucking little cunt," he said, wiping a trickle of blood from his nose.

Stampy snorted the blood out, his hand dipped into his pockets, and he spun out a balisong and came at me again, screaming,

"I'M GOING TO CUT YOU, YOU CUNT, EVERY TIME YOU LOOK IN THE MIRROR, YOU'RE GOING TO THINK OF ME!"

I retreated across the mire, my eyes glued on the hypnotic blade cutting an arc through the mist, separating it, lacerating, destroying it for good.

"No, come on, don't," I mewled at him.

Stampy laughed. "Even more like a cunt... Ooh, come on... Don't," he mimicked.

"Turn it in, Stampy. No weapons. If you can't take the wanker yourself, I'll do him," came a voice from behind him.

Stampy halted, shocked, turning on the dissenter.

"Yeah? ...And who put you in charge? Eh? Mathews?"

"Drop the blade... Just fucking do him, he's nothing."

"I said. Who put you in charge? How fucking dare, you?"

"Come on Stampy. It ain't about that."

"Yeah? ...So, tell me, what is it about, then?"

Mathews exhaled, "Little Dugs here, lost his brother because of weapons, just fucking do him. You can do him easily, he's nothing. Do him in a straight go, or don't do him at all."

Stampy cracked up. "Huh, these two wankers haven't got guns," he said, turning back to us, but all he saw was mist; we were about twenty feet away from them by then.

"Run, Danny, run," I said, sprinting back in the direction we had come from.

I thought, if we can get back into the maze of the estate, we can lose them, we'll be fine; then as the lights of the walkway leading out of the playing field came into view, through the mist. It filled up with a group of silhouettes. One of them clearly had a baseball bat in his hands; they saw the approaching Punks.

"Oi… You two. Come here, I what a word with you," shouted someone.

"Fucking hell. Danny, come on, this way," I said, pushing him in another direction, any direction.

"Who's been at my bird's, asking her for fucking dope?" Shouted Kipper, at our retreating forms, "Cocky cunts, get them!" He ordered.

Danny and me legged it to another walkway, leading us back into the concrete jungle of Berecroft, and we zigzagged around the back of a row of shops, where we stopped, panting like dogs, trying to get our breath back, near a long line of garages. I love all these walkways, I thought, changing my mind.

In a couple of deep breaths, I heard the harsh scrape of boots on concrete; our sanctuary was gone. Kipper and his mates were close now, we could even hear odd bits of their conversation. I thought, if we stay here, the chances are that we will be blocked in with no escape and get beaten to a fucking pulp. So, nudging Danny to follow me, we broke cover, trying to lighten our footsteps, fast walking, back towards the shops; but one of the searching pack saw movement in the engulfing mist.

"Oi, wankers, you're going nowhere, we'll get you!"

"The Punks are dead, oh yeah," sang one of them, paraphrasing The Exploited's track.

Danny and me ran around the back of the shops into a car park; they were right behind us now, slavering like rabid dogs. We should have stayed put. My frenzied mind bleated. Danny pointed out a staircase running up to a line of flats, above the shops, and we crept up the steep steps to lie low, await our fate. Knowing full well that Kipper knew this place like the back of his hand. It would only be a matter of time, until they worked out where we were hiding, and then we would be like lambs to the slaughter.

In the car park below us, we heard raised voices. Danny and me, peeped over a low wall that ran along the front of the flats, and saw Stampy and his mates standing at one end. Kipper and his mates walking towards them, coming from the other end.

"You alright Stampy? Mathews? Moley? …Oh, little Dugs as well? …You see any Punk Rockers around The Croft, tonight?" Kipper asked.

"Yeah, they're up on the balcony shitting themselves," said Stampy. "Which is where you should be you fucking cunt… You're Mark Harper's mate, aren't you?"

"Yeah, I know him, what's it to you? …Cocky cunt," he said, laughing to his mates; then, with a lightning bolt strike, he smashed his baseball bat down onto Stampy's shoulder.

Stampy screamed out in pain, fell to his knees, and the two gangs scythed into each other.

Danny grinned at me in the dim light, I snorted back. "Yeah… I suppose it is funny. Look at the fucking chimps. They would be perfect on the PG TV advert," I said nervously, watching the mayhem below. They were really getting stuck into each other.

"We need to get out here, because if we don't, whoever's left standing down there, is going to come up those stairs, and batter us," I said, standing up, looking for a way out, some way, any way out.

One of the flats at the end of the walkway was boarded up, seeming to be derelict. It was worth a go, anything was. I crawled along the short walkway, keeping my head below the parapet, so not to alert the battling skinheads in the car park, and saw the flat looked unoccupied. It was unlit, silent, and after looking inside the letter box, and seeing a mountain of letters stacked up high, I thought, it's uninhabited and maybe, we can hide until the storm blows over; it was all we had. I reached up, pulled at one of the boards over the window, slowly easing it from its housings, and felt a tug on my arm. It was Danny.

"What are you doing, Skinner?" He whispered.

"I'm not getting a kicking, that's what I'm doing, you coming?" I asked, lowering the board onto the walkway.

Danny gawked at me. I shrugged, pushed my torso up into the empty window frame, felt some pieces of glass, catching on my Discharge T-shirt. So, I slid back out, did my leather jacket up, gave it another try, and slid in through the window, over the sink and onto a black and white chessboard floor.

Danny looked at me blankly from outside. "I'm not going in there. Someone could be in there," he spluttered.

A scream of intense agony rang out from the car park below. Danny jumped up into the window frame, and slid, snake-like through, into the kitchen.

"What's that? What's that noise," he stuttered, creeping over, to the open kitchen door to investigate. He leant forward, looking into the dark hallway.

He tiptoed back, "Skinner, Skinner, there's a big fucking dog, in there," he whined.

"Bollocks, there can't be. If there was, it would have been on us by now," I whispered back, pushing him aside to take a look.

In the shadows of the hall, I saw the shape of a huge Baskerville-like hound, sitting upright, on its hind legs, head up, steadily surveying its territory.

Oh, fucking hell, I thought, I've really done it this time, now what?

"Good boy, he's a good boy," I soothed the beast, desperately, while slowly easing my lighter out of my pocket with one hand and plucking a letter off the mountain with the other. I thought, a bit of fire will see the monster off. Once he sees this, he'll leg it, then we'll have time to get back out of the window.

"He's a very good boooyyyy," I smarmed.

Seconds passed, I inhaled, put my thumb on the lighter wheel, tentatively spun it. The flint threw out a spark. It flickered. Died. I slowly repeated the process. The hallway lit up, and in the light of the dancing flame, I found myself looking at a massive stuffed Great Dane, its eyes shining blankly into nowhere.

Danny and me exchanged a glance. It was so realistic. It was taxidermy, at its finest. The attention to detail was incredible, it really looked like it was about to come at us at any moment.

I cracked up. Immediately shut up; a loud rasping emitted from one of the rooms off the hallway.

"That's what I was talking about. Skinner, there's someone sleeping in there," whinged Danny, from over my shoulder.

"Bollocks, come on… Beware of the dog mate," I grinned, tip-toeing ahead.

Danny didn't laugh, just ghosted forwards, nudging me towards the rasping.

I moved up the hallway, looked into the room, and through an open curtain, light flooded in onto a human shape sleeping soundly, totally oblivious to our presence.

"I mean it. Let's get out of here… Skinner, I'm going back."

"No way Danny, come on, there must be another way out of here," I said with little confidence, dropping onto my hands and knees.

One hand at a time I slunk, cat-like, past the bedroom door, leaving the snoozing figure behind, and came into a lounge area, and there in front of me was a door - a door leading out onto a small balcony.

In a second, I was up, ran to the door, twisted the key in the lock. The door creaked, shuddered, and I pushed through it, walked out onto a balcony overlooking the playing field.

On the other side, partially submerged under the blankets of mist, I saw the dark lines of the red spider highlighted by the bleaching lights of the walkways.

"Oh, nice one Skinner, is there a fire escape?" Asked Danny, coming up behind me.

"Nahhh, there isn't," I told him, with a heavy heart.

Danny and me looked over the edge of the balcony, and even though it was only a first floor flat, the drop must have been about twenty feet. Twenty feet into pitch black. Into the unknown.

I climbed over the side; Danny climbed over. I thought this is a leg breaker, maybe worse.

"I'm not doing it, Skinner," whimpered, Danny.

"Nor me Danny, fuck it, let's go back," I said, admitting defeat.

"Iris, is that you, dear? I knew you'd come back to me," called an old man's voice from inside the flat, "I knew you'd come, we always said, we'd never leave each other."

I looked into Danny. He looked into me. I nodded, he nodded.

"Aaaaaaaaaaaahhhhhhhhhhh!" I bellowed, letting go.

"AAAAAAAAHHHHHHHHHH!" Wailed Danny, as he let go.

A moment later I opened my eyes; realised I wasn't dead, realised I hadn't shat myself either. It was just the mud of the playing field on the arse of my bondage trousers. Wiping the mud from my eyes, I squinted at Danny. He was so covered in mud, he looked like The Blob. I cracked up laughing.

"Danny, let's get the fuck out here, man. If we miss the last train back, we could be stuck here," I told him, getting up, striding forwards, "We wouldn't last the night."

Danny cracked up, "So where is the station from here?"

"I don't know, but we can't retrace our steps, that's for sure, we'll get fucking Babe Ruth-ed. Let's go this way, it might take a bit longer, it should be alright. I'll tell you this now, Danny, I'm never coming back to this fucking shithole again," I said, making my position clear.

Danny nodded thoughtfully, and we sloped off, walking along in silence - lost in thoughts of what could have happened on this wild goose chase for something that grows quite naturally in most countries - stopping now and again, to brush some of the wet muck off us, before it set like cement onto our skin.

"Danny?"

"What?" he said, absently.

"Oi, Danny?"

"Whaaaaatt?"

"You got any cassettes?" I enquired, and we cracked our muddy faces into grins.

Chapter Nine

Suicide Was Painless

Dapper told me Chris Severn, the owner of The Feathers, was having a rare night off, and with Cerys working in the kitchen and Blo Jo on bar duty. It sounded like a night of free food and drink was in the offing. But before this night of free debauchery could begin, I needed to make a phone call. A call I had been putting off for far too long. In the days that followed our ill-faithed Hoddesdon gig, I had picked up the phone to ring Andy and Whiff on several occasions, only to put it straight down again. My thinking being, that last time I had put on my Henry Kissinger persona, been the diplomat, tried to sort out the bickering, it had been a complete waste of time. Andy and Whiff had told me there wasn't a problem between them, and not only that, Dave, had told me that I worried too much. I had my old man-ed back that 'some bugger has to', like it was a joke; but I felt stupid, like I had taken their 'near the knuckle sense of humour' way too seriously. It didn't sound like near the knuckle humour, to me, it sounded like the precursor to knuckle on cheek 'humour'. It was time to call them, find out where everybody stood.

Andy answered on the second ring. I took a deep breath, and Henry Kissinger took over again, "Oh, you alright, Andy? How's it going?"

"Alright, Skinner," he said, sounding happy to hear my voice.

"I'm good mate, been a busy week... You up for a practice tomorrow?"

"Yes of course. I'm a diligent singer if nothing else."

"Nah you're a Virus V1 singer Andy, and whoever The Diligents are, they can piss off."

Andy laughed, "I don't want to be in The Diligents, they sound like a lot of hard work."

"Yeah, meticulous too," I sniggered, then, holding back the urge to keep the synonyms going, I said, "So, you're OK then, Andy?" Awkwardly, trying to get down to business.

"Yes, why shouldn't I be?"

I inhaled deeply, dived in, "What's your problem with Whiff?" I asked, hoping that the stormy waters had calmed over the last couple of weeks.

"I don't have a problem with Whiffy," Andy countered.

"What?" I asked, incredulously, resisting the urge to smash the telephone receiver off my forehead.

"I have never had any problems with Whiffy. I've never had a problem with Whiffy!"

I snorted, sat up, waiting for the punchline to come. Surely this was some kind of joke, I thought, maybe some more of that Andy and Whiff near the knuckle humour I couldn't understand, but there was no punchline, just the dead air of the telephone line. A second led to a moment. A moment to more seconds, still no punchline. Nothing, dead air. Andy wasn't going to elaborate. Inwardly I groaned, turned my head, caught sight of myself in the fisheye mirror in our hallway. My badly drawn face, gawked back at me, distorted, bewildered, mishappen. Oh Jesus, I thought, he's not going to make this easy, is he?

"You two haven't got a problem, then?" I persisted, trying to keep my voice Kissinger.

"Whiffy's got a problem with me."

Once again, smashing the receiver off my distorted forehead seemed inviting. Inevitable.

"Why do you think that is?" I enquired.

Andy said, "Don't know…" then fell silent, allowing the dead air to rush back in again.

"You really don't know?" I asked, impatiently.

I heard a buzz and some nattering of a crossed line, then Andy finally declared, "If Whiffy takes the piss out of me, I'll take the piss out of him."

Oh my god, at last, I thought, now we are getting somewhere; now I can say some of the things, I've been thinking about saying over the last week. Kissinger could pull this off yet.

"Yeah, and that's fair enough mate, that's the way it should be, but listen Andy, Whiff's not like me and you, we just want to have a laugh all the time and piss about. Whiff likes to talk seriously sometimes, especially if it's about his girlfriends. You must know that by now?"

Andy laughed, "He does."

I sniggered back, "Andy, look, go around for him on your way up tomorrow, walk up with him, yeah?"

"OK, then," he said.

"And Andy, mate, don't mention his little stiffy."

Andy cracked up laughing, blowing the dead air out for good, "I won't."

"Nice one, Andy, see you tomorrow."

"See you, Skinner."

On a roll now, Kissinger replaced the handset, got up, stepped over to the fisheye mirror, and watched his melted face reconstruct itself. Then, feeling a lot better, he picked the receiver up to phone Whiff, to let him know that we were practising and Andy would be calling around for him tomorrow morning.

A couple of rings and Judy picked up, like she had been standing right next to the phone.

"Hello," she enquired, good naturedly.

"Hi. Is Paul there?" I asked.

"Oh, hello Mick, yes, hold on, I'll just get him."

I heard muffled scraping sounds, a loud sniff, a mumbled, 'fucking old slag'.

"You alright Skinner?" Said Whiff.

I resisted the urge to laugh out loud. It was time to talk seriously. "Yeah. I'm alright. Cheers," I said, keeping my voice neutral, thinking about how I was going to get around to it with him, hoping it would be easier than it was with Andy.

"Skinner… Listen I'm really sorry about Hoddesdon, I just lost it, it was a bad night, wasn't it?"

"It was shit, not good at all," I agreed, thinking, thank fuck for that, this'll be easier than the dead air.

"I want to forget about it, move on, concentrate on the band," he told me sincerely.

"Yeah, we all do mate, I've phoned Andy, he's the same mate, wants to forget it. We've got a couple of decent gigs coming up… Like you say, let's move on, say no more about it."

"What did he say?" Asked Whiff, saying more about it.

I sighed. "He… Errr… said he didn't have a problem with you," I said, quite truthfully.

"He said that? …What else did he say?"

"Oh, nothing much," I said, quite untruthfully.

Whiff said nothing. The dead air streamed in; Whiff knew a lie when he heard one.

"Whiff mate, it's fine," I said, back in full on Kissinger mode, "Look, we're practising tomorrow, and he said he'd call in on you on the way up, OK? …You can walk up together, talk to him, and sort it out."

"OK Skin, yeah. I'll walk up with him, talk it through, but I wish you'd have told me earlier. I'm supposed to be seeing Steph. It's alright though, I'll meet her later on."

"Sorry about that mate, I was going to phone last night, but I was on a quest, in Harlow."

"Harlow? Oh what!? I saw Harper in The Tap, lunchtime. He reckons Stampy, Moley and all that lot, got jumped by some of his mates over there, smashed them up bad. Little Dugs, you know Jamie's little brother? He's in a coma, he's only fifteen, someone smacked him with a baseball bat, he could die."

I thought, fucking hell, that could have been Danny and me lying in hospital beds, surrounded by machines, feeding us, helping us breathe, keeping us alive, and Mark Harper sent us there.

"Skin? You still there?" He asked my dead air.

"Yeah, yeah, yeah. What else did Mark fucking Harper say?" I asked, losing it.

Whiff went silent; the unexpected venom in my voice telling him something,

"What's that all about? What happened?"

"It's a long story, mate," I said, stalling.

206

"What happened, Skin?" He said evenly, wanting to know this long story.

I thought, no, telling him or anyone, the full story was not an option. Not now that I knew Little Dugs was in a coma, as it was Danny and me who had started the whole thing off in the first place, and sure, Mark Harper had played his part; but he was alright, he had his mates to back him up. Danny had no one. No one to back us up in this situation, and I knew the people around the Duggen family would not let this go unpunished, there would be repercussions. I didn't want to be any part of those repercussions.

"Oh, it was nothing really mate, some hippy knobend in The Tap told us that he had a mate, who had a mate, who had a mate, who could sort us out in Harlow… It was a complete waste of time," I said, quickly brushing it aside, telling the half-lie, the most believable untruth.

Whiff snorted, "One of those, eh?"

"Yeah, one of those, mate… Look, I better go. Chris Severn has left Cerys and Blo Jo to serve alone in The Feathers tonight, it's going to be a free-for-all. I'm going to see if I can drag Dave out of his new house, I haven't seen him for a while… You should come up. It could be a good night."

Whiff was silent for a moment; he knew there was more to it than that, finally he said, "Nah sorry, Skin, sounds good, but I've got The Woman coming around tonight."

I was pleased with the subject change, so I quickly weighed it up for him, "Hmm… A night of free snakebite and chips, or a night with

Steph. It's a tough one, have you by any chance got any sensimelia left?" I asked, remembering what he said about The Woman and what happens to her after a smoke.

Whiff cackled mischievously, "How did you guess?"

I cackled back, "I know you. You dirty git."

Whiff cracked up and sang, "Slip it, in, in, in."

"I don't want to know mate," I laughed,

"OK look, so Andy will come around for you on the way up as usual. He'll be at yours about twelve?"

"I'm looking forward to it already," Whiff said, sarcastically.

"I'm sure you are mate. See you later," I said, hanging up, and made my way to the door.

On the way down to my street, I thought about Little Dugs, or the baby-faced assassin, as some people called him, and the chain of events that led to him lying comatose in a hospital bed. It was sad to think that someone so young had taken such a beating, but Little Dugs had handed out a few beatings himself over the years, to younger and weaker kids. OK, Danny and me had been part of the chain of events that had got his head smashed in, but it wasn't our fault; we didn't swing the bat that put his brain to sleep. It had been his choice to hang around with Stampy and The Wolf Pack, and if it hadn't been this chain, it would have been another one. If you live in a world of violence, then there's always a price to pay.

I increased my pace, shook it off, thinking, fuck him, thought about the night I had ahead of me, then as I came to the two white fences at the side of the vicarage, I saw Doggy backing his mum's car out of the garage. I hadn't seen Doggy since the Thundridge youth club gig. It hadn't ended too well for him, so I gave him a cursory nod and carried on, expecting him to do the same, but no, Doggy wound his window down and asked me how it was going? I wandered over, and we started talking; he looked different. He had grown his hair long, was wearing an Afghan coat, and not only that, he sounded different too. The fake cockney accent had gone; he was speaking in his normal voice, he seemed confident, happy, like the kid I knew from The Junior Mental Institution. Doggy told me that he had dropped out of his Business Degree at Cambridge University and had actually persuaded his Mum and Dad to sign him up for a Sound Engineers course in Holloway. He said he couldn't be happier.

I thought that must have been a tough conversation, as his Mum and Dad had pretty much mapped out how his life was going to go. Posh school. Posh university, then afterwards, a job either in the civil service or the city; most likely the city, with his Dad. Doggy wasn't into that though, he was artistic. He was a dreamer, and just like me, he loved his music, wanted to be part of it, wanted to play it all the time.

"Bloody hell Doug, how did you manage to persuade them to let you do that?" I asked.

He smiled, "Oh, I… Er… Pretended to commit suicide…"

I scoffed, "How do you pretend to commit suicide!?"

Doggy smirked back at me, like it was the most obvious thing in the world, "I bought four boxes of paracetamol, opened them all, put one pill in my mouth, and flushed the rest down the toilet. I then shouted for my parents to come upstairs… Oh, and I left the empty paracetamol boxes and containers strewn across my bedroom floor, so they could see them."

I had heard a rumour in the village. It didn't go like this, though. I thought, this is bizarre even for Doggy and opening my mouth to speak and not finding the words… I let him carry on.

"When they came into my room, I told them what I had done, and why I had done it, and spat the one I had put in my mouth onto the carpet, to prove I had taken them…"

It took me a while to process what I had just heard, and a lot longer to find something to say, but eventually I got there.

"Why didn't you just tell them to fuck off?"

Doggy laughed at my silly logic, "I couldn't say that to them."

"No, no, no. I mean… Why didn't you just say, I'm dropping out of my business course; I'm not going to Uni anymore?"

He laughed again, "Oh, I didn't want to disappoint them."

Once again, in amongst this Doggy logic, this anomalous world of the upper classes I had managed to find a way out of, words failed me. I stood dazed, silent, cluelessly trying to find some sense in this madness while this total lunatic, gazed at me, rapping his fingers on the steering wheel of his mum's car.

Doggy smiled broadly, enjoying freaking me out.

"You see, Skinner, it's not how you get there, it's that you get there," he said, callously.

I stepped to walk away, "That's great news Doug, look, I better get on, I'm…"

"Oh, hold on," Doggy interjected, turning the red hatchback's ignition off, "I'm off to Cambridge Skinner, well not Cambridge. I'm actually going to a pub in Trumpington, I'm meeting a girl, would you like to come?"

"No mate, it's fine, two's company and all that."

"Oh, it's not a date. Well… It could be if I play my cards right… If I bring my cards, that is," he gibbered, laughing to himself.

Doggy wriggled in his seat, readjusted his seat belt, snag corrected, he continued, "I'm just meeting up with her, having a drink. I'm picking up Paul Sullivan on the way through, have you met Paul Sullivan?"

I smiled, thinking, yeah, I know Sulli the vocalist. Sulli the experienced vocalist. In light of recent events, I wouldn't mind having a word with him, and even though, it could be a long drive from here into the fen lands, well, as Doggy said himself, it's not how you get there, it's that you get there.

"I know Sulli, you introduced him to me. You remember?" I said, brightening up in fate's warming rays.

Doggy laughed, "Oh, of course you have, my brain must be destroyed. I must stop dropping acid!"

211

"Yeah, maybe, you know what, yeah, I will come along, it will be good to see Sulli again."

I opened the door, jumped in, he re-started the car, and we set off for the flat lands of Cambridgeshire.

On the way out of Thundridge, a fine early evening greeted us; slivers of red and crimson light gently manicured the growing expanse of dappled green fields around us. A congregation of small villages, hamlets and farms zipped passed the car's open windows, from which life-affirming air rushed in through onto our faces.

Doggy gave me a sideways look, leant forward, and began riffling through the mass of Pink Floyd tapes in the glove compartment. Plucking out 'Meddle' from the mass of tangled plastic, he pushed the cassette into the player in the car's console, and slowly but surely Echo's began.

Punks in general hated Pink Floyd. I didn't think they were so bad though, as Pete O' Shea, Danny's older brother, used to play a lot of their stuff when I used to hang out with him in my early teens, when the first wave of Punk was building up. Pink Floyd always brought back great memories for me, when we used to sneak into the local girl's convent school and the laughs, we had. I couldn't but, like them.

Pete's favourites had been Animals, Meddle, Relics, and of course Dark Side of the Moon. I knew them well, and enjoyed their heavy psychedelic rock, but some of Floyd's other more obscure albums like 'Atom Heart Mother' used to do my head in, though. So, Doggy being the accommodating kind of bloke, he was, had borrowed, his sister's Jimi Hendrix albums 'Are You Experienced?', 'Axis Bold as

Love' and 'Electric Lady Land' to play in the car just in case he 'overfloyded' me, as he called it.

Doggy, and me sat back and watched the soft undulating hills of Hertfordshire level out into the flat lands of Cambridgeshire in a million shades of green, while he told me more about his sound engineering course, and some of the characters he was working with. I thought not only did it sound like a good laugh; it was interesting too. Doggy steadily drove us through the fenland, happily chatting away, and as I listened, I watched the low sun beaming oranges and reds dipping ever nearer to the horizon.

Doggy flipped up his sun visor. "Oh wow, look at the colours," said Doggy, noticing it too.

I smiled, flashed him the peace sign, "Yeeeeaaah far out maaaaaan. Woodstock."

He grinned back, flashed one back, and said, "Beautiful… It's a beautiful world, isn't it?"

"Yeah. It is," I admitted.

Doggy and me, gazed in wonder at the greatest light show on earth.

"I'm sorry I told you about that earlier on, you know, the fake suicide, it must have shocked you," Doggy said, sincerely.

I snorted, "Yeah, it did a bit. I had heard something, though, there was a rumour going around the village."

Doggy laughed heartily, "Yes, I thought there could be, what was it?"

"Nah, you don't want to know, mate."

Doggy turned the stereo down, "I do, and I don't, but I think I do."

I sighed, "Hmm, if you're sure, mate?"

"I'm sure. I don't care what people say about me, every day, in every way, I'm getting better and better as a person. People hassle is all part of overcoming," he said, without hesitation.

I braced myself, "I heard that you decked one hundred paracetamols, and you spat one out."

Doggy snickered, "I decked ninety-nine paracetamols!? That's ridiculous."

I cracked up, "Well… Yeah, that's the old rumour mill for you, mate."

"I swallowed one hundred paracetamols and spat one out!" He said, incredulously, "What a load of buuuullshit, I didn't spit one out. It would have been a waste of good pharmaceuticals; I swallowed the whole lot… I don't waste pharmaceuticals, good, bad, or otherwise."

I spun around, peered at him, absolutely horrified; I didn't know what to believe now. He absolutely creased up laughing, and I soon joined him.

"Is there anything else?" He requested, knowing full well there would be.

"Some people are calling you The Ninety-Nine Flake, or The Ice Cream Man," I said, grinning, knowing full well, that, the old Junior Mental Institution Doggy was fully awake now.

Doggy repeated, "The Ice Cream Man," rolling it around his mouth, a huge smile tugging at the corners of his lips; eventually he cracked up laughing.

I creased up too, "Yeah, it's pretty fucking stupid, isn't it?"

"It certainly is," he said, trying to pull himself together, "You know what? The next time I drive through the village; I think I'll play Greensleeves at full volume, that will freak them right out."

I cracked up at the thought, "You could be like Cheech and Chong, in their ice cream van, selling nice dreams."

"I like it, Skinner. I'll drive through the village, playing Greensleeves, and you can sell Squidgy Black out of the back to the villagers."

I sniggered, "Yeah, they can stop me and buy one… Ounce."

Doggy and me cracked up, sitting back, thinking on our business plan, when we were disturbed by a huge flock of geese soaring above us, in the golden-crimson sky.

"Wow, Skinner, look at that, they're coming back from their winter retreat. Spring must be near."

I sniffed, looked up, watching the fast-moving triangle on their crimson background, "I see them, incredible man… Listen man, I don't think suicide is anything to joke about."

Doggy nodded sternly, completely open now.

"I know, I was so low, I couldn't see a way out."

"Doug mate… If you get down like that again, maybe you should talk to someone," I said, thinking of how Pete had helped me all those years ago, in my early teenage years. His humour, his music, and his infectious upbeat interpretation of what life could be, should be. Got me back on the right track.

Doggy pulled a tight smile onto his lips, "I wasn't really going to commit suicide. I don't think so anyway, at the time I thought of it as a ruse, but now… I don't know…," he trailed off.

"Jesus fucking hell, I hope not mate, we've all got plenty to live for… You know, life's not worth dying over."

Doggy chuckled, "Oh, that's very good, who's that?"

"I don't know, some cupid stunt." I shrugged, "Seriously though. If you do need anyone to talk too, just drop around, Doug."

Doggy nodded, "Thanks for that Skinner, I will," he said, then cranked Pink Floyd up again and put his foot down, like he was a man on a mission once again.

In the car, as Pink Floyd's 'Pigs (three different ones)' turned into 'Sheep', we crunched onto the drive outside of Sulli's house in Sawston, feeling mellow and at peace with the world. A world, which had not only entertained us, with its all-encompassing twilight show, and been a backdrop for our conversation. I thought it proved conclusively, that life certainly was worth living, no matter what one faces; who would want to miss something like that? I had hoped that

216

Doggy had realised it too. There would be no more sunsets after swallowing one hundred paracetamols, even if you spat one out. Just darkness. Silence.

It had been a long time since I had been up to Cambridgeshire to see my mates, way too long, in fact. I liked their attitude, the way they viewed life. It was totally different from the people down in the village, Ware and Hertford. They were more accepting, more laid-back, and when it came to laid back, there weren't many people around like Sulli. He was so laid-back; he was almost horizontal.

Sulli was a Punk Rocker or 'a career opportunities Punk Rocker' as he liked to call himself. He was tall with black spiked-up hair, was a few years older than me, and sung lead vocals with the Cambridge band The Sickos, a four-piece Punk outfit, who had been part of the original Punk uprising of 1977.

The Sickos, despite the many changes to their line-up over the years, Sulli being the only original member, were now well-established around The South-East with over forty gigs under their belts, including a couple of storming sets at Cambridge's Strawberry Fair.

In the five years that followed their inception, The Sickos had also made numerous demo tapes, sending them to the many independent labels that had sprung up to cater for Punk over the years; at one time they had been close to signing a major record deal. It had all gone wrong, though, when Sulli and their drummer had disappeared on a trip to Glastonbury in 1981 and didn't return until the end of the year.

I was about to walk up to his front door, when I remembered that he didn't live in the house anymore; he lived in a shed at the bottom of his parent's garden. On one of my trips up to Cambridge, Sulli had told me that, he had got so sick of his parents moaning about him smoking in 'their' house, that he thought fuck them, and had moved his entire bedroom into his old man's tool shed. Doggy didn't bother knocking his front door anymore; he was never there. So, I followed him around the house, down the long thin garden, past the languid lines of cabbages and brussels sprouts, straight to Sulli's shed.

Doggy knocked firmly on the wooden door, making it rattle. "Hello, hello, is there anybody there?" He said, spookily, like he was summoning up spirits on a Ouija board.

A while later the door edged open, letting out a cloud of sweet-smelling smoke.

Sulli's smiling face appeared amongst it. "Hi Doug… And Skinner, ay, come in, come in," he offered, gesturing with his hands.

Inside his old man's tool shed, Sulli had made it cosy, very cosy indeed, a proper home from shed, I thought, he had done a lot to it since I last came up. It didn't look like a tool shed now; all the tools were gone and knowing Sulli they would be up in his old bedroom, back in his ex-house.

Doggy and Sulli exchanged pleasantries, while I checked out his endeavours as a homemaker.

In one side, he had his bed, which was exactly the same length of the shed. I didn't know how he had managed to get it in there, again knowing Sulli, he had probably got it in by any means necessary. On the other side he had a couple of chairs, a table with a TV on it. Then in the centre, he had a small chest of drawers, on top of which sat his beloved reel-to-reel tape machine.

Doggy and me made ourselves comfortable on the chairs, and while Doggy filled Sulli in on his plans for the evening, I sat back and skinned up some Red Leb, I had got from Del.

Once the building was complete, I sparked it, took a couple of tokes, passed it to Doggy, who turned to Sulli, "So, how are the mighty Sickos these days?"

"Yeah, not bad Doug," Sulli replied, cagily, looking at me knowingly.

I had seen Doggy making advances towards joining The Sickos before, and I had seen Sulli knock him back on several occasions. I'll give him his due, though, it never stopped him trying, but I knew he would never get in, because both Sulli and me thought keyboards weren't for Punk bands. Psychedelic, reggae, yeah, but for Punk bands no, keyboards were way too subtle; would be lost under the torrent of guitars.

Doggy pushed on with his quest as usual, "Well… If you need any keyboards, just let me know."

"I don't know Doug. We might be able to use some sound effects for intros, but we don't really need keyboards in the band at the moment."

"Well, if you do, you know where to come," he said, passing him the spliff. "Here's some enticement for you," he told him, grinning like the Cheshire cat.

"Aaaah, yes that'll do nicely sir," Sulli beamed back at him.

"You got any gigs coming up, Sulli?" I asked.

Sulli blew out a ghostly plume of white smoke, "No… Not at the moment, we're… Well, it's not important. What about you?"

I smiled, "We got a couple of benefits coming up… We played to one man and his dog at our last gig. To be honest, it was shit, a total waste of time."

Sulli passed the spliff to me, laughing, "Oh no, they didn't let the dog in for nothing, did they!?" He Den Dennis-ed, grinning wisely; he'd seen Bad News Tour on TV, as well.

Sulli turned around to his reel-to-reel, looped a tape up, pressed play and continued, "We've done a new demo, check this out."

I hadn't seen The Sickos play live before, but I had certainly heard some of their demo tapes played on this very, reel to reel, in fact, and I thought they were decent enough; they sounded like a cross between G.B.H. and the Dead Kennedy's and like them, they were less serious in their approach lyrically than we were, even though their message was similar. The Sickos had tracks called, 'Over Idiot Educated', 'Jesus Saves at the NatWest', 'Spit in the Sky', 'When the Snake Bit the Sun', 'I Didn't Need Acid on the Falkland Islands (I got my mind blown for free)', and my personal favourite, the classically titled. 'I Wish I was a Dog Turd'. Sulli's band The Sickos were not only good musically; they were funny and thought-provoking all at the same time. I liked this new demo too. If anything, it was even better than their earlier stuff. It was tighter, more guitar-driven, and Sulli's vocals cut right into me.

"This is incredible man… You've got to be gigging this, haven't you?" I asked, enthusiastically.

Sulli inhaled a cloud of smoke, puffed it out of the right side of his mouth, shook his head sadly. "I wish I could Skinner, but we've got a problem. It's… Oh well, no harm in telling you. It's me and the bass player. We don't get along any mor… To tell the truth, it's all fucked up…," he trailed off, opened his arms, "I don't know."

Hmmm 'it's all fucked up', I thought, that sounds familiar, very familiar, "What is it about bass players and vocalists?" I asked.

Sulli laughed, "I don't know, maybe vocalists are extroverts who want to be introverts, and bass players are introverts who want to be extroverts."

"You could be right there, mate," I smiled, immediately getting his drift.

Sulli smiled serenely, passing the spliff to Doggy, who took a small last puff on it and dobbed it out in a rose from an old watering can that Sulli was using as a makeshift ashtray.

"You know I could play the bass root notes on my keyboards if you want. It would be easy to do," Doggy suggested, craftily.

Sulli smiled again, shook his head, seeing him coming a mile away, "No, it's OK dude, we'll be fine, there's plenty more bass players in the sea." He said, as he stretched self-indulgently. "So, where are we going again, Doug?" Asked Sulli, changing the subject before Doggy could make another obvious attempt.

"It's The Greenman pub in Trumpington, shall we go?" Asked Doggy.

Sulli stood up with purpose, looked at me, "Yeah, let's do it."

221

I nodded and after Sulli had padlocked his abode, we walked back up his garden, past the perfect lines of emerald, green cabbages and brussels sprouts, which glistened in the moon light, around the side of the quiet house, and crunched across the shingle drive out to the car.

Chapter Ten

A Trip With Doggy

On the short drive into Trumpington, Doggy told us that he needed to see his mate John Hinkley, so instead of parking up outside The Greenman he found a space outside his mate's house, just down the road from the pub, and left Sulli and me in the car. It had been a couple of hours since we had left Thundridge Village - one too many five-minute guitar solos meant I had hit my Pink Floyd threshold, and thankfully Doggy had noticed. So, he'd switched tapes from the solo wank-fest, that is 'Wish you were Here', to Jimi Hendrix's album 'Are You Experienced', which was a relief.

Sulli and me sat back listening to the psychedelic voodoo child do his thing, talking about our bands, what was going on in our lives and John Hinkley, while Doggy popped in to see the man himself.

John Hinkley and me had met on numerous occasions. On balance, I would say he was one of Doggy's more eccentric friends. In fact, I thought he was a nutter, not violent or dangerous - a complete oddball! John lived with his Gran in a three-story house at the edge of Trumpington, and his Gran got so fed up with being disturbed by the constant comings and goings of his mates 'at all hours of the day and night', she had given him the whole top floor flat to do with as he wished; he certainly made the most of it.

Inside the roomy attic flat, it had two bedrooms, a kitchen, a bathroom, and most importantly for his ageing, if unfortunately, not so hard-of-hearing, Grandmother, its own entrance at the back of the property, away from her bedroom, which faced the High Street at the front. In one bedroom, with our help, John had knocked the wall through, and was in the process of building his own twenty track studio, complete with vocal booth and something he named a sound cave, which was essentially an old airing cupboard that he had opened up into the loft that he used to create natural reverb. It was an impressive project to say the least, and it had to be, as John was a talented musician. He played anything from guitar to piano to the flute, and was making ready to record his first album.

In the other bedroom, John had converted it, again, with a little help from his friends, into what he called, 'The Maximum Head Room', which was entered through a series of beaded curtains. Once you had breezed in through all the silk and satin, you found yourself surrounded by dozens of lava lamps, throw cushions, and huge, towering hookahs. A record player connected to a P.A. system, feeding into two guitar amps serving as speakers, sat on an altar-like table at the top of the room. Six two-feet high brass candleholders surrounded the impressive Hi-Fi unit; then in the corner behind it sat his pride and joy; an original 1960s slide projector, complete with oil slides, that he claimed had once belonged to Syd Barrett.

On the occasions I had been allowed into its hallowed confines, I'd had some great sessions in The Maximum Head Room, as it was usually full of characters from Cambridge University and The City beyond. John could be weird at times, though; you never quite knew which John was going to answer the door. One day he would welcome you in like a returning friend; the next, quite literally, he wouldn't know who you were, and slam the door in your face. Being let in didn't guarantee you a sane John either, as sometimes, he would be open and chatty. Other times he wouldn't say two words to anyone all night, but I, like many others, thought the weirdest thing about John was, since he had left Cambridge University, he had stopped going out completely; Doggy told me he hadn't been seen outside for two years.

A few minutes later, Doggy re-emerged from the back of John's house, grinning like a maniac.

"Oi, Doug, is he coming to the pub then?" I enquired, as he sauntered up to the car.

Doggy snorted, "Yes. He'll be ready in five."

"What? Five years?" Sulli joked.

"Mmmm, maybe five millennia!" Doggy ventured, licking his dry lips, "I've got cotton mouth… Come on, let's go and have a lot of drinks. I can't wait to see Mia. I've got a good feeling about tonight, guys."

Sulli and me sniggered lecherously.

"Yeah. Go for it, man," I told him, getting out of the car.

Sulli nodded his head in agreement, and we strolled up the road to the pub, opened the solid wood door and entered. It was like a proper old coach house inside, with low ceilings, wooden beams, and a long, dark oak bar, lined up with taps sporting all kinds of specialist beers, ales, bitters and ciders. In the corner of the pub, there was a pool table, and standing in front of it, cue in hand, stood a good-looking girl with blonde hair, in a Jimi Hendrix t-shirt, wearing tight figure-hugging jeans and high black boots. Immediately, her face lit up when she saw us; she mouthed a hello to Doggy, waving excitedly.

Doggy waved back extravagantly, "That's Mia, I'll just go and say hi."

I looked to Sulli. "Well. Bloody hell!" I said.

Sulli smiled, nodded, and we left them to it, headed for the bar.

"What you having, Skinner, snakebite?" Sulli asked.

"Yeah, please mate."

Sulli nodded, knowingly, like we shared a secret, "Yeah good man, me too… They do a nice little still cider here called, 'Fenland Grog', it's twelve percent proof, you want to try that?"

I sniggered, repeated, "Grog!!!"

"It's the good stuff. There's no gas in it, so it doesn't go solid," he informed me, a grin tugging at his lips.

"Sounds good mate, I left my spoon at home."

I felt a tap on my shoulder and turned to see Doggy beaming incandescently back at me. Standing next to him, in the lights of the bar, stood a smiling Mia, who I noticed had purple streaks in that blonde hair. I couldn't believe how good she looked; she was a full-on Rocker with a full-on figure.

Doggy introduced us; she gave me a firm handshake.

Eying me up challengingly, she said, "So, Doug tells me you play pool, do you want a game then, Skinner?"

"Er… Yeah, I play a bit, OK, then, lead the way," I said, a bit taken aback by her confidence.

Sulli and Doggy grinned at my incredulous face.

"See you in a minute lads… this won't take long," I boasted, and she rolled her eyes at me; then led the way through the noisy pub-goers, towards the table.

Once over at the table, Mia reached down all business-like, grabbing the triangle from the ball return, and began filling it with the bright red and yellow balls. Then, job done, using her thumb, she smoothly flipped the black ball into the middle, removed the triangle, and stood back chalking her cue.

I smirked, "Your break, mugs away," I said, oozing belief in my abilities.

Mia snorted. "OK," she said, getting down on the shot, "You know you won't beat me. My Dad used to run The Robin Hood pub in Cherry Hinton. We had a table there. I used to play all the time," she declared, and to prove her point, she smashed the balls all over the table, sinking two yellows, got up, potted two more; then, running out of position, she left me tucked up under the cushion at the baulk end, and stepped back with a smug look on her face.

I snorted, stepped up, knocked in a long straight red.

"Oh, that's a good shot from under the cush!" She admitted.

"Cheers," I replied, evenly, and got down to take my next shot, "I used to have a half-sized snooker table at my house when I was a kid."

Mia smiled coolly, "Mmm… We've got a match on then, haven't we?"

"Yeah, we have," I replied, as I rolled a tight red into the middle pocket, which turned out to be the last ball I potted in the game.

A few minutes later, she smashed the black in to win the game comprehensively. I was surprised, disappointed, gutted, confused in fact, as I hardly ever lost and seeing my pained expression, she patted me on the shoulder, being the good sport, commiserating with the loser.

"Oh, bad luck. You played well," she announced, as another player fed his 10ps into the table.

I smiled back, feeling a bit better. "Cheers," I said, walking away.

"NEXT!" She shouted, making me spin around, and she giggled at my gawking face.

I thought, wow, as I trudged back to the bar with my tail between my legs.

Sulli grinned at my surly gait, "How did you get on, Skinner? Did you lose by any chance?"

I flopped my head up and down, despondently, "Is it that obvious?"

"Yep, it is. I knew you would, she beats everyone, you're lucky she didn't bet you."

"Oh what, I got hustled, didn't I?" I said.

"You did, I'm afraid, Skinner. Mia's an amazing girl, great-looking, great pool player, likes good music, a drink, even a smoke. She's what I call an all-rounder."

I chuckled, "I like that, yeah, she certainly is, it's weird though, I've known Doggy for a long time, ages, since we were kids, and I've never seen him with a girl like that before, they're usually a bit more… Er, well, let's just say, more conservative than her," I said, nodding towards her prone form on the table.

Sulli smiled, "Doggy?" he queried.

"Yeah, Doggy like Doggy Kennel, it's what we call him down our way, you know like Dougy Kinnell."

Sulli grinned, handed me my pint,

"Oh, I get it… You know, Doug's or should I say Doggy's a surprising bloke, I've underestimated him a few times over the years, I won't do it again," he said, picking up his pint, then taking a swig, "Aaahhh… Check out the still cider in this. It's well gnarly."

I nodded, took a swig, quenching my thirst, felt the warmth spread down through my body, appreciating the sweet liquid, and looked over towards the pool table where Mia was now playing Doggy.

Sulli waved to someone on the other side of the pub, "Oh yeah, did Doggy tell you about Steven Mackintosh?"

"What the actooorrrr?" I said, accentuating the end.

"Yeah, the actooorrr," he mimicked, back, laughing.

229

"Nah, what's the young Larry Olivier been up too now?"

Sulli set his pint down on the bar, "Well, he was in Maximum Head Room a few weeks ago doing bongs, and he threw a proper whitey; he was puffing on 'Big Bertha' you know the three-footer?"

I nodded respectfully; I was well acquainted with her; she could be a harsh mistress sometimes.

Sulli continued, "He took this massive cumulonimbus hit, slumped forward like a rag doll, and knocked Bertha over… The water went everywhere."

I sniggered, "Oh no, not the bong water… That stinks mate!"

"Yeah. It stains too, and you know what John's like about his flat? …He totally freaked out. And while we were picking Steven up, seeing if he was alright, he ran into the kitchen, grabbed some washing up liquid, and a scourer, came back in and started scrubbing at it, like a man possessed. He was going at it, scraping backwards and forwards, and if anything, it was making it worse. Then he starts running around the room shouting, 'fucking hell, fucking hell, fucking hell', at the top of his voice, and people started getting worried. Steven hears this commotion, comes around. His heads flopping this way, that way, he's all over the place, totally fucked up. Eventually he focuses, starts coming around, and sees John going mad, running about screaming, and his eyes go like saucers, scared that John's shouting at him… And he backs off, cringing away, like an altar boy in the presence of a sexually rampant catholic priest."

I chuckled, picked up my pint, took a decent swig, enjoying the story.

"Check this out, though, it gets better. John jumps up, still totally manic, leaves the room and comes back in again holding a Norman Bates psycho knife and a chopping board. Steven starts shouting, 'no, no, no, John, I didn't mean it, I didn't mean to do it', pushes us aside and runs for the door, straight into the beaded curtains, gets caught up in them, starts thrashing around like a fish caught in a landing net. Seriously, Skinner, I've never seen anything so funny in my life, I almost pissed myself laughing."

"What the fucking hell, what was John doing with a psycho knife?"

"I know it's unbelievable. I must admit, at the time I was looking for an exit plan too."

I creased up and drained my pint.

"Now this is the John bit… Once we had untangled poor Steven, who was still well agitated. John places the board over the stain, cuts around it, takes the piece out, gets up, moves one of his wardrobes over a few feet and cuts another piece out from where the wardrobe sat. He then swaps the pieces over, carefully smooths them in, and then moves the wardrobe back, sits down, grins, tells Steven to 'cut it out', and starts skinning up."

I cracked up laughing, "Jesus… I knew the guy was weird."

"I'll tell you what, unless you looked closely you couldn't tell the difference, the carpet looks immaculate."

"Well, they do say, there's a thin line between a genius and a lunatic," I said, picking up my empty glass, "I'll get these."

Sulli picked up his pint, "Cheers mate, I need to catch up," he said, before sinking his in two long drafts; then he banged his glass down on the bar, belching exaggeratedly.

I soon got the attention of the over-worked barmaid, ordered the drinks, and while we waited for our refills to arrive Sulli said, "I wonder how our lunatic genius is doing?"

"Who…?" I asked, confused for a moment, "Oh yeah, I wonder."

On the other side of the pub, near the pool table, Mia was talking avidly with Doggy, and he had this really weird expression on his face. His eyes were wide, almost peeled open, his head wobbled vigorously, up and down, left, right. He looked compliant, and attentive, to all the lady's needs. I thought, the poor sod, he's probably got a Mars Bar-sized lump in his pants too, throwing him even further off kilter.

"I don't know, mate. They're still chatting away," I said, grinning.

Sulli chuckled, "He looks like a nodding dog."

"I think he's in love. Oh. What? He's only shaking her hand now, and he's off to the bog…"

Sulli snorted, turned away to see how the drinks were coming along. "It's all physical contact though, Skinner, remember what I said? Never underestimate Doggy… Every Dogg has its Day," he said, wisely.

I sniggered, pulled out a creased-up tenner, paid the barmaid, and then I felt a light tap on my shoulder and there was Mia, and all of a sudden, my eyes peeled wide open too.

I reigned myself in quickly, "You alright, Mia? …You want a drink?"

"Yeah, I'll have one. Thanks," she said, going for her denim handbag, but I waved her away.

"I'll get them in, Mia, it's fine. It's the least I can do after you let me knock a couple of balls in earlier."

Mia smiled broadly, showing perfect white teeth; ordered herself a pint of Fenland Grog, and as we waited, she said, "OK, so let me get this straight, you're Doug's mates?" Sounding puzzled.

"Yeah," I replied, while Sulli lifted his untouched pint in the affirmative.

Mia looked towards the toilets, "Oh, come on, really! You two are Doug's mates?"

"Yeah, he's alright," I said, and took a gulp of my freshly delivered pint.

Mia snickered, "Mmm… He's a bit of a knobend, isn't he?" she opened her case with.

I was slightly taken aback… Then very taken aback, "Well… Yeah, apart from that."

"And what about that Afghan coat?" She pressed the case.

"Well… Yeah, apart from that."

"And what about the fake cockney accent?" She concluded, closing the case.

I slapped my forehead with my hand, "Oh, for fuck's sake, he's not doing that again, is he?"

She giggled, "Yes, he is, and it's bloody annoying. I don't know whether I'm talking to Prince Charles or that fucking iffy Dick Van Dyke character in Mary Poppins."

"Alwwiight mizz poppinnnz," I jeered.

Mia cracked up laughing, tossing her head back, her blonde hair scattering wildly. "I hope he doesn't think he's going to get off with me tonight. Some of my friends would like him, but no, he's not for me... He really is a knobend."

Doggy's head appeared, over her shoulder. "Mia? ...Who's a knobhead?" He enquired, not really wanting to know the answer.

Mia's face pulled itself into a tight grimace, she placed a hand over her mouth. "I didn't say knobhead, I said knobend," she said evenly, regaining her cool.

Doggy watched her all big-eyed, like a puppy that had just been chastised for pissing on the carpet. You poor sod, I thought, surely, she's not going to say that to his face. I remembered with trepidation our conversation on the way up in the car, a knock back like this could have devastating effects on him.

I cracked up laughing, way too loudly, "Oh what, no, no, she was talking about that wanker of a barman, BARMAID," I said, waving my hands around frantically, like we were standing in some dirty bastard's Vesta Chow Mein and lager, fart cloud.

Doggy smiled broadly from ear to ear, convinced his mate had just told him the truth, and carried on his pursuit of lovely Mia, by placing a protective hand on her shoulder.

Mia shrunk at his touch, edged away, crossed her arms. She was back in control now,"Doug, let's go outside… On our own, we need to talk."

"Come on, Doug, now," she instructed, already walking away.

Doggy's face lit up like a fruit machine on a win cycle, and turned to us, "Oh, my word, did you hear that, guys? …Skinner, is it OK if you get a taxi back to Sulli's and I'll pick you up in the morning? …Oh my god. I knew she liked me, but this is all happening so quickly, or maybe it isn't, maybe. Maybe, it was meant to be, I don't know, I, oh wow… I'll see you two later, a lot later."

"Doug, Doug, hold on, hold on, you might have got it wrong there," I pleaded.

Doggy's face switched from fruit machine to rotten fruit in a trice. He now viewed me coldly, searching my face, searching for the reason behind my ridiculous comment, the comment, that was now, holding him up from his liaison with the lovely Mia. He thought, he had it.

"I'm not stupid you know. I've seen the way you've been looking at her. You like her too… That's it… You're jealous. Aren't you Skinner?" He snapped.

"What? No, no… No… Doug, listen."

"No. I'm sorry, I haven't got time for whatever this is," he said, giving me a stormy sideways glance, and with that he was off.

"Sulli?" I mumbled, helplessly.

"Aaahhh just leave it, Skinner, he'll just shoot the messenger again, have another drink, he'll be back in a minute."

I couldn't do anything but laugh. Laugh at how cruel life could be sometimes, laugh at the stupid 99 flake, I tried to help him, save him a bit of embarrassment, and he had accused me of jealousy.

"She's right… What a knobhead," I said, finally summing it up.

Sulli shook his head, frowned, "No, she said, he was a knobend."

"What?" I said, absently.

Sulli necked his pint, belched again, "Skinner, I think you'll find she said knobend."

I smiled indulgently and picked up my pint for the draining, "Oh yeah, that's right… What's the difference between a knobhead and a knobend?"

Sulli paused, while thinking it over, and by the time I had downed my pint. Eureka, he was there.

"A knobhead is someone who has a cock for his head and, well… A knobend is someone who is just the end of a knob, you know like a bell end or a bobby Jelmet."

I cracked up laughing at this modern-day Archimedes, and Archimedes signalled the barmaid to bring forth more ale, for the issues of the day were truly taxing.

"Let's get a few in to save time," said the wise man.

"Good idea," I said, handing him a fiver for the next round.

Sulli paid the barmaid, and we got stuck into the precious juice. He was right about the Fenland Grog cider, it was smooth like a snake, and bit in very much the same way. The meaning of 'gnarly' I didn't know, but I was beginning to think it might mean, out of your fucking tree.

"Shit… Shit, talking of knobheads. Sorry I mean knobends," said Sulli, looking through the crowded bar to a bloke sitting with a Beki Bondage girl, on the other side of the pub.

I slammed my first empty pint down, "Who's that?"

"That's Sean… A fellow Sicko," said Sulli, ducking his head back behind the throng.

I nodded, picked up my next pint, drank deeply, and he continued, "Yeah he's our drummer, he's with his girlfriend, so he's told me to steer clear."

I put my half empty pint down, "Oh what, really?"

"He's a bit of a prat sometimes," he admitted.

"So, you don't get on with your bass player and the drummer's a bit of a prat. That's not good, mate."

"Yeah, tell me about it… And we are playing our best music now. I'll be honest Skinner, I'm sick of it all. Sick of the hassle. I don't know if I want to keep it going. I've had a good run, I'm the last original Sicko standing, I'm sick of The Sickos, maybe it's time for something different."

Whoa, I thought, fate's warming rays are really shining on me tonight, let's see what happens. I ventured, "I know how you feel Sulli, it's sad mate… Would you consider joining another band?"

Sulli stared at me for a while, thinking it over, "Hmm, yeah I might do," he said, carefully, "Why?"

I thought, you're beginning to sound like Doggy trying to worm his way into The Sickos here, then, no, am I bollocks. Virus V1 are a fucking guitar band. The Sickos are a fucking guitar band. Fuck it, keep going, what's the worst that can happen? So, I explained our situation in detail, right from the first inkling I had that, all was not well with Andy and Whiff, to the culmination of the row at our Hoddesdon one man and his dog gig. Sulli got it, he got it all, had been through similar things himself over the years he told me, and when I had finished, I drained my pint, and waited to see what he was going to do about it.

Sulli sunk his pint, too, matching me.

"I'm sorry to hear that, Skinner, Virus V1 are decent, really aggressive stuff. If it does go badly, then let me know, I'm very interested," he said, bumping my fist with his, "I can play bass as well, you know, if that's what you need?"

"OK, that's settled then, if anyone goes, I'll let you know, mate."

Sulli nodded, caught the attention of the barmaid, and produced another crinkled-up tenner.

"I'll drink to that, well I will in a minute."

A few rounds later, with The Sickos, Virus V1 entente thoroughly toasted, the alcohol began to really kick in, I felt woozy and not just a little bit sick, so excusing myself, from Virus V1's new vocalist or bass player, or the way I was feeling at the time, Virus V1's new triangle player, I stumbled off to the toilets. Once there, I went into one of the traps, where I stuck my finger down my throat, and after dry heaving a couple of times, I threw up a geyser of watery brown bile into the filthy toilet bowl. I repeated the process, then after wiping the sludge off my chin, I went to the sink to douse cold water on my face and gargle. A few splashes later and I began to feel better, so ready to go again, I pushed open the toilet door, returned to the bar just in time for the next round, and a grinning Sulli, who had already set them up.

On the bar in front of me sat another snakebite, shimmering under the lights. It was time to go again, so I put it up to my lips, and was about to drink, when Mia slunk up to us, taking us in, giving us both the eye. Her tight-fitting Jimi Hendrix T-shirt called out to me. A smile played on my lips, I couldn't resist it.

"Purple Haze, all in my Brain, lately things they don't seem the same," I sang, almost tunefully, quoting the psychedelic guitarist's ode to L.S.D."

Mia smiled back at me, gently bit her bottom lip, flicked her hair back, and strolled on, swinging her full hips, as she coolly, wandered past us, back towards the pool table, and another waiting mug.

Sulli burst out laughing, "Whoa, you're in there man."

"Nah, I'm with someone, mate, and she's with… Doggy!!!…" I said, fading out.

Sulli choked on his pint, coughed, spat some out onto the floor, "Oh. Shit. Where is he?"

"Mia, Mia," I said, grabbing at her arm, "What happen with Doggy? …I mean Doug, where is he?"

"Skinner!! Calm down," she said, placing an appeasing hand on my arm, "He went over to Maximum Head Room, don't worry, he said, he'll be back soon."

Sulli tapped me on the shoulder and right on cue there he was, Doggy, looking a bit sheepish, looking more than a little bit stoned, with his half-grin, and eyes straight out of The Chinese Embassy.

I trotted up to him, my face full of concern, "Doug, are you alright? …We wondered where you'd got to… Fucking hell man."

Doggy cracked up, his stoned face, smiling like a dinner plate. "Come, come, now, Skinner, don't worry… I wasn't going to string myself up," he laughed. "I told you it was a ruse, I'm not going to top myself, not now anyway, maybe later."

OK, I thought, you want to joke about it?

240

"Oh, that's a relief Doug, I need a lift home," I quipped.

Doggy and Sulli dissolved into fits of laughter.

"I'm going to give you a lift alright, Skinner, come on, let's go over there," said, Doggy pointing to a seated area on the opposite side of the pub and without waiting for an answer, he hobbled into the noisy hordes of people clustered around the bar, weaving left and right.

Sulli and me shrugged our shoulders, grabbed our pints and fell in behind him unsteadily.

Once we had navigated our way through the raucous pub patrons to our intended seats, the three of us sat down. I began to feel a lot better with my backside on Terra Firma; the shippy sea sickness in my legs abated some. Relaxing, I watched Doggy look around shiftily, to see if the coast was clear. Then nodding, satisfied, he pulled out a small piece of paper about the size of a postage stamp, grinning at us both.

"Hey guys look what IIIII'vve got," he sang in a high-pitched voice, placing it on the table in front of us.

"Yeah, really impressive mate. A postage stamp! Brilliant! Is that my way home? What you going to do? Write my address on my forehead, stick that stamp on my arse and leave me by the post box?"

Sulli and Doggy exchanged a glance; cracked up laughing.

"No, Skinner, if I'm not mistaken, there are three microdots on that postage stamp," said Sulli, looking to Doggy for confirmation, who in return bowed his head.

"It's LSD, Skinner, for, to trip out to."

Doggy leant forward, carefully ripped the paper into three separate pieces; looked meaningfully over towards Mia, who was still hustling the mugs on the pool table and lobbed it into his mouth. "Hmmm, vitamin L, vitamin S, and vitamin D," he smiled, washing it down with Sulli's drink, "I'm getting all the major groups now… What about you, Skinner? …Are you going to have your… Out o' Vits?"

"Nah, I don't know, I'm not really into all that hippy shit."

Doggy laughed, "I don't know about that, Skinner, you smoke dope, you like Hendrix, you like Floyd, like watching sunsets. I would say, you were a closet hippy."

I smiled at him, thinking, maybe he has a point, but I don't want to turn into one of those gibbering hippy wrecks that frequented The Tap. "Fuck off, man," I said, sort of proving his point.

Doggy looked over at Mia as she bent over the pool table, his face victorious

"Come on then, Skinner, let's see what you're made of."

"Nah. Seriously Doug. Fuck off, I'm not taking that from you," I said, raising my voice, sinking the hippy inside, disproving his point.

Doggy cringed backwards, moved his narrowed eyes to Mia's round backside, while I turned to Sulli, who was looking down at his tiny piece of paper; it didn't look like much, I thought.

"You dropping yours then, Sulli?"

"Yeah, I am. I do like a visit to Mars and beyond now and again… It's fine, Skinner."

"I'm pissed up enough already," I told him.

Sulli cackled, placed his piece on his tongue. "You won't be drunk after taking this, old chum. This will sober you up quick enough but listen it's up to you, Skinner. I'm not going to try and persuade you, I will say this though, it's fucking brilliant," he said, and with that, he clamped his mouth shut, trap door like, and swallowed exaggeratedly.

Doggy cheered, Sulli cheered back, I sat in the middle, staring down.

In front of me sat a tiny piece of paper, picking it up, I rolled it in between my thumb and forefinger, feeling a lump within it, no bigger than a piece of grit. I thought, how can this do anything? It's so small. Oh well, I'm well pissed up already, I doubt I'll even feel it, when in Rome, do as The Romans do.

"Oh well, when in Cambridge," I said, washing it down with a mouthful of Fenland Grog.

"Welcome aboard The Starship Enterprise, Skinner," said Doggy, shaking my hand. "To bodily go where no one in The Greenman has gone before," he said, dropping my hand, "Oh, by the way, before we launch, here's my car keys, whatever happens, don't let me drive,

243

not until I'm straight again, that is," he said, placing them on the table.

"OK if you insist," I replied, storing them in my pocket, safely away from the happy hippy.

Sulli shook my hand too, telling me, "You're a proper trooper, Skinner, I kind of want your band to split up, now. We would be great together, have a real laugh… We could bring even more anarchy and chaos to the masses."

"Yeah, we would mate, you'd love the rest of the band too, you'd fit in perfectly."

Sulli smiled, and the three of us sat back to await the effects of the microdots. I didn't know what to expect; what was coming my way. It was wait and see. I had seen The Beatles film Yellow Submarine late one night, last Christmas. In my drunken state I had thought it was a load of old hippy bullshit; I hadn't taken L.S.D. though, so maybe that was the key to understanding the soppy childlike cartoon.

A couple pints later, Sulli slowly turned in his seat to face Doggy. Examining him closely, he asked, "You alright Doug? …You getting anything yet?"

"No. Nothing," Came his reply.

Sulli snorted, grinned, shook his head. Yep, I thought, what a complete and utter waste of time, I wonder how much Doggy paid out for a piece of blank paper the size of a stamp.

I snorted, too, and looked through the mass of people to see how Mia and her mugs were doing over on the pool table. A Motörhead

T-shirt wearing rocker of around thirty-years-old, marched up to the table, and dropped his fiver down. Mia smirked, cat-like, added her own five-pound note to his on the side of the table and broke off. In a flurry of reds and yellows, the balls whipped around the table, two reds disappearing in the process. Mia stood back reading the table, nodded, leant forward, and then one by one she proceeded to clear the wool like, blue baize of the red balls. In a matter of minutes, she was done, and she picked up the two fivers, put them in her back pocket, then heron like she waited for another mug.

"You getting anything yet, Doug?" Asked Sulli, disturbing me from my reverie.

"No nothing… It might be a bad batch… John told me there's been a lot around recently."

Sulli nodded sadly, while I got back to the pool.

Motörhead T-shirt was replaced by a Slayer T-shirt, who, in turn was replaced by a Celtic Frost T-shirt. I couldn't take my eyes off the table. It was fascinating, illuminating, lucid. I was enthralled.

Sulli shifted in his seat next to me, "Doug? You getting anything yet?"

"Doug!!! …Doug!!!"

I swivelled my eyes away from the all-encompassing table, away from the soft, blue baize, lit from above, away from the hypnotic red and yellow balls, gaped at Doggy, and saw he was slumped back in his seat, mouth flopped open, eyes staring into some unknown galaxy.

Sulli and me cracked up laughing.

245

Sulli said, "Earth calling Doggy, earth calling, come in Doggy."

"I said, earth calling Doggy, come in Doggy, do you read me, over?" He repeated, Houston-like, grinning manically, his voice pulsing through the pub's merry hubbub.

"Oh what… Is he alright?" I asked, gawping into his vacant face, "DOGGY???"

Doggy shook his head. "Doddy??" Babbled Doggy, from his far away galaxy.

"Doggy… Not Doddy, you spoon," I said, creasing up.

Sulli toppled over backwards into the seat, laughing hysterically, "What is it, Skinner? Oh yeah, it's Dougie Kinnell, like Dog Kennel? …Doggy."

"I'm Doggy alright. Owooooo," he howled, wolf-like, "I see it now. I see everything. I am Doggy. I'm like Snoopy lying on the top of his kennel, out of his fucking treeeeeeeeeee."

Sulli and me fell about laughing. I looked around at them and both seemed to have become part of the red faux leather seat we were sitting on, sunken, moulded into it, which made me laugh even more. I thought, what the fucking hell is going on here, damage limitation, limit the damage, damaged goods. I tried to reign it in, limit the damage, stop laughing, like a mental case, in The Adult Mental Institution. It was impossible, though, unfeasible, something was coming; something building up inside me. It didn't make any sense. Deep inside the wetlands of my body, the alcohol was in full retreat, draining from every area, sinkhole, down the plughole; siphoning out, rip tides flushing it away, high tide, tsunami, and as it left, arid, dry, it was filled with something else; something a lot stronger was gushing in to take its place, something acidic, something that was going to keep me laughing, keep me laughing, maybe, forever.

"Whoa… What's happening? Jesus Christ," I said, watching my two seatmates laughing like hyenas, "You two look like you're connected to the seat," I gibbered.

Sulli and Doggy cracked up, wobbling backwards and forwards from their deep roots within the red leather seat, and with a feeling of foreboding, trepidation, and a million other stations of neurosis on the mainline to insanity, I dragged my eyes away from them, to see what the rest of the pub looked like.

I slowly raised my head, not knowing what to expect. The place was packed tight with human beings; different shapes, sizes, human beings filled every space. They moved normally, but the perception of time was slow. So slow, in fact, that even though they were moving at a normal speed, they were taking ages to do it. I couldn't believe my eyes. It boggled the mind. People were quite literally rushing around at a snail's pace - around the pub, around me, circling me. It felt like I was now at the centre of everything, the universe started and ended in my lap; I was the fisheye mirror in the hallway back at my home, the distorter of worlds, a vector redistributing light, sound, changing everything, I knew to be real.

Sulli gave me a gentle nudge. "You alright Skinner, you getting anything yet?" He enquired with a mischievous look on his warped face.

"I am at the centre of the world," I murmured incredulously.

"Check out the fruit machine," he advised me.

In the lights of the fruit machine, a group of lads stood, their faces lit up, but the more I looked, the more it seemed, that it wasn't the lights from the fruit machine that was lighting up their faces. It was their faces that were the lights, shining down onto the fruit machine. I was mesmerised, watching the undulating light faces as they disgorged their 10ps into the machine, which hungrily ate them up, giving scant return. It suddenly occurred to me, that this fruit machine is like life. In our short time on earth, with great hope in our hearts, we feed our 10ps; our heart, and souls into the great gamble of life, and as we slowly pour ourselves in; throw everything we have down the coin shoot to spin wheel plate to achieve that all-important win pay line, as to engage that jackpot feed, our star fades, as does our heart and soul in the quest for that win. Win or lose, we'll always keep on chucking the 10ps in.

Doggy sprang up from the seat. "NO, NO, no, no, fucking hell, I can't do it, I won't do it, AAAAAHHHH," he shouted, making a rapid slow-motion rush for the door, dodging the other humans, left grinning in his wake.

"What the fucking hell's up with him," I said, trying to keep my voice level.

Sulli sniffed loudly, craned his neck, elongating it, giraffe like, to two feet high, watching Doggy's escape, "Mmmm, I think that's what you'd call a freak-out."

I sniggered like Muttley on L.S.D., "Is he trying to run away from his trip?"

"Something like that… He won't get far, though, it's all in his head."

"Yeah, tell me about it. I'll be honest with you Sulli, this is fucking heavy-duty, man."

Sulli nodded, took a swig from his pint, keeping it together nicely, "I've had stronger, but this is pretty intense, especially on your first trip, you're doing well."

I snorted, blew my cheeks out, picked up my pint, "Cheers man, 'pretty intense' fucking is it! The way I'm feeling right now, I might be joining Doggy soon, I mean we necked those microdots, what? …About ten minutes ago?"

Sulli creased up, bending in half, falling up to his lap in the seat, "Noooo Skinner, we dropped them ages ago, more like an hour and half ago."

"Bollocks…… no way!!!"

"Yeah, seriously, you know what they say, time goes quickly when you're…"

"Oh what. Look, he's back," I said, cutting him off, seeing Doggy sashaying back towards us through the assembled humans, "What the fuck is he doing? …And why is he walking like that?"

Sulli perused the advancing Doggy, shaking his head ponderously, like a baffled Sigmund Freud, "I think he left his brain behind, Skinner, he's come back to get it," he diagnosed, finally.

I creased up, leaning sideways, for a different perspective, slapping at my forehead, knowing that wherever Doggy's brain was, mine wouldn't be far behind it, "Aaaah yeah that would be it, I know the feeling."

"I've done, I've done it," said Doggy, planting himself deep into the seat again.

Sulli smiled broadly at him, sighed, "What have you done?"

"I've got rid of it all, it's all gone now."

I stared at him, he really was a cause for concern, "What did you get rid of?"

"I chucked it all away. The microdots and the eighth of squidgy black I got from John early. I'm giving up, it's all gone, gone forever. I don't need it. In every day, in each way I'm… Er, … It's gone, now."

Sulli and me exchanged a glance; another Doggy classic had just manifested itself right before our very eyes, but this time it wasn't funny - far from it. I couldn't give a shit about the microdots right now, I was up to my eyeballs, but to throw away a whole eighth of Afghani Black, well, that was unforgivable.

"Oh, fucking hell, Doddy, where did you chuck it?" Asked Sulli, standing up with purpose.

"It's Doggy," corrected Doggy.

"Doggy, Doddy, Dodgy… Whatever. Where did you chuck it?"

Doggy paused, thinking it over. "You know what? I think I like Doddy better, like Ken Dodd, and there's my Diddy man mate, Mick Marmalised," he said, pointing at my still, disbelieving face.

I cracked up laughing; another Doggy classic had just been taken up a notch, but there still was the serious business of a missing piece of squidge to think of.

"Where did you chuck it, man?" I asked calmly.

"Chuck, Chuck Norris, who chucked Norris?" He gibbered back.

Sulli sighed, blowing out a hurricane. It was time to find out what we needed to know right now, he looked deep into the two black holes that were Doggy's eyes, "Doggy you are off your nut mate."

"I'm off my goose Sulli, off my dial, off the end of the scale," he grinned.

"Yeah, me too. I'm Mick Marmalised, and I'm off my fucking stork, mate," I gabbled, unhelpfully.

"You are mate, we all are. Now Doggy, where did you chuck the hash and trips?" Sulli persisted.

"In the car park round the side of the pub."

"Brilliant, brilliant, show me Doug, don't worry, we'll find it."

"Brilliant, I'm brilliant," declared Doggy.

I sighed with relief, went to stand up to right this great wrong, but my legs said... No, refused to move, I looked to my legs, thought

251

about them moving, they didn't; they were rooted, deep into the red leather.

"Er… OK, I'll see you out there in a minute," I said, to their retreating forms.

Sulli threw me a victory sign over his shoulder. Then standing behind Doggy, he drove him through the humans, using his shoulders a makeshift steering wheel.

Sulli and Doggy disappeared, and suddenly I felt very alone. Sighing again, I sat back, thinking about my legs. It was sort of funny being stranded, debilitated, on the short term like this, but what would happen if I could never use them ever, again. I couldn't stand up and play my guitar. Couldn't walk over to the bar, couldn't ride a motorbike, couldn't walk into The Anchor or The Feathers, couldn't drive a car, couldn't go anywhere. What the fucking hell would I do then? I couldn't walk over to the… I stopped. Mia, the goddess of the pool table, was still coining it in; another mug put a ten-pound note in her hand, and despondently walked away. I watched the poor sap. It was almost like, not only had she taken his money, she had taken part of him as well, his soul. She was like the fruit machine, taking people's souls.

Oh, what!!! Mia is a fruit machine!!! What are you on about? My conscience mind told me. No, Mia isn't a fruit machine; she's just a girl, a hustler, who uses the male belief that they are better than women at sport to take their money. A fruit machine!!! Bollocks. That's insane in the membrane. Inside, I felt something changing, something was leaving, something insightful. A door into this bizarre, yet real world was beginning to close. In some ways, it was a relief, but the piece of the intricate puzzle that had come on a postage stamp was withdrawing, taking its alluring secrets with it. On the seat below me, my legs began to detach themselves from the red leather, and the feeling grew back within them. Whilst inside my head, the once crashing waves on my brain, were ebbing, calming, slowly calming, into mill pond still waters. It felt like I had been on my journey; served my time, been to the outer limits, been to heaven and hell and every place in between, and finally it was time to dock, and as the ship came in to land, it was time for reflection and revelation. I was on a new plateau now, not so high, less confused, a friendly one, colourful, finite, intrinsically detailed, but it was of this world. I had landed back on earth, safely, to live with my fellow humans, felt the ticker tape parade of adrenaline flushing out the lysergic acid diethylamide, sense and reason rushing in to replace the alien rip tides, cleansing me, reeling me in, thankfully the world was still a beautiful place, and thankfully my legs seemed to work again, maybe even better than before.

I felt a tap on my knee, looked around, and Mia's face appeared before me. She smiled knowingly. She's come to save me, I thought; she was beautiful, she was an angel. She even had a purple halo.

"You alright Skinner?" She asked, squeezing my knee playfully, "You've been sitting here on your own for ages just staring into space, where's Sulli?"

"…Oh, my word, Skinner… You're out of your mind," she said, looking into my badly drawn face.

I cracked up laughing. "Nah, I'm alright," I told her unconvincingly.

"Mmmm… Yeah, sure you are. What did Doug fetch back from Hermit John's, I wonder?"

"Don't know, Miss," I said, smiling angelically into her pretty face.

Mia snickered, "Skinner, you shouldn't be in a pub tripping out…
Come on, I've got a bit of the squidgy black that's been going
around, let's go outside and have a smoke. That will level you up a
bit. I've got one here, all skinned up and ready to go. All you've got
to do is light the white touch paper."

"Nah, I'm alright, let's play another game of pool, double or quits," I
quipped, standing up a lot easier than I thought it would be.

Mia smiled broadly, shook her head, "Really? …Well, OK, if you're
sure, the pubs closing soon, but yeah come on, I can't refuse a
challenge," said, my fellow earthling.

On the way to the pool table, the scene of my early slaughter, my
eyes were drawn to her; my tripped-out brain just couldn't help itself.
I was hypnotized by the way her blonde streaked hair ghosted
deliciously from side to side on her narrow shoulders. By the way her
curvy thighs wriggled in her tight jeans as she sauntered across the
pub like she owned the place. Mia knew I was watching too; she had
probably seen it a thousand times with pool mugs over the years, and
she half turned, glancing at me indulgently. I looked up, suddenly
finding the oak beams on the ceiling even more enthralling, and she
laughed knowingly.

"Oh, so you're not that out of it then, Skinner?"

"What?" I said, absently, examining the finely crafted load bearing
beams.

Mia snickered, strolled up to the table, began to rack up.

"Now are you sure about this?" She asked me, her tone telling me, she wasn't.

"Are you alright?" She pressed on.

"Yeah!!! I'm more than alright, I'm Jimmy White, alright," I said, grabbing a cue, chalking up.

Once she had set the table up, she stepped back with an amused look teasing her face, allowing The Whirlwind to make ready, and waited for the master class to begin.

"OK, mugs away," she said, edging away, as I drew my cue back.

I snorted, I felt good, like I had just conquered another planet, so what's a game of pool? I thought, this time, I'm going to beat her, the cocky cow and threw my cue at the ball, slicing it horribly, and gawked in amazement as it leapt off the table onto the floor where it rolled off under the blazing fruit machine.

Mia sniggered, put her head in her hands. "OK come on, let's get you outside, Jimmy Shite," she said leaning her cue against the table.

"Oh what. Nah, I'm alright," I told her holding onto my cue resolutely, "Well, I would be… It's just the balls are egg shaped, and some of them seem to be melting, a bit!!"

"Yeah, and whose faults that then?" She said, taking my arm as she drove me through the dwindling pub users to the door, just like Sulli had done with Doggy.

"You'll feel a lot better out here, Skinner, a bit of fresh air will do you a world of good."

I hesitated at the door; The Greenman had been my world. In fact, my galaxy, for what felt like a lifetime, a lifetime that had begun with Doggy and Sulli melting into a seat. Now it was all about to end. I had been The Green Man at the start of the evening, the greenest of men, when it came to L.S.D., and now The Green Man was about to leave The Greenman, go outside. I wondered what I was waiting for.

In a second, I put my weight on the oak door, felt it relent, broke on through to the other side, pulling Mia along with me outside. Immediately another door opened, above us; the lights from the city had painted the sky a light magenta, above us trees towered, tinged with oranges, reds, and yellows. In slow motion, a car zipped passed us, at its front, headlights beamed out a yellow jet of liquid light.

"Oh wow, this is amazing, Mia," I said, feeling the pavement beneath me acquiesce with my every step, I thought, bloody hell, I'm walking on a sea of marshmallows,

"I'm the Michelin man walking on marshmallows. This is great," I said, cackling, like a mad bastard.

"I told you," said Mia, taking my arm.

I smiled at a yellow tree, its low branches waved at me, "You seem to know a lot about tripping. You done it before?"

Mia snickered, pointed at her boobs.

"Ooooh, yeah," I said, checking them out.

"Jimi Hendrix," she said, in explanation.

"Yeah, yeah… of course, Jimi Hendrix."

Mia eyed me suspiciously, "I did one of those microdots, with
Hermit and the actoorr, in Max Head Room last week. Very good
they were too, but for the life of me, I can't imagine why anyone
would drop one in the pub. Even The Greenman, maybe pop in for
a pint, when you've levelled out, like you have now, but peaking. No
way."

A car raced by, doing about five miles an hour, I grinned at the
vapour trails it left behind, and the car's crimson rear lights smiled
happily back at me, from its boot.

"Hi man," I said, waving a peace sign at my mechanical friend.

Mia laughed and increased her grip on my arm, as I took this new
world in.

I noticed how the street lights seemed to radiate heat inside their
spheres of light, warming the marshmallow-like pavements beneath.
It was crazy. It's a crazy, mad, fervid, beautiful world, I thought, a
world I didn't see on a normal day, today isn't a normal day, though,
today I had seen so much more.

Mia slowed off, loosened her grip on her arm,

"I'll tell you what… I've got a new Jimi Hendrix album, Lifelines…
Why don't you come back to mine, and we can smoke some black? I
only live just down there," she smiled, pointing towards John's
house.

"Nah… I don't want to go inside now, it's amazing out here… I can't believe it. Hold on," I said, feeling the shape of Doggy's keys in my pocket, "I've got Doggy's car keys, let's go have a puff there."

"Doggy?" Said Mia. "Oh, I get it, Dougie. Doggy," she laughed.

I pulled his keys out, waving them in front of my eyes, studying the shiny, shiny, totally in awe.

"Oh, OK, it's up to you?" She said, sounding surprised.

In the sky above us, a Cessna light aircraft, eased its way through the magenta lake of clouds, and with its lights blinking, like it was signally down to us, it slowly lost height, in preparation to land at Cambridge Airport. I smiled to myself, thinking E. fucking T. has come home after all, and marvelled at the way it leisurely cruised across the sky pool, cutting a trail. I tilted my head, tuning into its sound, as it phased out into the distance, then disappeared completely as it dropped down to land. It could have come from anywhere, I thought. The whole universe was its oyster. London, Liverpool, Manchester. Ganymede or Titan; anywhere, in the Milky Way seemed local tonight. All was alien, allusive, exciting. Inevitable.

I strolled up to Doggy's car, feet still deep in marshmallows, pressed the button to open the door, and the lights flashed up, casting a warm aura around the car.

Mia wandered around the passenger side, "You just locked it," she told me, pulling at the now rigid door.

"Oh what," I said pressing the button, and the lights flashed, once again.

Mia rolled her eyes, gave it another pull, flipped it open, and slid in. "Mmmm where's that lovely squidge hash stick," she said, as I jumped in next to her.

Mia flicked the internal light off, going for her pockets. "You never know around here Skinner, people can be right nosy bastards, especially with all the people going in and out of John's place," she explained.

A moan resonated from the backseat, then a pale hand plopped onto Mia's shoulder.

"AAAaaahhhhhh," screamed Mia, jumping out, flooding the car with light.

Doggy rose up like a dead man awakening in his coffin, stretched his aching arms, yawned, flickered his eyes, flipped one of them open onto me.

"What are you doing in my car Skinner?" He enquired, then his blood-shot red eyes switched to Mia, standing at a safe distance, away from this maniac.

"Fucking hell, Doggy," I exclaimed.

"And, what are you doing with my girlfriend? …In my car?" He accused.

"I'm not your girlfriend… You knobhead," Mia spat.

Doggy scratched his withered head, "I thought you said I was a knobend?"

259

"What…?" She said, irritably.

I snorted, I was confused now, "What's the difference between a knobend and a knobhead?"

Doggy didn't hesitate, "A knobhead is a dickhead, whereas, a knobend is a Helmet Schmidt."

I creased up; Doggy creased up. Mia jerked her head back into the car.

"I'll tell you what… You're a knobhead," she said, pointing at me, "AND YOU'RE A FUCKING KNOBEND!" She said, foaming at the mouth at Doggy, "How does that sound? …WANKERS," and with that, she pounded away from the car.

"Bloody hell man. You scared the life out of her," I said, watching hurricane Mia blow away down the road; she was going to take a long time to blow out. She was so enraged.

"Skinner," Doggy cackled, mistily from the back.

"WHAT?"

"Are you getting anything yet?"

I fell back in my seat, laughing, convulsing, like it was the funniest thing I had heard in my whole life. Then I felt a strange presence. Something was wrong, someone was close. A mangled face appeared in the off-side window about two inches from my head. I ducked, jolted away from it, then looked back in horror. It's John, I thought. No, it can't be. It was him, though. He grinned insanely, ungluing himself.

Sulli appeared over his shoulder, in fits of laughter, "Ha, ha, got you there, Skinner. Classic freak out."

"I almost shat myself, come on, get in… Who's got the puff?"

Sulli jumped in next to me. John hopped in next to Doggy.

Doggy viewed John like he had just beamed down from another planet. It took him a while, but when it finally dawned on him who it was, he sat bolt upright, put his hand out, "Doctor Livingstoned, I presume."

John nodded, breaking up, at his babbling mate. "Doug Kinnell, I presume," he returned.

"I used to be… I'm not exactly sure now," said Doggy poignantly, not knowing if he would ever be the same again, deep down, hoping it to be true.

Sulli lounged back in the passenger seat, took a sharp intake of breath, "So how was your first trip, Skinner?"

"It's not finished yet, Sulli… I like this bit the best, I know what's going on, but what I'm seeing now… The what, would you call them?"

"The visuals?" Offered John.

"Yeah, the visuals, they're fucking brilliant."

"The start though, the lift-off, fucking hell man, that was intense. You could lose your mind out there," I said, looking pointedly at Doggy.

Sulli sniffed, "Yep, the launch is pretty fucked, man. Do you reckon you'd do it again?"

"Nah, not in the pub, I reckon I'll go to Maximum Head Room, if that's all-right John."

John held up a freshly wound spliff from the back, "Sure, why not."

Doggy sobbed, "I'm never doing it again, never."

I thought, oh, here we go, I knew this would happen. His old man will have to take him off to the funny farm when we get back, if we get back. I turned, to calm the bloke down, surveying the acid casualty. He was hunched forward, head in hands, then through his fingers I could see a big grin on the nutter's face.

"I'm never doing this again, and again and again and again and again," he said, laughing manically. "I'm off my rainbow dome," he announced.

I said, "Yeah, me too, mate," turning the key in the ignition, bringing his car to life.

Jimi Hendrix sang, 'and the wind began to howl', and started his massive guitar solo on 'All Along the Watch Tower' from the speakers in the back rack of the car.

Sulli rocked towards me, "Er, Skinner? You sure that's a good idea?" He shouted, through the psychedelic rock.

"I'm fine, Sulli fine, fine, fine mate," I said, disturbing a memory of falling timber, wrecked reindeer, and wiped out wisemen, cackling exponentially, to myself.

"I've had a few lessons," I told them, confidently, depressing the clutch, putting it in gear.

I slowly let the clutch out, and the car shot forwards, veering to the right. I spun the wheel hard left, and it carried on right, so I threw the wheel right and pitched right. Whoa, fucking hell, I thought, now this is suicide, stamping on the brakes, bringing us to a halt. I couldn't work out what the hell was going on. The car was listing to the right. It felt like a flat tyre. So, I got out to investigate, have a look, check the tyres, but when I got out, I couldn't tell whether there was a flat or not, as all the tyres were shaped like eggs.

"I'll drive Skinner," offered John, from the backseat.

I nodded, jumped in the back, edging Doggy over, and he made room for his new backseat pal.

Doggy bopped his head to Hendrix. I soon joined him, the drums, and bass thumping behind us, the guitar bouncing around inside the car. It felt good being in the back, away from responsibility, finding myself in the music. John deftly spun the sunroof open, and the wind rushed in; this time the rush was refreshing. It fed into me, cleansing me, blowing out the dust. I was still tripping, but it was light, head-friendly, invigorating, and sensual. I thought about Cerys, and what we would do the next time I saw her and wondered what would have happened if Doggy hadn't risen like Dracula from his tomb with Mia and me alone in the front of his motor.

263

Or what would have happened if we have gone back to her place.

I had liked Mia. She was a good-looking girl; funny, confident. A Rocker too, and if I had met her a few months earlier, I would have behaved differently, but sometimes in life, timing is everything. A week here, a week there, even, a minute here, a minute there, it could change anything. No matter who you are. I was with someone now, a someone that, I had worked hard to get. It just wasn't worth the hassle, and that feeling of waking up, the morning after the fucking whisky time debacle, wasn't going to go away soon.

Into my soft seat, I eased myself, stretched my arms out extravagantly. John whooped like a cowboy, flooring it, pushing me in deeper. A world of colours scrolled past my window, oranges, reds, pinks, blues in flashes, and as my tired eyes tried to find purchase in the scrolling cosmic rainbow, I saw that we weren't the only ones out and about, having a night to remember. There were other groups of late-night revellers out in Trumpington, having a laugh, living it up, making the most of their Friday night.

Sulli saw them, too, jumped up from his seat, weaved his thin torso snake-like up through the open sunroof, raised, both hands high in the air,

"IT'S GOOD TO BE ALIVE, IT'S GOOD TO BE ALIVE, IT'S GOOD TO BE ALIVE!" He yelled at the passing revellers, and they laughed, waved back, cheering at the friendly mental case, standing proud, upright, in the speeding car, chanting his Shaman-like good vibes at them.

Sulli cheered back, repeating the mantra. It's good to be alive. I thought, yeah. Yeah. It. Is.

264

Chapter Eleven

The Clash

Doggy dropped me off at mine early the next morning, and even as I said goodbye, thanking him for the lift, I knew that a combination of L.S.D., Fenland Grog and T.H.C. coursing through my veins, coupled with an amazing night, would mean there was no way I would sleep, not for a long time. In the first tentative rays of sunlight from the approaching day, unsteadily, I walked around the back of my house, carefully unlocked the kitchen door, and crept into the kitchen, half expecting the old man to be waiting for me. The coast was clear though, his steady snoring radiating from his bedroom upstarts. I paused at the sink to drink a glass of cool water, and immediately began to feel the munchies gnawing deep in my empty stomach. A couple of pieces of cheese on toast would do the trick, I thought, so I quickly put it all together and crept upstairs to my bedroom with another glass of water. Devoured it all, and satiated, I grabbed my open leaf track file from my bedside table and began thumbing through it. I felt inspired, wanted to write music. Right now. Something explosive. Whiff and Dave's words of encouragement for the new crossover tracks came back to me. So, I skipped through the forty Virus V1 and thirty Horror Tape tracks and went to the unfinished lyrics at the back of the file. Picked out the best of them, found a sheet of Venom, Slayer, and Celtic Frost inspired thrash/Black Metal riffs, and got to work.

In the early morning light spilling around the curtain edges in my bedroom, I played and sung quietly to myself, trying to find the right combinations of lyrics and riffs, and after juggling them around for an hour or so, I had the bare bones of 'Life in A.D'., 'Crucified Again', 'Child A Is Born', 'Revenge', 'City of the Damned', 'Legion of the Dead', 'Leviticus' and 'Syndicate' all of which would sit perfectly with our other new track 'Exhibition'. I didn't know what was going to happen to these new tracks though, as none of them would fit into our set as it was at the moment, so I put them aside and turned my attention to Virus V1. I thought, we've got loads of decent tracks ready for us to work on, so why not change some more of the set. It would be good for the band, as not only would we all be working together, helping each other out. If we had to play any more of those Hoddesdon/Founder's Hall type gigs again, it wouldn't be so bad, as everything would feel fresh and new. Picking up my file again, I spun the pages back through to the Virus V1 tracks; soon picking out 'Let Your Slaves Go', 'Apathy', 'El Salvador', 'Spoils of War', 'On the road to Babi Ya' and 'No Revolution', which would sit perfectly with our other new tracks 'Church War' and 'IRA Ireland'. 'Christ Fuckers', 'No more Genocide', 'Horrors of Belsen', 'Suffer Little Children', 'Protest' and 'V1 Bomb' would be the only tracks to remain from our original set. Stretching back, getting comfortable on my bed, I began visualizing what our new set might look like…

1. V1 Bomb
2. Christ Fuckers
3. Spoils of War
4. Church War
5. Let your Slaves Go
6. Horrors of Belsen
7. IRA Ireland
8. No Revolution…

I saw light, warm, clear; it called irresistibly. I acquiesced. Into it, I walked.
In front of me lay a beach, sun-drenched diamond white sands; behind me a cool shaded palm grove.

I looked out into the azure waters of a lagoon; white caps rode high, breaking onto a distant reef. I took a deep breath like I wanted to take the image down into my chest, keep it close to my heart forever.

Inside the palm grove, a shout had me spinning. A young girl of about fifteen, with long sun-bleached blonde hair pointed up into the high branches of a palm tree, giggling; her laugh full of wonder, excitement, full of love. Next to her stood another girl of about eighteen, her hair also long, but the colour of light ginger. She looked up, her face beaming, searching the branches at the top of the fleshy leaved palm.

One of the girls called out, waving widely. Returning her wave, I padded across the rich white sands, feeling the grains massage my feet, some gently rising up between my toes, to the two girls. I took them in, and although they were not alike, they could have been sisters. The younger one giggled again, pointing upwards. I raised my head, focusing on the shade of the high canopy, and marvelled. A dozen fruit bats looked down upon us with their dark, jewel like eyes. Pointing up, I laughed too; they were hilarious.

A sound of a closing door, had me spinning once again. Cerys appeared out of a hooch at the edge of the palm grove, wearing a red swimming costume. She looked different. Her figure was fuller; I liked it. She eased her sunglasses back up into her chestnut locks and gave me a smile that put the sun in the shade.

I smiled, waved, walked into her light...

I'm in heaven, I thought, then, slowly coming to, my eyes focused onto that same life-affirming sun, which now, played at the edges of my curtains. I was back home; Mum standing over me.

"Did you spend all night like that?" She asked.

"Oh. Hi Mum," I said, sheepishly,

"Er… Yeah, I had a bit of a late one."

"Mmmm, so I see," she agreed, looking me up and down, still fully clothed in my black bondage trousers and Discharge T-shirt,

"What are you doing today? Are you practising?"

"Yeah, that's the plan," I said, sitting up stiffly.

"How's it all going? …You haven't said much recently."

"Ahhh, not so good, really."

"Oh?"

"…I don't know mum; I'll find out later today… One way or another."

"I'm sure everything will be fine, Mike. Now come on, get up, you need to get a move on. It's getting late," she chided playfully, turning to leave.

"OK, OK. It's still early, though, Mum… Early, afternoon!" I joked, looking at my bedside clock, whose red slits told me it was half past twelve.

Mum snorted, and left me on my own, to get a move on.

On my bed, I sat scratching at my bristle, thinking, I'm glad the football season has ended; we now have three weeks of practising in the afternoon before the cricket season begins. Still, I needed to get myself moving, as Andy and Whiff would already be walking up by now. Into the bathroom, for the first part of the reassembly job I headed, leant forwards and doused my face in cold water at the sink. It was beautiful; like a chain reaction, everything reconnecting, and my groggy feeling was soon rescinding.

In the bathroom mirror, I gave myself the once over now my mind was clear, and body reinvigorated. There was only more thing left to do now to become whole again, pull up the spikes on my head.

"And who is the most spaced-out Punk Rocker, of them all?" I asked the mirror.

"Why you are, you fucking sky pilot," it grinned back at me, and feeling satisfied, I left its silly grin behind, and decanted for the kitchen, to rustle up some breakfast.

A couple of pieces of toast later, I was ready to go, so I grabbed my gear, said goodbye to Mum and Dad, who both said good luck – I thought, Mum must have said something - and set off for Dave's. It felt like a lifetime since I had been down there, and I was looking forward to seeing them all again.

Into Anne's kitchen I walked, where I smelt freshly baked bread, eggs and bacon. It was its usual hive of activity. Anne was at the sink with Hayley chatting away, Jo and Vicky were cleaning the sides down, while Dave and Alan were sitting in the dining room, with steaming cups of hot tea set in front of them.

"Ah, Baker. Here he is, Thundridge's answer to Romeo… You got her, then?" Asked Alan.

"Who?" I asked back, cluelessly.

Alan chuckled. "Who?" He repeated, "Bloody hell, Baker… You know, Cerys? The girl you've been chasing for years?" He expanded, rolling his eyes at the grinning Dave sitting beside him, "Bloody hell mate. Keep up."

I chuckled back, "Oh yeah, cheers Alan. I got there in the end."

Alan eased into another huge grin, "Oh, the poor girl, she doesn't know what she's let herself in for!" He told everyone, sending us all into fits of laughter.

Anne picked a spud up, out of the sink, introducing it to her psycho knife. "Well, I think they'll make a lovely couple," she said, slicing into its muddy skin, "I thought you might have got together with Jill though, you always liked her, didn't you?"

"Nah, I couldn't compete with Benson."

Alan smiled, "What's this?"

Dave smiled and explained to them that I thought I had been in competition with Jill's dog Benson, and once the tale was told everyone dissolved into laughter at the ridiculousness of it.

I stifled a laugh, "Yeah, but I don't care… Bentsod may have won the battle… But he lost the war… The little shit's dead now. He overdosed on full-cream, milk," I told them, sending them off again.

Hayley furrowed her brow, "I thought Cerys was going out with Mark?"

"Yeah, she was. But she chucked him!"

Alan grinned, "Bloody hell. It's a cruel world, isn't it, Baker?"

"It certainly is, she took him somewhere quiet down by the River Lee and chucked him."

Alan cracked up. "She took him somewhere quiet and chucked him," he repeated.

I ran my hand through the spikes, "Yeah. Cerys reckons when she told him, he slouched forward on the bench, and kept shaking his head, saying no, no, no, no."

Anne said, "Oh no… That's terrible. The poor bloke," laughing, despite her concerns.

"Oh dear, have you seen him since then?" Alan asked, in an amused tone.

I shook my head.

"Oh dear, oh dear, oh dear. That could be awkward, Baker."

I shrugged, "I'm not worried about him."

"You know what, I doubt you are," said Alan, nodding his head. "Baker," he chuckled to himself.

Alan picked up his teacup, took a hesitant sip of the hot fluid, his mind now on this afternoon's job.

One solitary spud remained in the washing up bowl. Anne pulled an amused face, grabbed it, raised the psycho knife menacingly, and began slashing.

Dave slumped forward in his chair, shook his head slowly from side to side. "No, no, no, no," he said, mimicking the forlorn Mark, and the kitchen rang out with laughter again.

Dave repeated his impromptu Mark impression a few more times, to more raucous laughter, and once the mirth had finally died down, he said, "Come on, we better get on."

I nodded in agreement, and we said goodbye to everyone, grabbed the last couple of pieces of Dave's kit, loaded them into the van, and we were away.

One of those bright, beautiful, spring is on the way, crisp afternoons greeted us. I sat back, taking it all in, while Dave drove us down the A10 and onto the little dirt track that led down to the pavilion.

Dave changed down to second, and we crawled along; the van pitching haphazardly from side to side as he navigated our way through the multitude of deep potholes.

"Oh, by the way, Skin! Do you want to buy some cassssseeeeettes?" Dave asked, reaching over to the glove compartment, dropping the door down, revealing a whole load of them.

I picked one up, laughing, spinning it in my hand, examining it, saw that it was Discharge's 'Hear Nothing, See Nothing, Say Nothing' album.

"It looks like the good shit, maaan."

Dave concurred with a nod, then pulled down hard on the steering wheel to avoid another crater.

"You look happy today, mate," I smiled.

"I couldn't be happier," he pronounced, excitedly, and went on to tell me that he had exchanged contracts a week early; his house-warming party was now on for tomorrow.

"Oh what, that's great news, man," I said, after he had explained what exchanging contracts meant.

I thought, nice one, another night on the piss.

Dave spun the wheel hard left, to dodge a huge crater, only to go straight into another.

"Oh yeah, I meant to say, did you know, my Uncle John's moved in with Tess?" he asked, crunching down from second to first to negotiate the mini-crevasse, "Skinner, we could be sort of related after all… Cousin Skinner," he told me, grimacing, playfully.

I snorted, "I heard mate, Cerys said he was moving in. I didn't know it was happening so soon, though… What did we use to call him when we were kids?"

Dave laughed, "Big Bad John."

"Oh yeah… We used to sing that country and western song, didn't we? How did it go, now?"

Dave took a breath and sang, "Big John, big Jooooohn," in a deep baritone cowboy twang.

"Big Bad Johnnnnn," we both crooned, completing it.

"Big Bad John, that's it. He is big, though, isn't he? The bloke's absolutely massive. I remember when we were kids, we were so scared of him. I used to look up at him, thinking, blimey, he's so tall, his head's touching the clouds."

"I remember… Anyway, look, he was up my house last night, asking the old man about you."

I stopped grinning, "Oh. Shit… That doesn't sound good."

A smile played at his lips, letting me wait.

"You worry too much Skin," he said eventually. Setting us both up for the tap in.

"Well, some bugger has too," we both my old man-ed in unison, cracking up.

Dave steered us through another caldera, "No, it was fine, didn't hear everything they were saying, but I heard the old man say that he and mum really liked you, and that you had a good heart."

I breathed a sigh of relief; let it all sink in, as Dave concentrated on dodging the milliard of deep crater-like potholes in front of us, and we pitched and yawned along the track in quiet contemplation.

"Your old man's alright, you know," I told him.

Dave smiled warmly, laughed, and said, "Yeah, he's alright."

Once we had ridden the perilous gravel track and got set up in the pavilion. Dave told me he had worked out a variation of the 'Dutchmen' drum beat that we could use on 'Church War'. So, we quickly powered up, went through it, and unsurprisingly, just like he had said, it was excellent and fitted the track perfectly. A couple of run-throughs later, feeling satisfied with our work, we pulled out a couple of chairs, set them in the window looking out towards the hill, sat back, and let the early afternoon sun wash over us, waiting for the others to show up. I took a deep breath, shut my eyes, felt the healing rays on my face.

"I wonder if Mark would do anything, Skin?"

"Nah… What's he going to do? Drown me in his fucking hair gel?" I jeered.

Dave chuckled, "I never really knew the bloke. He was pretty vain, though, wasn't he?"

"I don't know if it's true or not, but, Cerys reckons, he used to spend more time in the bathroom getting ready than she did," I said, digging a knot out of my neck, in the healing rays.

Dave laughed, clicked Andy's mic on.

275

"No, no, no, no, no," boomed through the pavilion.

I cracked up, opened a sleepy eye and Dave was sitting slouched forward in his chair, bottom lip sticking out, looking all heart-broken and sorrowful,

"No, no, no, no, no," Shook the pavilion again.

In a high-pitched girl's voice, I replied, "Oh, Mark. You've nicked my blusher once too often, you're chucked," pointing an accusing finger.

"No, no, no, no, no!" Boomed back at me, and we both fell about laughing.

I sighed, closed my heavy eyelids again, felt the warmth of the sun on my face and slowly started to nod off listening to the steady hum of the amps.

Dave tapped me on the shoulder, "Skin. Oi, Skin, I think I see them… Yeah, they're coming. Look."

In the blaze of the sun, I could see two figures at the top of the hill, heading down towards us. I put my hand up shielding my eyes, and like Dave said, it was Whiff and Andy.

"Oh what. Are they walking together? …Dave, look. They are," I said,

"Halle-fucking-lujah."

Dave moved out of the glare.

"Nah, Skin," he said, regretfully, "Whiff's walking behind him, mate…"

I moved into the shade, squinted, "No way, they're together, look."

"No, it just looks like that. Whiff's about a foot taller than Andy," Dave snorted derisively, "Jesus, will you look at that… It's like they're racing… Racing each other. Oh my god they are, but they're not running. They're trying to out fast-walk each other," he said, slapping his palm onto his forehead.

"You're fucking joking?" I snarled, filling up, with that overfamiliar, sinking feeling.

Dave squinted, "No I'm not, they're trying to out-walk each other, Skin!"

"What is the matter with those two? Look at them, it's like fucking ladies' day at Ascot Races," I said, raising my voice, anger flaring up.

The mic crackled behind me, then Dave announced in a clipped English accent, "And welcome to glorious Ascot on this fine afternoon… I say!!! It's a spiffing day, wot? …And they're orf…"

I cackled, watching our vocalist and bass player trot down the hill towards us, while listening to Dave's commentary, "Aaand… It's vocalist who takes an early lead in the Queen Jubilee Stakes… Vocalist from bass player. Vocalist from bass player… And, oh, I say, bass player is moving up on the outside. Yes, he's challenging, moving up fast… And they, yes, they're neck and neck on the final furlong and… Oh, my golly, gosh… Vocalist is fading. Yes, falling back, dropping away, and bass player strides ahead!"

Whiff was now about twenty paces in front of Andy and half the
way across the cricket pitch.

"Oh, my golly gosh. What a race… And vocalist is falling away now.
I say, it's a real turn up for the books. The favourite has muffed it…
And he is. Oh, crivens."

Whiff and Andy pulled up in unison, then raised their heads up,
staring quizzically at the pavilion.

Dave dropped the mic into my hand, and collapsed against the
nearest wall in hysterics, his flailing hands, clutching at his aching
stomach as the laughter ripped through his torso.

I could hardly move, I was laughing so much, too, but I steeled
myself, knowing what both Dave and me were both thinking. It had
to be said. I drew the mic up, and for all the world to hear. I
bellowed…

"WWWANKERSSSSSSSS!"

Dave mewled in pain; he was done now, he dropped to the floor,
totally destroyed. I exploded into laughter, my chest heaving,
convulsing, my legs weakened. I made a futile attempt to grab one of
the chairs to stay upright, but only managed to push it over; then I
too was rolling on the floor.

A few moments later, the outer door of the pavilion crashed open.

Dave and me jumped up, trying to pull ourselves together, and Whiff
marched into our practice area in pole position,"I've had enough.
He's doing me fucking head in," he said, belligerently, striding over
to his amp, and then opening and closing his thumb and forefinger

278

like Rod Hull's Emu puppet, he spat, "Andy. Andy. Andy…
Fucking, ANDY!"

I peeked over at Dave, to see what he was making of all this, and he
had his hands tightly wrapped around his chin, trying not to explode
into laughter again.

"What?" I said, distractedly, trying to keep my voice neutral.

"Fucking Andy!" Whiff shouted, and he sparked up a readymade,
took a huge toke, then we heard the outside door crash again, as the
back marker made his way in.

Andy appeared, red-faced and angry, strode purposefully up to
Whiff, and squared up, "What have you been saying about me?
Whiffy? Whiffy? Whiffy?"

Whiff took another toke, viewing him steadily, "I ain't said nothing,"
he let him know, and blew out a massive cloud of smoke into his
anguished face.

Andy looked over at me and my laughter was gone.

"Oh, for fuck's sake. Alright, you two, give it a rest, will you?" I told
them, angrily.

Andy nodded slightly, slowly wheeled, walked over to his amp near
the window, while Whiff's eyes steadily burned into the back of his
head.

I sighed internally, relieved that they hadn't come to blows, this time
anyway, and sneaked a glance at Dave, and although his face was

unreadable; his eyes were still sparkling. He was still back at the races.

"Dave? Shall we just do the set?" I asked miserably, picking up my guitar.

Dave nodded back, smashed the intro drum beat to 'Everybody's Boy', and we all came in, and as our music filled the high ceiling of the pavilion, I realised I wasn't in the mood for this anymore. I hadn't realised how much this thing had been gnawing away at me over the last few weeks, either. I thought, what a couple of wankers, you are ruining it; we are supposed to be working on new songs today. New songs that I've spent a lot of time and energy writing, and now because of you assholes and your silly little feud, it isn't going to happen. I scowled at them both, shook my head thinking, nope, there is no way I'm going to work with these two in an atmosphere like this. Being in a band is supposed to be fun, a good laugh, and once again, because of them. It wasn't a laugh. It was no fun at all.

Whiff kicked his amp away from Andy at the end of 'Everybody's Boy'. In retaliation, Andy slid his amp over towards the pavilion window, then nodded at his handy work. I thought Jesusss. Dave and me exchanged a glance. Dave snorted at the absurdity of it, hit the intro to 'Christ Fuckers', and when we all came in, the pavilion began to shake. It was Déjà vu time again, and just like the last time they had rowed at a practice; they were right on it and giving it their all. Whiff was chucking his bass around all over the place, digging into his bass strings with real venom, and even though Andy, for all intents and purposes, was now singing to the cricket pitch, he was still giving it his all too. If anyone's not playing well, I thought it's me, so I was relieved when we eventually finished the set up and the whole farce was over.

In the silence of the pavilion, Dave and me noticed Whiff was moving slowly, taking his time, packing his gear up, holding back. So did Andy, who eventually took the hint, and decided to leave on his own.

Andy smiled at Dave and me, "See you later," he said, and paced to the inner door, then turned contemptuously towards Whiff, "Now you can talk about me, Whiffy," he said, laughing uncertainly.

Whiff held his look, viewing him with distaste, "Yeah, I will Andrew," he said, his voice full of scorn.

Andy waved sarcastically, "Huh, bye, bye, Whiffy," he said, and slammed the door shut behind him.

Andy pound back off across the cricket pitch, and once he was out of earshot, I spun on Whiff, "I need you to tell me what the fucking hell's going on Whiff?"

Whiff shot back, "I've had enough of him. I can't take him anymore, he does my fucking head in, Skin."

"I thought we'd sorted this out. What happened on the way up?"

Whiff shook his head, embarrassed, "Oh, nothing. He… He, just does my fucking head in!"

It wasn't enough for me, nowhere near enough, so I insisted, "Whiff. Come on man. What happened?"

Whiff exhaled, deflating, letting the frustration out, "OK, OK."

Dave puffed his cheeks out in the oppressive silence, and we waited.

"OK…" Whiff began, "We were about halfway up, near the bypass, and I was talking about getting a motorbike, and doing me test. I said, I was thinking of getting a Yamaha 100cc, and he said something like, 'Oh you can't wear bondage trousers on a motorbike Whiffy, you'll get all tangled up,' and burst out laughing, like he'd just said the funniest thing in the world. It wasn't funny, so I didn't say anything, and then he says something like, 'Oh, and what about your bum flap? It could flap you to death,' and starts flapping his hands in my face… I thought, are you taking the piss out of me? I didn't say anything. I couldn't be arsed, and we carried on walking in silence. Then he says, 'My little brother Steven's got an Action Man armed car at home, and when I pass my driving test, I'm going to get a car and bolt it onto the car's roof.'"

Dave and me fell about laughing.

"Is that it?" Dave asked, unbelievingly.

"I don't know why you take him so seriously. He's only messing about. Why do you take him so seriously?"

Whiff held his hands up, like he'd proved his point, "Yeah, well, exactly, there you go. I laughed just like you two did, and he got pissed off, says, 'Well, I think it would be smart, I'm going to do it, and drive to all our gigs in it' and I said, 'Oh shut up Andy, you'd make us look stupid,' he said, 'Oh, Paul, what's the matter Paul can't you take it?' I thought fuck this and walked ahead of him and he just kept saying, 'Oh, Paul, Oh Paul, Oh Paul, Oh Paul', over and over again. He must have said it ten times, so I turned around and I swear I was going to punch him in the mouth, and he says, 'Ooh calm down, see I can wind you up too, Whiffy. It works both ways, doesn't it?'"

Dave scratched his chin, snorted cynically at the thought of it, "You were going to hit him?"

Whiff nodded, "Yeah, I was. He just… FUCKING HELL!" He said, through gritted teeth, and gestured with both hands, like he wanted to strangle the life out of him.

"Calm down, Whiff… Jesus."

 "I'm sorry, I can't be in any band that he is in," he mumbled, his voice full of regret.

"WHAT!?" barked, Dave, incredulously.

"Oh what, come on Whiff. You're joking, aren't you?" I implored, "We've got gigs coming up."

"I've tried Skin… I can't do this anymore. It's no good, I can't be in this band, if he's in it… It's the things he comes out with," he said, still flexing his fingers.

"Nah, come on, we can work this out… He's just younger than us, mate, that's all it is!"

Whiff dipped his head forward, like he was expecting me to say that, "Yeah, he is… And that's the problem… He's our frontman, Skinner. You've seen the interviews in Sounds, and NME. They always talk to the vocalists more than anyone else. He'll be our spokesman. I mean, if we ever do an interview, what the fucking hell is he going to come out with?"

Dave and me nodded.

Whiff saw he was making some progress,

"And what about the Ware college gig? It was embarrassing, Harper and his mates were laughing at us… You remember he told them about me liking women that were like men?"

A smile pulled at my lips, "I remember, that was just an in-joke."

"Yeah, exactly, an in-joke. An in-joke, that he told everyone. Don't laugh, but when I introduced Harper to Steph, he said, 'You alright, Stephan. What are you? West Ham or Spurs, mate?'."

I resisted the urge to fall about laughing, and even though I knew it could be fatal, I glanced at Dave and his eyes were glinting malevolently back at me.

Whiff saw it; held his hands up, "Yeah, yeah, yeah. I know it's funny, but it wasn't funny for Steph. She didn't know what he meant. She was upset. I had to tell her, and, I had to say something to Harper. In front of his mates. I don't want to have a barney with Mark Harper, you know what he's capable of… And it all came from one comment, a comment he made. What would he say in an interview…? He'd make us into a fucking laughingstock."

"OK, fair enough. I know what you mean. That was embarrassing," I acknowledged.

Dave looked out the window, thinking. "I must admit, that was embarrassing, Whiff…" he declared, "I like him, I get on fine with

284

him, he's alright… He's not someone I would hang out with normally, but he's a decent vocalist."

"Yeah, me too, he's alright, and he writes some good tracks as well," I chipped in.

Whiff agreed, "I'll give him that, he does, and he's an OK, singer… But he's not a proper frontman, a proper spokesman, someone who could speak on behalf of the band."

I nodded again, and Dave added, "And he got us all of those gigs, didn't he?"

Whiff countered, "No, he didn't, Dave. He got us Richard Hale, Founder's Hall, and that total waste of time over in Hoddesdon, which was basically a gig for his mates."

"Oh what, that's not true." I exclaimed.

"OK, well, maybe not. It was still a waste of time. Dave got us Thundridge Youth Club, and the other gigs we both got them. It only looked like he did because we gave out his phone number."

I looked to Dave, he looked neutral.

"It's not about the gigs Dave, we can get gigs without him, no problem, this is about him. I think he's alright, but sometimes, well. I haven't told you this, but when I phoned him, and asked him to sort his problems out with you, Whiff. He denied he had a problem with you. Said he never has. I wanted to smash the telephone phone off me head. I pressed him further, and he got all arsey, says it was you that had a problem with him. I thought, problem with you? Problem with him? What's the fucking difference? It was stupid, just a turn of phrase, it wasn't meant to be an accusation. I tell you. It was really frustrating, like I couldn't talk to him properly."

Whiff threw his hands up victoriously, like he had been vindicated, "Yeah, that's exactly what I feel like every time I'm with the… The little chipmunk."

Dave snorted, repeated, "Chipmunk."

Whiff nodded to himself, clear in his mind that there was no going back. He'd made the right decision now, and he was sticking to it, "I'm sorry, I've been thinking about this for a long time… I cannot be in any band, that he is in."

"OK, OK, I get it," I sighed, dropping my head into my hands thinking it over. "What do you think, Dave?" I implored, through a gap in my fingers.

He shrugged his shoulders, "I don't know… It's your band, Skin, it's up to you."

Oh, fucking hell, I thought, it's on me. Whiff's right, he's going to make us look bad, and it might not just be in front of a few mates, next time. Nah, fuck it, we can't have that.

"OK, he's out. Andy's out."

Whiff let out a long sigh of relief, "I'm really sorry, Skin, I just can't be in…"

"Don't worry about it mate," I said, cutting across him, "It's probably for the best. Better now than later. You probably did us a favour in the long run, I'll give him a bell tomorrow, get it over with."

"Oh brilliant, that'll get you in the mood for the party then," Dave groaned, "What about today?"

"Nah. I can't Dave, I need time to think about what I'm going to say to him, it won't be easy," I said, turning to Whiff, who looked off up the hill.

I swept my hands back through my spikes, "Anyway, why do today, what you can put off till tomorrow? Give him another day as Virus V1's singer," I told them, trying to make light of it.

Dave and Whiff and nodded in unison.

"I'm sure he'll appreciate that Skinner," said Dave, absently checking his watch, "Oh well, that's done then… Shit. I've got to go. I'm meeting one of Jo's mates in Hertford."

I couldn't believe that the subject had changed so quickly. It was doing my fucking head in.

"Is that a female mate, by any chance?" I dived in, happily.

Dave smiled lewdly, "Yeah, as it happens, her name's Abbie."

I bobbed my head, eyed Whiff provocatively, "I hope she's not like a man."

Whiff smiled indulgently. "I bet he doesn't," he said, pointing at Dave, "I bet, he'd like a bit of the old meat and two veg."

287

Dave protested. "Oi, leave it out, that could be the next love of my life… Bloody hell, have a heart mate, bloody old boy," he Alan-ed, and we all dissolved into a relieved, yet raucous laughter, like everything was back to normal again.

Once we had loaded up the van, we wished Dave good luck on his date, told him that we would see him at his party tomorrow night, and he waved back, telling us to bring a bottle, and drove away.

Whiff and me stood in silence, watching the bright yellow van glinting in the late afternoon sunlight, slowly edging back up the hill trying to avoid the potholes, until just like Andy before, it disappeared.

I hoisted my guitar onto my shoulder, Whiff did likewise with his bass, and we padded off across the pristine grass of the cricket pitch, enjoying the sunshine on our faces.

"I'm sorry, Skin," Whiff conceded, once again.

"OK, you can give it a rest now, mate," I protested.

He pulled his bottom lip over his top and exhaled, "Skin, look it was me that made this happen, so I'll sort it, I know a few people who would love to be in our band."

"Yeah, like who?"

"Gobber's interested."

"Yeah, I thought of him. He's a good laugh, got the right attitude, we'll give him a try."

"I can see one problem. He hangs out with his brother all the time."

I countered, "Mark's not going to show up now though, is he? Not unless we're giving away free hair products at the audition."

Whiff laughed, shaking his head slowly from side to side, "No, no, no, no, no," he drawled, doing a decent impression of the broken-hearted Punk Rocker.

I smiled at his effort, then beamed, as he flourished a half-smoked spliff from his leather jacket pocket,

"Ha, ha, ha, ha, ha... Look what I've got."

I nodded my head like a nodding dog, "Yes, yes, yes, yes," I mimicked, doing the opposite impression of the love-lost lonesome Mark.

Whiff sparked it up, took a pull, considered our options, "Dave Cowling's interested."

I creased up, "What? Custer!? Fuck off man, I'm not having Custer in the band!"

Whiff looked affronted, "Oh, leave it out, he's alright," he told me, passing the spliff.

"You should have passed me that before you mentioned the cowardly Custard, he's a poser man. Next!"

Whiff shrugged, "OK fair enough, what about Markus Crosswell?"

I billowed out a cloud of smoke, "You mean Mucus? The guy at Tarnia Gorden's piss party? Yeah, he was alright. Let's give him a go."

Whiff smoothly plucked the fast-dwindling spliff from my hand, "I'll have a word with them. I know it's only two, but it's a start," he finished, like the conversation was over.

"I know a couple of people."

He turned to me, mouth gaping.

I chuckled, "Don't look so surprised mate, I've had a plan B for a while now, in fact I've a plan C, D, and E, since the bullshit at Ware college, mate."

Whiff smiled, holding my look.

"Yeah," I smiled smugly back at him, "I think Basher would be good."

"What, the tea-leaf?"

I snorted, "Yeah, that's him, Ronnie Biggs," accepting the proffered spliff back, took a last blast, "Nah he's alright. He wouldn't nick off us, if he does, he knows I'll kick his fucking head in," and to illustrate my point I dropped the spliff onto the ground, flattening it under my boot.

"Hmm, I must admit, he looks right for us… I talked to him at the Hoddesdon gig, and he seemed alright… Yeah. Let's give him a go".

"One problem though. It could be six months till we can audition him," I cackled.

Whiff cackled back, "…and is the other one Sulli by any chance?"

I pulled a huge grin and tipped my head back, "How did you guess?"

"I thought there must be some reason why you suffer Doggy's company."

I smiled, "I can't think of anyone better. Sulli's a good vocalist, done plenty of gigs, demos, the lot, and he's a proper frontman with stage presence. You can talk to him too… And I reckon if we wanted to try something different, some of that cross over stuff, he'd be well up for it."

"You reckon he'll leave The Sickos, then?" He nodded enthusiastically.

"I'm not one hundred percent sure, but from what he was saying the last time I saw him, I'd say yeah, yeah he would."

I looked down into the valley towards the river as we left the potholed gravel track and crossed the A10. You know what Skinner, me old mate, I thought, it's just another perfect day.

"OK, Whiff, I'm going to run my guitar home. I'm meeting Cerys in The Feathers after her shift. I'll see you tomorrow at the party, yeah?" I said, stopping at the gravel track leading up to the graveyard.

"Yeah, and look, Skin… I'm…" said Whiff wryly, walking on.

"Oh what, you're not going to apologise again, are you mate?"

"No, sorry," he quipped, throwing up a hand.

"It'll be fine, mate. One of them will come through for us and we'll be even better."

Whiff turned and beamed back at me, "See ya Skin."

I stepped up the hill, crunching over the loose stones, and I thought Custer, fucking Custer on vocals! Custer Cowling, the cowpat dropper. Nah, he's no leader, laughing to myself.

Once home, I shot upstairs, propped my guitar safely up against my bedroom wall, and on the way back out I popped my head into the lounge, and heard my old man say, "Oh shut up, you scruffy bastard."

"I'm off out, I'll see you later." I announced, presuming that he was having a political debate with Michael Foot.

"You're not a politician. You're a bloody tramp! Michael Heel, more like," he told the moving pixels on the cathode ray tube, proving my presumption to be correct.

"Oh bye, Mike," Mum called brightly, her head edging out, owl like, from behind the safety of her book.

I could still feel the warmth of the spliff channelling sweetly through me as I sauntered back down my road, on a mission to get to the pub. A car approached from the bottom end of the road. It was Doggy's Mum's Golf, so I stuck my thumb out, like I was trying to get a lift from my nutty mate. Only to see it was his mum, Victoria

Kinnell, whose austere look told me, I was to blame for everything. I smirked at the stupid cow, looked up, gazed into the blue sky until she had disappeared around the corner at the top of my road, as even to acknowledge her presence would be a waste of my precious time and energy.

Andy? What about Andy? I thought. Once I had told him. Now, that would be my fault, and through my stoned haze, I started feeling sorry for him. Andy was a good bloke, really, always up for a laugh, never talked behind anyone's back, and for the most part, was positive, and only had good things to say about people. It was the ultimate irony that he had brought Whiff into the band, and now because of him, he was being booted out. I knew he'd be OK, though, as his original band, Necro were still going, and when he had left, they had said that they 'missed his solid guitar playing', so I was sure they would take him back again. It still didn't sit well with me, though, but when it came down to it, he was just too young to be in a band with us; there's a lot of difference between a sixteen-year-old and a group of eighteen-year olds, and unfortunately for Andy, he was going to pay the price for that. In the end, I was always going to side with Whiff, as we were closer in age, so we hung out together a lot more than Andy and me did. Whiff and me, also shared a lot of interests outside the band, namely, motorbikes, drink, drugs, and of course girls, the touch paper for a lot of their squabbles, all of which Andy seemed to have little or no interest in at all. I didn't know whether Whiff knew that I would side with him when he gave us his ultimatum or not and when it got down to it, I didn't really care, as far as I was concerned. If Andy wasn't right for us on a personal level, couldn't get on with everyone on a day-to-day basis, then he wasn't right for the band either. And even though we had gigs coming up, I was going to relieve us of that problem.

293

Into The Feathers I strolled, feeling less confused, feeling more at peace with the world than I was an hour ago. I thought, there is nothing like half a spliff and a bit of country air to get you back on track, and on the subject of spliffs there's Dapper sitting at the bar, looking Dapper in his usual Ted Baker suit.

"Hey, Skinner," he said, waving me over.

"Alright Daps? I didn't see your car outside," I said, smiling broadly.

Dapper smiled back, "I've got a new one now… And it's not bright red," he said, illuminatingly.

"Oh yeah, you thinking of taking a road trip?" I asked, catching his drift.

Dapper slapped the bar with his hand, "Well, yes, I am, as a matter of fact."

I smirked, "Anywhere nice?"

He shook his head, "No, not really. It could be fun, though."

"I'm up for that, I do like a road trip. When you going?"

"I can do any night next week."

I smiled, "OK, me and Danny will be outside here Wednesday night, yeah?"

"I'll put it in my Filofax," he laughed.

One pint of lager, and a pint of snakebite, appeared like magic before us. Blow Jo, smiled pleasantly, and gave Dapper a peck on the cheek, before slinking off down the bar. I watched the regulars ogling, checking out her tight curves as she passed them by.

"Don't you mind that?" I asked.

"No. Not at all, actually. I take it as a compliment... It's as close as those dirty buggers will ever get."

I cracked up at the logic, "Yeah, I like it, they can look, but... But what about Jo?"

Dapper tapped his temple with his finger, his Rolex, glinting under the bright lights of the bar,

"Oh no, she doesn't mind. Not a bit. She says she likes the attention, says it's all part of a barmaid's job... She told me the mugs buy her drinks all night long in a vain attempt to get into her knickers... And then at closing time while they bugger off back to their two dirty kids and ugly wife, she cashes up all the drinks she didn't have, and she's minted. It's funny, most days, she makes more in tips than she does in wages, especially over the weekend. Blo is very funny. She told me. 'The more perverts, the better'."

I cracked up at the logic again, "Bloody hell... Well, if she's OK with it... Good for her."

"Skinner, she's more than OK with her admirers."

"The dirty bastards," I scolded, having a shifty myself, as Blo Jo poured another glass, for a mug.

Dapper clinked his glass on mine, "I'll drink to that. To all the dirty bastards. Oh, that and road trips."

I nodded, picked up my pint, took a long draft, and saw Chris Severn, the owner of The Feathers, strutting towards us. He stopped in front of us, simpered, and thrust a brown envelope into my hand.

"Ah, Skinner, here you are, here's your beer money," He guffawed.

"What's this then?" I asked, turning it over in my hands.

"It's Cerys' wages, I thought I'd cut out the middleman, or in this case the middle woman, so to speak."

In a second the whole bar creased up laughing, seeing the Punk had been ribbed so perfectly, and satisfied with the killer line, its delivery, and particularly with its reception among the regulars. He fixed a smug expression on his face and strolled off like he'd just made the funniest joke in the world, while the fly skating ring on his head shone invitingly to any nearby bluebottles, underneath the bright lights.

Once he was out of earshot, I theatrically pocketed Cerys' wages, making sure everyone could see.

I sighed, shook my head, "I tell you what, he's right. Cerys is generous to a fault when it comes to getting a round in… But on balance, I reckon Chris Severn pays for more of my drinks than anyone else," I said, to the collected regulars, who threw back their heads laughing at the riposte.

Dapper agreed, "Yes, me too," tapping my glass with his, setting everyone off again.

I thought, this night is warming up quite nicely. I'll have a couple more here, then walk Cerys back to hers, go home, and try to catch up on some much-needed sleep. I'll need to be on form tomorrow, as not only will it be a late night at Dave's house party. I've got to tell Andy he's out the band.

A few moments later, Del and Joyce entered The Feathers, waving happily in my direction. I knew what that would mean, so immediately, I readjusted my plans, and beckoned them over. Not long afterwards, Cerys joined us and once I had given her, her wages, and she'd bought the first round, much to Chris Severn's amusement, the four of us settled in for another nice little Saturday night session.

Chapter Twelve

Dave's House Party

Inside the fug of my bedroom, I woke up late the next morning feeling dry mouthed, hungover, and my first thought of the day was… Food. It wasn't going away, so I hastily hopped out of bed, pulled on my black bondage trousers and Discharge T-shirt, dodged the bathroom, and went downstairs to find Mum and the old man in the kitchen having lunch. Mum greeted me with her customary call of 'good moaning', while the old man stayed hidden behind his broadsheet, or 'bored shit', as I called it, or 'that wretched rag', as Mum had begun to call it.

George sat on the chair next to him, eyeing him provocatively, impatiently waiting for his lunchtime game of 'gimme paw' to begin. All to no avail, though, as suddenly, from nowhere, the old man slapped his paper onto the table for all of us to see, declaring in no uncertain terms, that 'this country is finished'.

"Bloody finished," he told us again, and with that chilling declaration, he got up and took the paper into the lounge to read all about it.

Mum sighed, a big Mum sigh, leant forward, and lowered a couple of pieces of buttered bread scraps onto George's chair, who dived in, like it was his lucky day; no paw work, and food!

I poured myself out some Crunchy Nut Cornflakes and slopped some milk over the golden flakes.

"What's the matter with him, Mum? …Why's he like this all the time?" I asked, crunching away.

"Oh nothing. He's just bored, Mike. He hasn't adjusted well since leaving work, there's nothing for him to do, around here. He's fixed everything. Everything's been painted, there's nothing."

"Why doesn't he go out then?"

"And do what, Mike? There's nothing for people of our age around here."

I snorted, thinking your age? …Try being eighteen.

"He could go to the pub, anywhere but The Feathers or The Anchor," I joked.

Mum smiled, took a deep breath, "The truth is… He wants to move, Mike."

I stopped crunching, Mum took another breath, "There's nothing around here for him anymore. He is bored, and there's been a lot of talk in the parish magazine about them running a bypass across the fields at the top of our road. It's absolutely shocking what they are planning to do. They are going to run a four-lane road, right across the River Rib valley… He doesn't want to be here to see that, and w… W… Well…"

"What do you want to do, Mum?"

Mum sniffed, stiffened her resolve, "I want to go too Mike, there's nothing around here for me either, well, apart from you, of course."

"You should go then Mum. If you're not happy, go."

Mum reached forward, placed her hand on mine, a smile pulling at her lips, "Dad said he won't go until you are settled."

I squeezed her soft hand, "I'll be fine, Mum. I can look after myself now. You know that," I said, looking deeply into her eyes, she nodded, and I nodded back, pulling a smile myself now, "I'll do what I need to do. I'm not a kid anymore. I'll tell you what, just let me pass my driving test, get my licence, then I can get a job, rent a room somewhere. I've seen landscape gardening jobs, in the Ware no job centre now spring's coming. All I need is a driving licence, and with my experience I'll be in."

"Do you think so?"

"Yeah, of course, Mum," I assured her, thinking hopefully.

"What about your music?"

I shook my head, "Don't worry about that, I'll have plenty of time… Listen, if you could move anywhere, where would you go?"

Mum smiled broadly, let my hand go, and tickled George under his chin, who lifted his head for more, "Well, I was stationed at Falmouth in Cornwall, when I was in The Wrens. It really is a lovely place. The scenery is spectacular… I would love to go back there."

"If you can do it, you should do it, do it while you can, live your dreams, Mum," I told her.

"Mike, you could come with us."

I snorted, put my hand up, "No, no, no, you two must have had enough of me by now. You go. I know what Dad's like about beaches, maybe he could get that boat he always wanted, do a bit of sailing again. Seriously, Mum, talk to him about it, if he stays around here. He'll end up in the funny farm."

"I know, and I won't be far behind him," she laughed.

"You should have been put in one, years ago, Mum," I said, giving her another laugh.

George looked up at the humans, sniffed the air, then spun around on his chair, before docking his tail with his nose, and shut his eyes for his early afternoon snooze. Mum and me shared a glance at the talented little ginger and white furball, smiled, and got back to our respective lunch and breakfast.

Once I had filled up, feeling a lot better, I slouched back up to my room and waited until Mum and the old man went for their usual Sunday afternoon walk. Peeping out from behind the curtains I watched them steadily hike to the top of our road through my bedroom window, thinking surely, the powers that be, aren't going to rip those beautiful fields to pieces, roll them flat, and pour concrete from one side of the valley to the other. Of course, they fucking will, all the little drones need their roads to get to work, to keep the powers that be where they want to be. On top of the heap.

On seeing their heads disappear at the top of the valley, I marched downstairs. It was time to make the call, put this thing to bed, once and for all. I picked up the receiver, dialled Andy's number, and waited, and as I waited a swarm of butterflies woke up in my stomach. Oh shit, I thought, this is going to be horrible, what the fucking hell is he going to say? Andy loves Virus V1, maybe I should leave it, maybe we should talk about it again, maybe Whiff's calmed down. Fuck it. Maybe I should let Whiff tell him.

"Hello," It was Andy's old man.

"Hi… Is er, Andy there?" I asked, hesitantly.

"No, sorry, he's out at the moment."

Now what do I do? I thought, feeling the frustration rising.

"Oh, is that Skinner?" Andy's old man enquired pleasantly.

I said, "Yeah, Hi."

I thought fuck this, I want this done now, "Can you tell Andy he's out of the band?"

In the hum of the phone line, he shifted, "I think that's something you should tell him yourself, don't you?" he told me coldly.

"Yeah. I, OK. Cheers," I said, uncertainly, hung up.

Immediately it rang again, hands shaking, mind racing, I picked it up slowly, put it to me ear,

"Hello???" I asked, tentatively.

"Mick, is that you? It's Martin, I'm your brother. I'm your blood… You've…"

"FUCK OFF!" I shouted, smashing the receiver down, almost taking it off the wall.

Into the lounge, I pounded, sat down, trying to calm down, and felt a lot of different emotions welling up inside me. Sadness was probably the biggest one of them all. It was bad news, I hadn't had the chance to tell Andy myself, as I thought he deserved that, at least. I knew his old man would tell him, though. So, my overriding feeling was that of relief. Relief that all the bullshit was over. Now we could get back to what being in a band was all about, making music and having a good fucking laugh while doing it.

I stretched back on the sofa, pressed the zapper, found some snooker on BBC Two to while away the hour or so, before I expected Whiff to show up, to walk down to the party, and soon fell asleep.

In the twilight of the evening, a long time later. I'm not sure how long, but the snooker had finished, so it must have been a very long time. I opened my weary eyes to see the old man sitting in his rocking chair, and seeing me stirring, he rocked forward.

"Is that how you're going to spend the rest of your life? Getting drunk and sleeping it off?"

"No, I work," I said, defensively.

He pulled an amused face. "Work!?" He said, chuckling to himself, "It's hardly a living, is it, Mike?"

I sat up, "I do alright, give mum housekeeping," while wiping the gunk from my eyes.

"OK, OK, calm down. I need to tell you something."

Oh, fucking hell, no, I thought, I've had zero sleep in two days, had to chuck a mate out of the band, and now I'm going to be lectured on my career prospects. Oh well, on the bright side, at least I won't be hearing from that slimy wanker Martin in the near future. FUCK OFF! Brilliant; the perfect answer to an imperfect wanker. I couldn't have put it better, even if I had thought about it.

The old man smiled at the dread written across my face, "It's not that bad. Listen, I had an audience with Lady Victoria Kinnell, last week, and she told me Douglas likes pop music. So, they've paid for him to do a sound engineer's course in Holloway. It's a three-year course, costs about ten thousand quid. I was wondering if you would like to do the same, money's tight now I'm retired, but it would be worth it, in the end, it could lead to some big money."

Bloody hell, I thought, that would be brilliant. Not only would it help the band, it would help me, and it would give me something to fall back on, like they've been going on about, but hold on.

"What about my bed and board?" I asked.

"What bed and board? You'll still live here. You can commute, it only takes an hour on the train."

"I thought you two wanted to move away?"

"Oh, you've been talking to mum, have you? …Mmmm, well, we don't need to go just yet."

"If I'm being honest Dad, I'm not interested, those sound engineering courses… They don't deal with the kind of music that I'm interested in, not my thing Dad, but thanks for the offer though."

"Oh… You… Right. OK. Well, that's up to you, the offers there," he said, totally shocked, swivelling his head back to the bleating TV.

"I'm fine Dad, seriously, once I do my driving test, I'm going to get a job, move out, get my own place, that's what I want to do."

He nodded minutely, keeping his eyes on the rapidly strobing screen.

I heard the doorbell ring; I couldn't get out of the room quick enough. I thought, if I stayed, I might change my mind. It was such a good offer, but I had taken a lot from them over the years and given them precious little in return. It was now time, not only, to give them something back, it was time for me to move forward, and to do that, I had to get out of the village. I had outgrown the place anyway.

A Whiff sized shape presented itself, through the frosted glass of our front door.

"Whiffters, old chap. You alright?" I said, pulling it open.

Whiff, grinned, "Mr. Baker. You ready to party, then?"

"As always! Mr. Hammersmith."

"See ya Mum. See ya Dad," I called back into the house, and Mum said a cheery bye from the kitchen, but I heard nothing from the lounge.

Whiff and me exchanged a glance.

"I'll tell you about it later," I exclaimed.

"Oh. Another one of your old man's classics?"

"Nah, it's nothing like that, it's… Well, come on, let's go," I said shutting the door, and we set off for Dave's house-warming party.

On the way down my road, in the twilight of the evening, we were greeted with a refreshing, life-affirming early spring breeze. I sucked it in hungrily, taking in our surroundings, as Whiff puffed away on his rollie. In the distance, a rose like sun, perched on the horizon of High Cross Hill, while a million and one insects gambling on an early summer, cast themselves gently in the air around us.

Whiff and me walked down past Doggy's, on through the two white fences passing Hilary's house, then after vaulting over the wall into the graveyard, we walked down the hill towards the all-night garage and Dave's soon to be, old house. I smiled at some memories coming back to me, and then turning left at the bottom of the hill, we carried on down the A10 towards the river. In time, we passed the village hall, and the whole valley opened up before us in a multitude of greens and browns. Above it all, the sky shone in the purest shades of magenta, fuchsia, folly, and flame, as the day relented, and the night crept in.

"It's going to be alright, isn't it?" I asked, breaking our silence.

"Yeah. It's only the end of a chapter, isn't it?"

"I don't know, mate. I see it as more than that. A chapter is like a life in a day, this… Virus V1, well, it's been like a million chapters, you know? …I think it's more like the end of a book."

Whiff laughed knowingly, "Reckon another one's about to start."

"I suppose stories never really end, Whiff. It's just a passage of time, and once that passage is over, another one connects to it and the story continues. It's not an end, there's never an end. Life is perpetual. It just keeps on going. It's just people that change… Maaaaan," I said, flashing him a sarcastic peace sign.

Whiff laughed, flashed a V back, "Yeah maaaan, but it's true, Skin. In a few years we'll be gone and someone else, maybe our kids, will take over the story."

"Yeah, Virus V2?" I said thinking it over. "I tell you what. You'll be gone in a few months' time if you don't get off the whiskey."

"Oh yeah, look who's talking, microdot man," he returned.

"Microdot Man! I like that. It sounds like a superhero. Microdot Man! Speeds faster than a locomotive. Leaps off tall buildings, and dies, like a stupid cunt," I said, sending us both into fits.

One step at a time we paced, taking it all in, enjoying the moment, enjoying the comfortable comradery of two people who are completely on the same wavelength. A chilled breeze gently blew over us as we passed the top of Ermine Street, and at the far end of the street, Dawkin's house was just about visible in amongst the thick vegetation of its front garden. Next door, I saw protruding through a group of conifers, the roof of the house, which I had helped Dave to re-tile, and remembered how we were The Superheroes that day, crawling around like Spider-Man up there on the high rafters.

Into the valley we continued, approached the river and the bridge, and we saw Tarnia Gorden's House, as another chapter in our passage of time passed us. On the bridge Whiff stopped, smiled, put

307

his hand to his ear, and hearing the steady thump of music coming from the house-warming party, he beamed at me, nodding his head along to a distant beat. In the water below us, I saw that although the traffic lights were visible in the depths of the river, they were long since extinguished. I thought about the orange glow and the beautiful translucent body underneath it, then right on cue, the empty Deacons' house appeared on the right-hand side, as we cleared the bridge and came up to another chapter in this book of our lives.

"You alright, Skin?" Whiff asked, disturbing me from my ruminations.

"Yeah, sorry about that, I was zoning out."

Whiff saw a group of people standing outside of Dave's house, raised his hands in the air. "Wheyyy!" He shouted, and a cheer came back from the throng, "No time for that, Microdot Man... Come on. It's party time," he told me.

I cracked a smile, thinking, Whiff mate, you are such a party animal, "OK man, I'm going to pick up Cerys, see you later. Save us a couple of beers, will you?" I called out to his back, and watched him strut confidently across the road, up to Dave's door; where he shook someone's hand in the group, patted another on the back, pushed the door open, and in he went.

A few more chapters later, I was knocking on Cerys' door. It swung inwards, and there was Big Bad John looming in the doorway, looking down from his high tower. He slowly took me in. Up, down, left, right, middle, and centre like I was a curiosity in a visiting freak show.

"Oh… Hello," he said, in a formal tone.

"Oh Hi… Is Cerys ready to go to the party?" I asked.

"I don't know…… I'll go and see, wait there," Big Bad John replied, business-like, pushing the door to.

Tess shouted, "Is that you, Michael?" from deep inside the house.

"Yeah. Hi Tess!"

Her head appeared at the top of the stairs, "Oh, let him in, John," she chided.

John had vanished though, and with a 'tut', she beckoned me to come in. So, I wiped my DMs off, went into the lounge to wait, and found Taddy and his new girlfriend Ali, sitting watching Bullseye on TV.

"Alright Taddy, Ali," I said, taking a seat.

Taddy took me in, "Bloody hell, you look tidy, Skinner."

"Had to be done. I'm meeting Big Bad John today," I replied.

"Big Bad Joooohn," he sang almost tunefully.

"Big bad Johnnnn!" Ali finished, sending us into fits of laughter.

I said, "I'm in the shit here, aren't I?"

"No… Don't think so. He was just worried about your reputation, that's all," Taddy assured me.

"Oh what! …Look who's talking, Mr. Petrol Syphoner," I smiled back.

"I know, but he's got no choice with me, has he?" Said Taddy, wisely, tapping his temple, "I'm part of the package, aren't I?"

"I'll have you know," said Ali, warming to the theme, "That John said that one of the reasons he wanted to meet Tess in the first place, was because he used to see Taddy at football, and he thought he was a really nice lad."

"Well, fuck me, I might be in with a chance after all," I said, in mock wonder.

Ali and Taddy burst into infectious laughter, then abruptly fell silent as the door slowly edged open. I grimaced in anticipation, my mind singing, "Big Bad Joooohn, Big Bad Johnnnn."

Cerys strolled in, "Hiya," she said, and walked over to the big mirror above the fireplace. Took a brush from off the mantelpiece and ran it through her lush brown hair.

I was stunned, Cerys looked incredible, I drank her in. She wore a figure-hugging red dress, pulling tight in all the right places. It plunged at the neckline to reveal her smooth dark cleavage. A black leather belt criss-crossed jauntily over her hips; the dress cut short at the leg, showing off the beginning of her deeply tanned thighs. I shook myself out of it, I walked over to her, took her hands in mine.

"Wow, you look fantastic," I said, kissing her full on the lips.

Ali and Taddy cackled madly, "Ooohh," they chorused, and we pulled back from each other, smiling.

A while later, Taddy, Ali, Tess and John left for Dave's, leaving us alone, and as they walked off up the path, I couldn't help myself, I kissed her again, rubbing my hands gently up and down her smooth thighs.

Cerys beamed a smile at me, seeing the effect she was having, "Oh, not now Skinner, I'm all made up," she said, without much conviction.

I beamed back, "OK… But you've got to wear that again."

She nodded, "I will," she said, pinning me with her green eyes.

I kissed her full on the lips, lingering this time, "You promise?"

Cerys said, "Yeah, I promise,"

"Now come on, let's go before I change my mind."

"No change your mind, let's stay," I retorted, grabbing her waist. She pushed me away playfully, creasing up laughing, at my dog in heat face, and headed towards the door. She didn't quite make it, though, and a full two minutes later, after she had retouched up her make-up, we linked arms and set off for the party.

Cerys and me strolled down her road arm in arm chatting away, and as we came out onto the A10. A driver tooted at Cerys in front of The Feathers, and I thought, yeah, I know mate, you can toot, but you can't touch, you dirty bastard. I can, though, and pulled her closer to me, and we carried on to Dave's.

Dave's new house was rocking on its foundations by the time we stepped up to its front door. Danny and Phil were loitering outside, having a crafty smoke. I gave them a wink, then followed Cerys inside, once again checking out her curves, and we found, a party that was in full swing. The front room was packed out with revellers, all the village's young people were in, drinking, dancing, chatting, laughing. Whiff was near the front room window, in conference with Hayley, and next to them Dave was chatting with Jo and a short, cute looking blonde girl, I assumed to be Abbie, the girl he met the day before. Hello, I shouted, trying to get their attention, but no one could hear me through the pounding music, so I looked around.

Alan and his older brother, John, were standing in the opposite corner, away from the pumping stereo system. Alan saw me, smiled, gave me a friendly wave. John just glowered. Alan grinned at his older brother, gave him a friendly nudge, then smiled, that Alan floodlight smile back at me.

I waved at them, put my mouth to Cerys' delicate ear, "Come on," I said, raising my voice, "Let's go and say hello to Dave," I said, and she nodded.

Dave had already seen us, though, and walked over, "Alright Cerys, alright Skin, glad you could make it," he said brightly, looking at his watch theatrically.

"Sorry mate, we got delayed…" I grinned.

Cerys smiled self-consciously, handed him a bottle of Blue Nun, "I brought this for the party, Dave."

Dave took it, "Cheers Cerys, that's very kind, thanks," he responded, spinning it over in his hands, then looking at me seriously, he said, "So did you do it then?"

"What!?" I cried, absolutely mortified, thinking he was talking about me and Cerys' quickie before we left hers.

Dave frowned, "Andy, the phone call… Andy, remember him? Bloody hell mate! Keep up," he Alan-ed, exasperatedly.

"Oh yeah. Yeah, yeah, it's done, mate."

"Well, I think you're mean, I liked Andy," Cerys interjected.

Dave nodded thoughtfully, "So did I, but… Well…" and trailed off.

"Oh well, it's done now, time for a drink or two. Where's the booze?" I said, putting it to bed.

Dave cackled, pointing to a small hallway leading from the lounge, "It's through there, in the kitchen, there's plenty, get stuck in, mate."

"Cheers Dave, by the way, I like the house, it's alright, isn't it?"

Dave scanned my face sceptically, "It's not really your thing, though, is it?"

"I'll have my own place one day Dave, maybe, sooner than you think."

Dave cracked a smile, "You're a clever bloke Skin, I wouldn't put anything past you."

Cerys smiled, "Skinner owning a house? Can anarchists have houses?"

I snorted, shook my head, asked them what they were drinking, left them to talk houses; while I slipped out of the front room into the kitchen, and found Tess and John were just leaving with their glasses full.

John smiled, put his hand out, "Oh hello, Michael. I expect we'll be seeing a lot more of you now."

I carefully took his big shovel-like hand, feeling only warmth in his shake. "I hope so. Cheers, thank you," I said, totally dumbfounded.

"Yes Mike, come and see us again soon, won't you?" Added Tess, smiling sweetly.

I smiled nervously, "Yeah… Yeah, I will, thanks," I told them, and they returned to the front room.

Bloody hell, I thought, I wasn't expecting that, and whistled Big Bad John to myself, while I grabbed a can of cider, a can of lager, mixed them up in a pint glass and took a long draft of the sweet amber drink, then pouring Cerys, a medium white wine, snatched a lager for Dave, and ambled back into the party.

Whiff had joined Cerys and Dave now and saw me coming.

"Wheyey, you alright Skin?" He said, holding a short, aloft.

"It's… Fucking… Whiskey… Time!"

I cackled, "Oh yeah, maybe for you mate, my whiskey days are long gone."

"Yes, they are!" Cerys warned, giggling.

"Whoa, you'd better watch it there, Skin," said Dave, throwing his arm out, making a cracking lasso noise.

I saluted her, "Yes, m'lady," I fawned, passing her a glass of wine. "Oh, and will there be anything else, m'lady in red?" I fawned, sticking to my posh waiter's voice.

Whiff snorted, took a couple of paces back, admiring Cerys' steep curves, "Oh lady in red, she's dancing with me," he sang tunefully.

Cerys sniggered at the nutter.

"I don't mind if I do," I said, taking her hand, placing my other firmly around her tight waist, guiding her towards the dance floor.

"Ooooh Skinner, you're so masterful," she said, pretending to melt in my arms.

"I know I am darling, I know," I Trevor Howard-ed back, and took her for a spin around the room and as my eyes passed over the front room window, Andy's face peered back at me.

"Fucking hell, it's Andy," I said, dropping Cerys like a hot coal.

Dave burst out laughing, "What's he doing here?"

"I don't know… It's not fucking funny, Dave."

Dave looked down, with a huge smile playing at the corner of his lips, while Andy steadily watched us through the window, his breath frosting the glass. He then made a move towards the door, and I gestured for him to wait, stay where he was. I would be out in a minute.

"Oh, for god's sake, Mike, you said you told him," Cerys said, anxiously.

"I did, I did. I told his old man… Ohh, fucking hell," I said, zigzagging my way through the party-goers to the front door, and then with one backward glance at a horrified Cerys, I walked out into the street.

Andy stood upright under a street light, bathed in the orange glow. He put his hand up in a small wave, when he saw me coming out of the house. I replicated, slowly walked up to him feeling a lot of different emotions. When I noticed him wearing his Virus V1 T-shirt, I added guilt to the collection.

I steeled myself, there was no going back now, even if I wanted too.

In the most conciliatory tone I could muster, I said, "I'm sorry, Andy. You're out of the band, mate."

Andy's eyes immediately welled up.

"I left a message with your old man. Didn't he tell you?"

Andy shook his head, looking devastated, then turned and walked away quickly, with his head down.

On the way back into the party, I pushed a few random people out of the way to get to Dave and Whiff, who were exactly where I left them, silently looking down, lost in their own thoughts.

"Seriously, that was fucking horrible," I said, giving them both a tight smile.

Dave sighed, "What did he say Skin?"

I shook my head.

"He didn't say anything, Dave. He was fucking destroyed," I said, putting my hand onto my forehead, rubbing it up and down, like I was trying to erase the image of Andy's face. It wasn't working, though.

Dave and Whiff exchanged a glance, I didn't know what to say, nor did the others. So, we stood in silence as the party raged all around us, watching everyone enjoying themselves like nothing had happened. I thought Alan was right, when he said, 'sometimes it's a cruel world', seeing him now surrounded by his girls, Anne, Hayley, Jo, and Vicky, you wouldn't have thought he would have known something like that, he looked so happy, but he did. In the end, I supposed it was all about moments, moments of sadness, moments of joy, and when it came to life. It's about enjoying those good moments.

OK, so Andy was having a bad moment now, but this was Dave's house-warming party. This was one of his good moments, so I picked up my drink, pulled a grin, and toasted my mate's full glasses.

Dave got it, he raised his head up, "Come on lads, this is a party, and it's not just any old party either, this is my house-warming party! Come on!" He said, giving Whiff a gentle shove out of the way.

Dave rushed over to his stack system, grabbed a record, set it onto the already spinning deck, dropped the needle, and Lemmy's bass intro on Ace of Spades blasted out. I began nodding my head; glancing to Dave, to Whiff, back to Dave, back to Whiff, who both beamed back at me.

"Yeah, come on, it's fucking party time…," said Whiff throwing his head back, cackling like a mad bastard.

Dave and me responded, "Yeahhhh," in unison.

Cerys came up behind us. "You lot look happy, what's happening?" She asked suspiciously

"I tell you what's happening, Cerys… It's a party, that's what's happening," I replied, smiling broadly, grabbing her around the waist again; getting back to where I was before.

In the middle of the party-goers, I raised Cerys up, and she wrapped her long-tanned legs around me, her red dress rising dangerously up over her thighs. I spun her around, around, around, gazing up into her smiling, green eyes, and I thought, this isn't a problem. It's an opportunity. Music is changing again, and this time, we're going to change with it. Virus V1 is finished. It was a laugh, we learnt a lot, but it's time for a fresh start. A new beginning. Our new band will be called, Legion of the Dead; we will be a Punk Black Metal crossover band, be on the crest of the wave, instead of being behind, following in everyone's footsteps. I'm not going to stop doing this. No way. Not now. I've got no choice. It's simple really, when it comes down to it, music is my past, music is my now and, whether it'll be my final destination, I don't know, but one thing I do know is. It's the path I've chosen, and I'll follow that path to the end.

Printed in Great Britain
by Amazon

11658051R00190